The K Wave

Profiting from the Cyclical Booms and Busts in the Global Economy

DAVID KNOX BARKER

IRWIN
Professional Publishing®
Burr Ridge, Illinois
New York, New York

ISBN 1-55738-881-4

Printed in the United States of America

BB

1 2 3 4 5 6 7 8 9 0

HCC

Dedicated to all who enjoy the challenge of K Wave theory.

CONTENTS

Part III: The Intelligent Investor

Part IV: Looking to the Future

ACKNOWLEDGMENTS

This book has been written over a period of ten years. Many have contributed to my thinking and learning along the way. A very special acknowledgement goes out to Dr. Edward Allen, whose love of teaching was largely responsible for my developing a love of learning. The mark of a great educator is the admiration, respect, and love of his students, which Dr. Allen selflessly inspired year after year. Appreciation must also be extended to Dr. Ray Jones and the many others whose academic influence over the years has been helpful. A particularly important acknowledgement must go to P.Q. Wall, whose writings, along with our many lengthy discussions and friendship, have had a significant impact on my thinking on cycles. The writings of Robert Prechter, Jr., have also had a profound influence on my views. The editors at Irwin, especially Pamela Sourelis and Kevin Thornton, made this a far better book. Last but not least, I readily confess that without the support of my entire family, particularly the patience of Berdjette, this book would never have been written.

Nikolai D. Kondratieff   1892–1938

INTRODUCTION

Recent years have witnessed a significant number of prominent national and international financial and business publications running articles discussing the potential existence of a long-wave economic cycle of prosperity and depression: boom and bust. Among the publications carrying such articles have been *The Wall Street Journal, Barron's, The Economist, BusinessWeek, National Affairs, Forbes,* and *The London Financial Times.*

To the surprise of many readers, these articles always mention a number of prominent economists, financial analysts, and academic institutions that take very seriously the evidence of a long-wave cycle—a cycle that passes through the global economy at regular intervals of 50 to 60 years. However, in the end, most of the articles typically conclude that, although compelling, the theory is outdated for our modern high-tech economy with built-in government safety nets.

Economic and financial crises have devastated the global economy and financial markets along with unsuspecting investors on a recurring basis throughout history. This fact is undisputable. The real question is whether there is a long-wave pattern to such unfortunate events, a pattern that wise investors should heed. A closer look at the evidence reveals that those who take the long-wave lightly are making a mistake with potentially severe financial and economic consequences. The accounts and portfolios of most savers and investors are reduced to mere fractions of their previous values, often to nothing, when the periods of depression inevitably come knocking at the door of global prosperity.

This introduction will touch on the highlights of long-wave theory and build a case for why the theory of the long-wave shouldn't be dismissed. This book was written to consider the past evidence and future prospects of the long-wave cycle and how you can benefit from such information.

Among the respected institutions that are interested in the long-wave is the prominent Massachusetts Institute of Technology in Cambridge. The System Dynamics Group in the Sloan School of Management at MIT is dedicated to studying the dynamics of economic, political, and business relationships. The program's computer-generated National Model provides powerful evidence of long-wave cycles that is truly sobering.

The System Dynamics National Model program is sponsored by dozens of major corporations, who for very obvious reasons are concerned with the evidence, pro and con, of a long-wave economic cycle of boom and bust. Businesses are keenly interested in any solid research on a possible economic long wave, its origins and effects, especially in relation to their particular business operations and profitability. This book will take a brief look at the work being done at MIT.

The man credited with discovering the long-wave cycle in the global free-market economy was, ironically, a Russian economist by the name of Nikolai Kondratieff. Kondratieff was studying Western grain production and prices in the early 1900s when he stumbled onto some disturbing evidence. His findings ultimately led to what has come to be known as the Kondratieff long-wave theory; thereby popularly referred to as the K Wave.

After taking a close look at the agricultural data he had collected, Kondratieff began to see the emergence of a 50- to 60-year cycle in the rise and fall of agricultural prices and production in the market economies of the West. Fascinated with this phenomenon, he began to study other segments of the economy and markets, such as interest rates, land prices, debt, industrial production, and labor prices. He saw that they too followed a distinct long-wave pattern of boom and bust.

Kondratieff did extensive research on what he found in the data and published his findings in a paper in 1926, which he delivered in a speech at the Moscow Institute of Economics. Kondratieff's research showed distinct long-wave cycles rising and falling in the global market economy from 1789 until his research ended in the mid-1920s.

Kondratieff became convinced of a long-wave cycle of prosperity and depression in the capitalist system. He postulated that if his theory was correct, the free-market system was headed for a crash and depression in the 1930s. But he also concluded that the bust and the changes it spawned would in time give birth to a new advance of ideas, inventions, growth, and prosperity for market economies that would far surpass the previous advance.

Stalin was pleased with the notion of the impending collapse of the Western world's economic system as projected by Kondratieff for the 1930s. However, he was not happy with Kondratieff's predictions that the system would rebound stronger than ever.

Something else troubled the Stalin regime even more than Kondratieff's prediction of the West rising to new heights after its next purifying fall. Kondratieff also concluded that lacking a free-market for finding appropriate price and production levels, the planned communist/socialist system would naturally and of necessity become inefficient and stagnant. Kondratieff argued for more freedom for prices and production in the economy. In time, logic dictated that a planned communist economic system would fail because of the fundamental contradictions, basic economic relationships, and lack of market forces. The recent history of Soviet demise tells us Kondratieff was onto something.

Kondratieff's struggle for more economic freedom in Russia (he opposed Stalin's agricultural collectivization programs) coupled with the idea that the free-market system in the West would come back even stronger than ever during its next long-wave advance was intolerable for the authorities. Kondratieff's research was, in effect, praising the inherent self-rejuvenating, long-wave nature of the free-market system, while predicting trouble, and in time failure, of a rigid, planned economy.

Kondratieff was rewarded for his research with imprisonment in a slave-labor camp, where he died in 1938. Alexander Solzhenitsyn recorded the death of Kondratieff in his book, *The Gulag Archipelago*. Kondratieff's death came only after his predicted economic and financial collapse in the West had occurred in the form of the Great Depression. The foundations for the new economic and financial beginning in the West, which Kondratieff predicted would come after a depression, were already being established when he died. The ultimate victory in the struggle of global economic and political ideas was already being won by the West.

In light of the collapse of the Soviet Union and the recognized superiority of the market system over the planned communist system, Kondratieff's work takes on prophetic dimensions. His research is now finding new respect within Russia and in other countries around the globe.

But don't start the celebration just yet. If the past gives any clues to potential financial crises and economic trouble in the future, the validity of the free-market system will be brought into question and challenged again—just as it was by communism and socialism during the Great Depression.

A dangerous new world of international bureaucratic interventionism, or what some would consider the threat of a global New Deal, may well be the next utopian dream to challenge and potentially stifle capitalism. It will be argued during a crisis that there wasn't enough intervention and government control. It will be argued that the pain created by the market demands even more government involvement, but on a global level. If the long-wave theory is valid, we face another troubling crisis in the Kondratieff long-wave cycle in the years immediately ahead. If the past gives us clues, the market economy may well face even greater challenges in the years ahead than it ever did against the hollow dream of communism.

An interesting thing about the long-wave cycle is that during every new cycle a new core nation appears to lead the next cycle up and therefore experiences the greatest speculative bubbles in stocks, real estate, and industrial expansion. Evidence would indicate that France was the leader of the long-wave cycle peak in the 1810s; England was the leader of the peak in the 1870s (although England wasn't as speculative as other leaders, the empire was lost during the decline); and the United States was the leader in the 1920s. It is clear that Japan was the leader of the most recent long-wave economic advance and financial speculation.

The leading nation of the advance is often the first to suffer the bursting of the speculative long-wave financial bubble. The Japanese stock market peaked in December of 1989, marking the end of an era, and has since declined following a similar pattern established by the U.S. market six decades earlier. There are always great bear-market rallies within long-wave market declines in financial markets and there are economic recoveries, but the trend is down—just as the trend is up during a long-wave advance.

Japan faces more serious trouble in the years ahead. K Wave theory would say that historians will one day look back and see the Japanese market and economic peak as the beginning of a global financial and economic shake-out that will reach bottom by the early 2000s.

All nations do not move down together. However, in the end, they all realize they are in the same mess. Some nations make final peaks late in stocks, real estate prices, and corporate profits, but they all enter the decline eventually. However, the leading nation during the advance will typically suffer the most devastating decline. This time around that appears to be Japan.

Many nations in the global economy will recover before Japan begins its next K Wave advance, although others may actually lag behind Japan. The K Wave decline has always proven to be far less severe in some nations than in others. Hopefully the United States, or the reader's particular country, will be one of the first to recover and get on with emerging in the new and exciting economy of the next long-wave advance.

In the final chapter, I will speculate as to the new economy that will begin to emerge beyond the year 2000 and what nation or nations will be the leader or leaders of the next K Wave advance. You may be surprised by who the new leader(s) could be. Eventually the entire global economy may experience the long-wave expansion and decline in perfect unison as the nations of the globe become more interdependent, but that may be a cycle or two away.

A brief review of how the K Wave unfolds is appropriate here. The Kondratieff long-wave cycle has distinct periods of development. The two most basic periods are the advance and the decline. However, the K Wave can be broken down even further into four distinct seasons. This seasonal approach to the long-wave was first advocated by Harvard economist Joseph Schumpeter and refined by market analyst P.Q. Wall. The advance is made up of the spring and summer seasons, while the decline contains the fall and winter seasons. Looking at the K Wave from this seasonal approach helps us to understand and interpret the characteristics of the cycle. Each season is from 12 to 16 years long; therefore, the advance and decline average 24 to 32 years each for a full long-wave cycle of 50 to 60 years.

This first half of the long-wave advance should be considered the spring season of the long-wave cycle, during which early inflation is seen in the global economy. This is when the new global economy is emerging. New technologies are being implemented. Runaway inflation occurs in the second stage of the advance, which is the summer season of the long-wave. This is when the global economy is overheating. The fundamental long-wave advance peaks at the end of the summer season with what is known as the primary long-wave recession; for example, the deep recessions of 1920 and 1980–1981.

After the primary recession, the long-wave decline begins with the fall season. The 1920s and the 1980s were both part of K Wave fall seasons. While the global economy booms on the financial-market surface of the K Wave fall, it is going through major structural changes. The most notable part of the cycle is the second phase of the decline, which is the winter season. A K Wave winter is noted by late runaway deflation. Winter begins after the peak and collapse of the financial speculation at the end of fall. It is between fall and winter seasons of the K Wave that the global economy suffers the secondary recession/depression and begins the global winter season. The Great Depression came in a long-wave winter. The winter phase typically sees runaway economic deflation and global economic crisis and restructuring.

Some long-wave winters are worse than others. The 1930s decline was worse than the late 1800s and early 1890s. We can only hope that the latest global long-wave winter will be less severe than the 1930s. Unfortunately, some evidence indicates things could be worse this time around. Both scenarios will be reviewed in this book.

It is important to note here at the outset that although the K Wave is concerned to a great extent with prices, the economic inflation and deflation of the K Wave cycle is far more important than price tags on your favorite goods and services. The long wave represents the inflation and deflation, rise and fall, of the real economy. By real economy I mean, real personal income, real global growth, and the real standard of living. The real rate makes adjustments for price changes.

Prices typically inflate and deflate with the K Wave expansion and contraction of the real economy, but it is conceivable that prices rise in a decline. You could have inflation or even hyperinflation, while the real economy is in the fundamental economic deflation of a K Wave decline. This would be the worst possible scenario.

In past cycles, inflation or hyperinflation in a K Wave decline has been extremely rare. Germany in the 1920s and early 1930s is the primary exception to the rule. It is most likely that the economic deflation of the latest decline of the K Wave will also see price deflation—as it already has in many segments of the global economy, especially Japan. However, a K Wave global economic decline with inflation or hyperinflation in a particular nation, as was the case with Germany last time around, is a possibility.

If a nation's government and central bank are determined to destroy the currency to try in vain to avoid the inevitable K Wave decline, they could create the nightmare of an inflationary depression. This book will examine inflation versus deflation in detail in Chapter 15.

Personally, I don't believe the United States will take the path of high inflation or hyperinflation in the latest K Wave decline, but such an occurrence must be considered possible. Germany lost World War I and then had hyperinflation. Since Russia lost the Cold War, it may be the hyperinflationary example this time around, which could produce a similar political environment to Germany in the 1930s.

There is a fascinating dimension to the idea and evidence of a K Wave cycle of boom and bust that the skeptics in the international press and financial community seldom discuss. I present it for the unique insight it provides to K Wave theory. It certainly helped me personally to understand and conceptualize the K Wave cycle. The theory strikes me as missing a critical piece of evidence if this unique perspective isn't included.

Over 3,000 years ago, forces were acknowledged and defined that if left unchecked in an economy would eventually lead to a severe depression and financial collapse approximately every half-century. The source of these early warnings gives the K Wave theory an unexpected yet prominent and respected endorsement for many observers.

There is a clear outline of the natural economic forces and ingredients that create the K Wave cycle presented in the Book of Leviticus in the Old Testament. The year of Jubilee was to take place every 50 years, according to law. In the year of Jubilee all debts were forgiven, prices were to be discounted according to the years left until Jubilee, and all land, the means of production, was returned to its original owners. It was to prevent the build-up of inefficient and dangerous elements in the economy that lead to economic collapse—specifically debt, overproduction, and high prices.

This book does not attempt to define a strict relationship between the year of Jubilee and our free-market economy's K Wave cycle. The principles presented by the year of Jubilee are used to gather insight into our subject and provide analysis.

The reader should know that this book was not written to suggest a radical change to the structure of our economic system. In a real sense, this book will applaud a true free-market system as being very close to the best humans can hope to achieve—as long as we stick to a true market economy and not one choked by government on every level.

This book will attempt to present and underscore the inherent elements within our global market system that were acknowledged by Levitical law, and which of necessity eventually lead the global market economy into systematic decline and depression after long periods of prosperity. Evidently the author of Leviticus had the foresight to see that human competitiveness would eventually cause a market system to get ahead of itself and out of control—on an unstoppable collision course with an economic and financial reckoning. It is this reckoning that brings a new beginning much like the desired effect of a year of Jubilee.

It is reasonable for you to ask how a predictable K Wave period of depression could be a new beginning for the global economy. Fortunately, there is a very optimistic side to the theory. Kondratieff himself, and the Levitical rules for the year of Jubilee, seem to have acknowledged that the K Wave cycle is not all bad. There is a bright side to the gloomy picture the theory paints, even if there are those who like to dwell on the bad news of the theory. There is a highly positive message for investors and the average employee. The fact is that the same inherent elements that cause the economic/financial decline are what give our market system its vitality and strength.

The natural forces within our market system will always bring it back stronger than ever after its predictable decline. Indeed, the free-market economic system would not be able to fully develop and advance without periods of crisis that wake up and stimulate all participants in the system. Mistakes must be weeded out. A decline, due to its very nature, brings new life to the economy and markets, and purges the mistakes. It is precisely what winter does for the spring in the natural seasons.

The year of Jubilee was to be a time of celebration, second chances, new beginnings and bold new dreams. This is the case in many respects with a K Wave decline in our modern global economic system—even if it doesn't feel like it at the time.

As we begin our study, it should be remembered that just prior to the Great Depression, financial markets around the globe were reaching all-time highs and the investing public was in a state of euphoria. Great profits were being realized by global investors as the world's stock markets reached levels never before dreamed possible. Very few had the insight to see what was just ahead, and not even those few realized the depth to which the global economy would soon sink. Nikolai Kondratieff was one man who had seen and predicted what was to come—but the world did not listen.

The Great Depression vindicated the work of Kondratieff. Once again the economic prophecies of the forgotten Russian are coming to fruition—on schedule—in the global economy. And once again, the world is not listening.

When studying an all-encompassing subject like the K Wave cycle, we must realize that the global economy is much like a great work of art. Standing too close while viewing a masterpiece, one gets a distorted view of the message the master intended. A specialized and shortsighted view tends to emphasize one aspect while diminishing the value of the whole. We are all products of a system that, while at times attempting to deliver a holistic experience, fails miserably. Most of us find a niche in which we feel at ease and seem to have all our needs and desires taken care of. Whether an accountant, lawyer, mechanic, minister, writer, farmer, scientist, doctor, banker, broker, teacher, reporter, historian, poet, or homemaker, we are all guilty of underexposure to the whole of life. This distorts our perception of the global economy and the vital role played by the sum of its diverse elements.

After a long hike through rugged terrain, a hiker once found himself standing on the edge of a river observing a fisherman who had waded into the center and was casting his line. Unsure of his location, the hiker called out to the fisherman and asked which direction the river was flowing. The fisherman replied, "Sir," with a satisfied smile, "I couldn't tell as it is really of no concern to me. I am here simply to catch my limit for the day and return home."

In terms of the K Wave, we are all guilty of making our daily catch with no concern for the directional flow of the global economic river that is providing for our existence. Within the confines of our well-known fishing hole, we are not able to ascertain that earlier there was flash flooding in the plains upriver, and at this moment there are high waters making their way down to our undisturbed fishing hole. We are equally unaware that just downstream there is the precipitous drop of a giant waterfall and that if caught unprepared we will be carried on the rising water to our ultimate ruin and downfall.

I do not seek a reputation as a prophet of doom. Rather, I am an historical realist who also happens to be an incurable optimist. This book is an effort to show the reader that, if you are fully aware and prepared for the K Wave cycle, you can use it to your advantage.

This book was written to make you consider your current position and the shape you would like to find your investments in, in the long term. There is no reason to fear the K Wave cycle. If used correctly, obstacles only enhance and advance one's position. A true winner is sharpened by adversity and is made all the stronger through trials.

Quite obviously, I have personally become convinced that the theory of the global Kondratieff Wave cycle of global expansion and contraction is valid and I will seek in this book to relate to you how best to understand and deal with it. But, even I will acknowledge that the Kondratieff wave is only a theory. There is historical and current evidence, but the validity of the K Wave will rest in the coming years of real-life experience. Will we experience a global winter season frought with risks and opportunities that appears to have already begun in many respects? If so, will this turn out to be a mild or severe K Wave winter as compared to the past?

The flip-side of a global meltdown is whether we will witness the beginning of a powerful new global K Wave expansion in the early years of the new millennium. Will the new economic expansion bring breakthroughs and advances in all areas of science and technology exceeding anything dreamed possible at present? Will you be prepared both mentally and financially to survive a K Wave winter, no matter how severe, and will you be ready to participate fully in the new era of prosperity that emerges in the years ahead? This book will address these probing questions and many more.

The economic and financial picture that this book paints is obviously not a pretty one for the duration of the latest K Wave winter season. However, as surely as winter follows fall, bringing death and decay, so the winter, of necessity, gives birth to spring and new life.

Part I: Laying a Foundation

1

A HAUNTING PAST

"Every generation, no matter how paltry its character, thinks itself much wiser than the one immediately preceding it, let alone those that are more remote."

Arthur Schopenhauer

"Study the past if you would divine the future."

Confucius

Any theory that attempts to put forward the notion that history will undoubtedly and of necessity repeat itself must first acknowledge history as its primary instrument of research. Clearly this is the case with the Kondratieff long-wave cycle. Observation of history plays an all-important role in our study. We will readily admit that our chief concern in attempting to prove the existence of the long wave lies in the history of the past 200 years. However, to limit our observations to modern history alone would be close-minded and shortsighted.

This chapter is to be a brief and hopefully entertaining overview of the Ancient, Roman, Medieval, and Renaissance history of human conflict with the economy. We will look at a number of fascinating facts and stories. This chapter is meant to help build a framework for our study of economic cycles.

There is clear evidence that the rise and fall of the economic forces wrought by human interaction have been with us since the history books have been kept. The rise and fall of economies within societies and civilizations in many ways appear to be subplots in the entire story of human development. To assume humanity has become immune from such historic tendencies may be the height of human arrogance.

This chapter takes a look back into history so that we may gain a broad-based perspective and have a clear and well-rounded understanding of the issues of prosperity and depression; boom and bust. The economic advances and declines we will review in this chapter played an all-important role in molding the economic world we live in today. Recorded economic declines of ancient history have haunting similarities with modern declines and depressions.

Many have a hard time imagining the Pharaoh of Egypt in the year 2500 B.C. pacing his gold-laden throne room, worried over the current trade imbalance or the dwindling of the treasury due to extravagant public works projects. Whether due to our preoccupation with the present or simply a lack of education, it would seem there is a prevailing view that ups and downs in the economy are a fairly modern problem. The fact of the matter is that for thousands of years humanity has been plagued with the seemingly uncontrollable economic downturn—just when life was beginning to seem comfortable.

What are the forces that cause kings to fall from their thrones, banks to shut their doors, and previously sane men to leap from tall buildings? Are there natural laws that govern the rise and fall of economies and financial markets, or does humanity hold the key that controls the forces that can and will bring whole nations and civilizations to their knees?

The late publisher and noted historian Otto C. Lightner (1922) wrote a major work titled, *The History of Economic Depressions.* Lightner owned and managed a number of successful newspaper and publishing companies. During the Great Depression he was publisher of *Hobbies* magazine based in

Chicago. He said that since very few people had money during the Great Depression they should have a hobby. The public agreed. His magazine did very well and Lightner prospered during the period.

The Lightner museum is located in what was the Alcazar Hotel in St. Augustine, Florida. The Alcazar sits across the street form what was the famous Ponce de Leon Hotel. St. Augustine was considered the American Riviera in the late 1800s. The Alcazar Hotel was one of the most lavish and opulent in the country in its day. The Great Depression proved to be more than the hotel could endure. It closed its doors after the winter season of 1931.

During the Great Depression Lightner became a collector of everything form rare art work to musical insturments. He bought fascinating items at greatly reduced prices from the estates of former millionaires during the Great Depression. Many of the items were relics of the roaring 1920s. His collection became so large that in 1946 he bought the vacant Alcazar Hotel for $150,000 and turned it into a museum to store his collection. Lightner's book (1922) gives an insightful perspective into the problem of changing economic forces and the havoc they played on humanity's plans over the centuries.

We will begin our quest for answers on the ancient shores of the Mediterranean Sea. Going as far back as 6000 B.C., the Mesopotamians made incredible economic advances. They appear to have experienced the peak of a great civilization around 4000 B.C. They engaged in substantial trade and commerce, and some historians say they had banks similar to those of the present day before vanishing as a culture. Around the year 2000 B.C., the Egyptian civilization dominated as a commercial empire on the scale of one of the few major empires.

Egypt is the first clear example in recorded history when the economy of a civilization repeatedly rose and fell in cyclical fashion yet maintained its identity. It is recorded that ancient Egypt reached incredible levels of economic development, which then declined. During periods of depression, the rulers put armies of hundreds of thousands of unemployed to work building pyramids. Egyptian history was scarred by four severe economic declines and subsequent revivals. During these ups and downs, the empire was never conquered by its enemies. Other civilizations probably experienced such swings from prosperity to depression, but the historic evidence of such economic shifts is missing.

Babylon emerged as the commercial leader in the region of the lower valley of the Tigris and Euphrates Rivers. But in time even the Great Babylon succumbed to the forces of economic decline, and the empire crumbled. In considering the decline of Babylon in the first half of the final millennium B.C., we see this clearly. According to Lightner (1922),

> It was only when the Europeans found a new path to India across the ocean and converted the great commerce of the world from a land to a sea trade that the royal city on the banks of the Tigris and Euphrates began to decline. Then, deprived of its commerce it fell a victim to the two-fold oppression of anarchy and violence and sunk to its original state—a stinking marsh and barren land.

The Assyrians emerged from the carnage left by the Babylonian demise and built an empire that also stretched into Egypt and Asia Minor. In time, disorganization and then anarchy brought down the Assyrians as well. After the Assyrians, the Persians, led by Cyrus the Great, became the dominant and ruling people in the region.

During the Heroic Age of Greece, the city states rose to commercial and artistic supremacy. The Greeks are known for their innovation in politics and philosophy and for their openness and creative spirit in dealing with the issues and obstacles of life. For thousands of years, leaders had attempted to avert the erosion of faith in commercial systems unsuccessfully; but in the year 594

B.C., Solon, Athenian statesman and lawgiver, took radical measures never before recorded.

The plan Solon used to bring order to Greece's economy is very much like the plan laid out for the year of Jubilee. Whether Solon borrowed the plan or came upon it spontaneously, its application as a cure for a worsening situation was unique. While the year of Jubilee was to be applied as preventive medicine, Solon was applying his plan as Athens lay on its financial/economic deathbed.

Lightner (1922) wrote of how a great depression struck Athens in 594 B.C. Solon produced a bold plan during this time of public panic and rescued Athens from a dire predicament. It is said that debt and poverty oppressed the poor of Athens at the time. Selfishness and greed were considered normal and expected behavior on the part of the higher classes. Extracting the last dime in interest from the poor for their debts seemed the highest aim of the wealthy. By birth, Solon was a member of the aristocracy. However, during the course of his life he had learned the ways of exploitation by merchants through interest on debt. He understood the plight of the common people and he knew the cure. The situation had grown so bad that neighboring city states were planning to attack Athens in its weakened state of economic depression.

Solon saved Athens by taking drastic actions. Every citizen who had been sold into slavery was restored. All debts secured by individuals and property were canceled. All debt on land was canceled. Looking forward in history from the time of Solon, we find that the laws enacted by him have been re-enacted by many nations and leaders during times of economic depression right up to the present day. No doubt we will see similar actions in the future as well.

It was many years after Solon had saved Athens from distress with his radical changes, debt cancellation, and innovations that Greek civilization finally fell from dominance in the ancient world. Alexander the Great ruled the remnants of Greek civilization through the Macedonian Empire in the fourth century B.C. He led the overthrow of the then declining Persian Empire in 328 B.C.

It would be fascinating to have a documented and detailed historical account of the demise and destruction of these ancient empires. Perhaps it was a few dry years and the devastation of the wheat harvest that brought the Assyrians to ruin; possibly the Persian leaders had an extravagance for villas on the Mediterranean and a weakness for wine and women. Even without perfect records, we know that there were major shifts taking place in the commerce of the world and market forces that led to the fall and decline of these empires.

It would be easy to drift into the dangerous game of finding one villain for all the problems and afflictions that bring about the rise and fall of civilizations. But every factor plays its role and is only enhanced and strengthened by other factors as they slowly weave their way together and around the very life of the civilization they are seeking to destroy.

The rise and fall of empires and civilizations beyond the control of the men, and occasionally women, at the helm was not confined to the Mediterranean region and Southwest Asia. Counterparts of the Far East were not immune from the disease of decline that in time infects all cultures who have come together to form both political and economic ties in their quest to build a stable society.

Evidence indicates that from the first Chinese dynasty around 2200 B.C., its people experienced periods of great prosperity and, in turn, trade decline and depression. The cause of these declines is not completely known. We do know, however, that the printing press and mariner's compass were discovered and used by the Chinese and were then lost and forgotten during periods of economic crisis and chaos.

The Roman Empire began to emerge as the dominant political and economic force in the world in the first century B.C.

Eventually, Rome expanded its borders to engulf most of the civilized world. In its prime, Rome reigned supreme as the seat of world government. The *Via Sacra* was the Wall Street of the world.

We can gain a number of insights into today's problems from an account of a Roman crisis in the year A.D. 33 as told by Lightner (1922, p. 20–22).

> When we make a hasty survey of the Roman Empire to find the symptoms of decay there is brought to light as the outstanding feature industrial stagnation and commercial ruin. The year 33 A.D. was full of events in the ancient world. It marked two disturbances as the outgrowth of the mob spirit. The first was in the remote province of Judea where one Christus [Christ] was tried before Pontius Pilate, was crucified, dead and buried. The other event was the great Roman panic which shook the empire from end to end. The consternation accompanying the latter died down and it was soon forgotten, but the murmurings of the former swept down the centuries until, bursting into flames, it enveloped the world.
>
> A description of the panic reads like one of our own times: The important firm of Seuthes and Son, of Alexandria, was facing difficulties because of the loss of three richly laden ships in a Red Sea storm, followed by a fall in the value of ostrich feather and ivory. About the same time the great house of Malchus and Co. of Tyre with branches at Antioch and Ephesus, suddenly became bankrupt as a result of a strike among their Phoenician workmen and the embezzlements of a freedman manager. These failures affected the Roman banking house, Quintus Maximus and Lucius Vibo. A run commenced on their bank and spread to other banking houses that were said to be involved, particularly the Brothers Pittius. The *Via Sacra* was the Wall Street of Rome and this thoroughfare was teeming with excited merchants. These two firms looked to other bankers for aid, as is done today. Unfortunately, rebellion had occurred among the semi civilized people of North Gaul, where a great deal of Roman capital had been invested,

and a moratorium had been declared by the government on account of the disturbed conditions. Other bankers, fearing the suspended conditions, refused to aid the first two houses and this augmented the crises.

Money was tight for another reason: agriculture had been on a decline for some years and Tiberius had proclaimed that one-third of every senator's fortune must be invested in lands within the province of Italy in order to recoup their agricultural production.

Publius Spintler, a wealthy nobleman, was at that time obliged to raise money to comply with the order and had called upon his bank, *Balbus Ollius*, for 30 million sesterces, which he had deposited with them. This firm immediately closed their doors and entered bankruptcy before the praetor. The panic was fast spreading throughout all the province of Rome and the civilized world. News came of the failure of the great Corinthian bank, Leucippus Sons, followed within a few days by a strong banking house in Carthage. By this time all the surviving banks on the *Via Sacra* had suspended payment to the depositors. Two banks in Lyons next were obliged to suspend; likewise, another in Byzantium. From all provincial towns creditors ran to bankers and debtors with cries of keen distress only to meet with an answer of failure or bankruptcy.

The legal rate of interest in Rome was then 12 percent and this rose beyond bounds. The praetor's court was filled with creditors demanding the auctioning of the debtor's property and slaves; valuable villas were sold for trifles and many men who were reputed to be rich and of large fortune were reduced to pauperism. This condition existed not only in Rome, but throughout the empire.

Gracchus, the praetor, who saw the calamity threatening the very foundation of all the commerce and industry of the empire, dispatched a message to the emperor, Tiberius, in his villa at Capri. The merchants waited breathlessly for four days until the courier returned. The Senate assembled quickly while a vast throng, slaves and millionaires, elbow to elbow, waited in the forum outside for tidings of the emperor's action. The letter was read to the Senate then to the forum as a breath of relief swept over the waiting multitude.

Tiberius was a wise ruler and solved the problem with his usual good sense. He suspended temporarily the processes of debt and distributed 100 million sesterces from the imperial treasury to the solvent bankers to be loaned to needy debtors without interest for three years. Following this action, the panic in Alexandria, Carthage and Corinth quieted.

And so, under conditions very similar to those existing in the Twentieth Century, business of the Roman Empire resumed its normal aspect and the *Via Sacra* went its normal way, the same as Wall Street has done on many an occasion after the storm has passed. How similar was the business of the world in that year of the crucifixion of Christ to that of present time!

The Roman Empire dominated the world with the longest period of peace and prosperity ever recorded. But eventually, under the Caesars, corruption and decline set in. Rome's decline as a world empire was scarcely noticeable for the first few hundred years. But in the year A.D. 476, Rome was finally sacked by the Barbarians and the Empire came to an end.

Many attribute the fall of Rome to overtaxation, which disgruntled the people and caused unrest, allowing the Barbarians easy victories as they moved toward Rome. The overtaxation and growing inefficiencies of the great bureaucracy had dramatic effects on trade as the volume of the Empire's trade began to slow.

There is a popular belief that moral decadence and the erosion of a nation's value system are the cause of decline. The decline of Rome is often attributed to this erosion. There is definitely evidence that supports this hypothesis. Too much success can remove the competitive edge from a society and lead to a lazy, pleasure-seeking mentality. There is no doubt that an erosion of values destroys the internal structure of an economic system, which will eventually lead to the fall of the civilization. But we must be cautious as we look for the cause of decline and not narrow our vision to any one element. All factors must be taken into consideration as we study the forces that move the global economy and turn even the greatest civilizations into forgotten heaps of rubble.

History shows us that modern humans are not the first to be afflicted with the changing tide and fortunes of trade. As the world moved from the glory days of the Roman Empire into the period known as the Middle, or Dark, Ages, it is hard to track the rise and fall of commerce. The years of Greek and then Roman dominance of the world were marked by great advances in art, science, literature, and commerce. But starting around the year A.D. 500, culture took a radical turn for the worse, a turn that lasted a thousand years.

The ruthless reign and rampaging of the Barbarians stifled any hint of a resurrection in business or the advance of past civilizations. While areas of the Arab world flourished during this period, in Europe there were virtually no books written, and the scant trading that existed between tribes of western Europe was more often than not interrupted by wars and infighting among the various peoples. The study of this period goes far to show the depth to which humanity can sink. Lightner (1922) noted that simply not being killed and having a sheepskin coat in winter was the height of luxury for most people during the tenth century.

During the stagnant years of the Middle Ages, a new component to the economic equation was introduced. Religion, taking control of the politics of the day, soon began to have an enormous impact on commerce. The Catholic Church was becoming more and more powerful during this time; it was, and is still, often blamed for holding the world in economic bondage during this period. Wealth that was generated during this time seemed to find its way into the treasury of the Catholic Church and was spent on the extravagance of the Pope and his pious few.

However, late in the Middle Ages the tables began to turn, and an extraordinary era in the economic progress of the world was ushered in. The Crusades were military campaigns from 1096 to 1291 that were financed by the Catholic Church and government to free the Holy Land from Islam for the Christian cause. The Crusaders did more to stimulate world trade than has any event in history before or since.

Many of the crusaders were motivated by a desire to wrest the Holy Land from the "infidels." However, most of the crusaders were homeless men who had nothing to lose and everything to gain. The economic distress was such at the time that most of the warriors were willing to fight for bread and future reward if they were victorious.

Troops traveling from west to east and back ignited the economies of the nations they passed through. New ideas on world affairs were floated as a result. Money was put into circulation. A new system of trade and commerce emerged.

Civilization was slowly working its way out of its darkness, stagnation, and decline, and slowly but surely a new day was dawning. The many regions and countries of the world were once again beginning to associate and trade with one another, while at the same time domestic business activity was on the rise. Art and literature were beginning to emerge, and there was a growing support for education.

Late in the Middle Ages, Holland and Spain emerged as the leading commercial countries of the Western world. Something unique was beginning to happen in these countries. The guild, the predecessor of today's union, was coming into being. As early as the 15th century, depression was attributed by historians to the monopolistic, price-fixing, and protectionist policy of these guilds. The association of commercial interest as a unified front that had its beginning at this time is one of the many elements that play a role in today's rise and fall of the economic cycle. Modern debit and credit banking can be traced to the last few centuries of the Middle Ages.

During this time, the doctrine stating that it was sinful to take interest lost its force. Economic leaders convinced the clergy that money secured through loans could be put to good use. The financiers convinced the Catholic Church that borrowed funds through debit and credit banking would lead to legitimate development.

During this period, Antwerp was recognized as the financial center of the world. However, lending money to royal debtors who then proceeded to lose their wars and were thus incapable of repaying their loans was a grave mistake. These bad loans led to a panic and depression, during which the center of the financial world moved to London, where it remained for five centuries, until the first world war, when it moved to New York. Tokyo was passed the torch of financial leader and speculator of the world in the 1980s.

As the Middle Ages gave birth to the Renaissance, enormous changes were taking place in every area of life. Renaissance means "rebirth," and indeed this period was just that, as sweeping changes came to politics, religion, and commerce. Humankind was beginning to play with the ideas of individualism and human freedom during this period as the idea of self-rule surfaced for the first time since the Greeks.

During this time, the industrial and commercial classes began to emerge. Before this period, laborers had been slaves. The quality of their breeding or intelligence didn't matter. Sometimes it was the fortunes of war and sometimes the changes in trade that made them join the ranks of laborer. It didn't matter. They automatically became slaves.

Things were changing at the end of the Medieval period. Humanity was struggling upward to a state of freedom. Whereas trade and commerce had once been considered degrading for the ruling classes, now it was becoming dignified and of growing importance. Lightner (1922) postulated that the world emerged from feudalism due to the demands of commerce. He believed that a need for stronger central government emerged in an attempt to ward off the evil effects of trade declines and local depressions.

Early in the 16th century, with the rise of the Renaissance and mercantile era, economic declines and depressions began to take on new characteristics. Previously, depressions were on the order of trade declines, which moved slowly and gradually into a state of economic despair and confusion. Political folly was often the cause of these declines, as is still true today, but not to the same degree as in previous centuries.

When the personal gains of individualism and freedom began to emerge with the Renaissance, there also emerged a willingness to take a chance and speculate. The art of speculation that arose during this time has stayed with us to the present. The propensity to speculate is another one of the strands that weaves its way into the rope that time has shown will eventually choke the life out of an economic system. One of the first and certainly one of the most fascinating escapades in speculation history occurred around 1630–1635 in Holland.

Lightner (1922, 37–39), quoting Selfridge, relates the story of the tulip mania.

> The tulip was a rare flower which had been introduced into western Europe from Turkey and grown in the horticultural collection of Counselor Herwart of Augsburg. The plants were seen by the collectors' neighbors who desired some of their own. The blooms became their pride and others were infected with the desire to possess them. Before long the single little flower had turned everything topsy-turvy; the public had caught the fever and started speculating in tulips. All Europe became involved and the flower gradually found its way at first into the gardens of wealthy people and later to all classes. Holland was the center of the tulip trade and in that country, as well as most others, it became the requisite of society to possess a collection of tulips.
>
> But the speculative side was probably the most romantic. The state of the people's mind was such that they wanted excitement and speculation. We read of a trader of Harlem who gave half his fortune for a single bulb . . . Stock jobbers

made the most of the mania. Few kept their heads and fewer kept aloof from the mania. At first—and it was at this immediate period that the disease reached its virulent form—everyone had infinite confidence in the values and the speculators gained. The market broadened and, as is so often prayed for nowadays by Capel Court and Wall Street, the public came in. Everyone seemed to be making profits from tulips and no one dreamed that prices could fall. People of all grades converted their property into cash and invested in the flowers. House and lands were offered for sale at ruinous rates or assigned in payment of purchases made at the tulip market. Foreigners became smitten with the frenzy and money from abroad poured into Holland. The fever of speculation was superseded by an equally intense fever of pessimism. The whole country was involved and it became imperative that something be done to prevent general bankruptcy. The Government was appealed to. The Government did the usual thing. They discussed the matter for three months and concluded they could not solve the problems. Those who had tulips must lose and lose they did. This applied to nearly everyone. Holland suffered fearfully. Her people, many of them at least, had to begin the accumulation of savings or of fortunes all over again and for years the commerce of the nation languished.

There were numerous economic upheavals throughout Europe during the remainder of the 17th century. In 1640, Charles I sent British commerce into a tailspin by seizing the bullion deposited in the Tower of London. France in 1661 was in great distress due to an enormous trade imbalance with England, Holland, and Spain. In 1672, Charles II sent shock waves through the business community by refusing payment out of the exchequer. The first modern-day "run" on banks occurred when the Dutch fleet sailed into the Thames. Consternation reigned in London at the sound of their guns. Anyone who had any money at the time had it deposited with the goldsmiths—the bankers of their day. Unfortunately, the government had borrowed the money. The government didn't seem to offer a great deal of security at the time.

In the 18th century, the crisis of 1720 was the first general crisis throughout all of Europe. This crisis was precipitated by the collapse of speculative companies, the South Seas Company in England being one of them, supposedly organized for development in the New World among other ventures. This is known as the South Seas bubble era of speculation. Fortunes from all over Europe were lost as the companies proved to be ivory towered. Economic activity and speculation were muted for decades.

December 6, 1745, is known as "Black Friday." A rumor of French invasion touched off a panic. Citizens rushed to withdraw their money from the Bank of England. Virtually all businesses were forces to close down due to the crisis. Merchants hurriedly met and agreed to accept bank notes. A resolution was passed urging the citizens and all merchants to do the same. The resolution was signed by 1,140 businesses and depositors.

England was the victim of another crisis in 1772, which brought with it 525 corporate failures. After the signing of the treaty with America, England found itself again in crisis in 1783; Cornwallis had surrendered to Washington, and the British fleet had been conquered by the admiral of France. Peace brought new markets and a strain on British gold reserves and finances. The year 1789 brought with it the French Revolution and the commercial demise that was inevitable for that nation before its next great advance of Napoleonic conquest.

There were certainly also economic expansions and collapses in the Orient, Africa, the Middle East, and South America, about which we know little or nothing. Coming to the close of the 18th century of global economic history and looking back since the demise of Rome, we see that crises and depressions tended to be local or national in their scope of influence. Occasionally these downturns crossed national borders, but this was the exception, not the rule.

Most argue that there was not sufficient data available to show distinct economic and financial cycles until the end of the 18th century, although booms and busts have long been a reality of economic relations. Some argue that there was sufficient data to demonstrate regular cycles in early periods.

Evidence indicates that there has always been a rise and fall in the world's economies. Since late in the 18th century, when better records have been kept, the evidence is even more compelling. A disturbing and fascinating long-wave cycle of expansion and contraction has become increasingly obvious for those willing to take the time to examine the evidence.

Works Cited and Additional Sources

Lightner, Otto C. 1991. *The History of Business Depressions.* New York: Burt Franklin.

Bernstein, Jake. 1991. *The Handbook of Economic Cycles.* Homewood, IL: Business One Irwin.

Selfridge. *The Romance of Commerce.* John Lane Company.

2

A FASCINATING DISCOVERY

"He who floats with the current, who does not guide himself according to higher principles, who has no ideal, no convictions—such a man is a mere article of the world's furniture—a thing moved, instead of a living and moving being—an echo, not a voice."

Amiel

"The long waves, if existent at all, are a very important and essential factor in economic development, a factor the effects of which can be found in all the principal fields of social and economic life."

Kondratieff

Nikolai D. Kondratieff, born in 1892 in Russia, grew up and was educated during the turmoil of the fall of the Russian monarchy and the emergence of a communist totalitarian dictatorship. Kondratieff graduated from Petersburg University School of Law in 1915. Before radically changing his views, Kondratieff was a member of the left-wing Socialist Revolutionary Party in 1917.

Early on, Kondratieff's interests were turned toward the study of economics and markets, which proved to be his livelihood as well as contributing to his premature death. It was reported in an article on Kondratieff in *National Affairs* (1988, 56), that soon after the revolution, "Kondratieff was no longer a student with socialist-revolutionary leanings, but an eminent scientist, a shrewd and accurate analyst."

At some point, Kondratieff's interest turned from Soviet economic planning—he had worked to develop the first five-year agricultural plan—to the more fascinating analysis of the regular rise and fall of the international capitalist system. Kondratieff became the director of the Institute for Market Studies under the People's Commissariat for Finance.

Early on in his career, as Kondratieff looked over the history of the capitalist system and the data on developments in the global economy since the late 1700s, he saw something quite different from what his peers and predecessors had seen. Kondratieff saw emerging from prices, interest rates, production, and human nature the rise and fall of what has come to be known as the Kondratieff long-wave cycle. Just as most economists of his day and today, Kondratieff had limited his vision and study to short-term analysis and had never stepped back and taken in a sweeping, all-encompassing view of global economic history. His discovery surprised him.

Kondratieff formulated his views over a number of years. In a footnote at the end of his famous paper, "The Long Wave in Economic Life," which first introduced the notion of long waves to the world, Kondratieff (1951, 42) wrote, "I arrived at the hypothesis concerning the existence of long waves in the years 1919–1921." He noted that he had written the article during the winter and spring of 1925. In February 1926, Kondratieff read a paper on his findings at the Moscow Institute of Economics.

Kondratieff wrote of what he observed to be long-wave economic cycles (see Table 2.1). He observed two and one-half cycles. The first cycle began in a trough (economic low point) in 1789 and ended with a trough in the 1840s. He wrote of a plateau period, the long-wave fall season, that followed the advance or peak of the cycle. History indicates that the plateauing fall season always gives way to a long-wave winter season. Kondratieff himself never used the seasonal analogy.

To gain a clear understanding of the long-wave plateau, it might help to conceptualize a geographical plateau. You have a steep and lengthy climb to the top of a plateau, an area that brings apparent stability for a time. After crossing the plateau, you come to the edge where you face a steep drop and decline. In like fashion, the economy builds up and expands through the years with rising prices and increasing debt levels, climbing to great heights of output, production, and efficiency. After moving through great advances and expansion, the economy has outdone itself, quite literally. The economy then makes a gallant effort at trying to adjust through capital restructuring. This is the disinflationary fall plateau season of the long wave.

It would be nice if we could stay at these lofty heights forever. The problem is that the economy has been pushed too far and is producing too many goods in every area. With too many companies producing too much, you begin to see falling prices in raw-material sectors of the economy. The shift from an inflationary advance to a disinflationary plateau marks the changing of the long-wave season from summer into fall.

Falling raw material and commodity prices are first welcomed after coming through a period of inflation. During the fall there is the illusion that the economy is improving and becoming very stable since inflation is under control. The fall offers really only an Indian summer boom before the bust. The financial markets are flooded with cash during the fall because economic growth slows and expansion is no longer demanding as high a level of capital commitment. Almost every area of the economy has been stimulated beyond the world's true needs and demands.

Sure there is still some substantial development and real expansion going on in the fall, but overall the free-market system has taken the advance too far. Because of the great amount of cash

in the economy with no place to go, and due to increased corporate efficiency due to falling prices of raw materials, the fall season always sees booming stock markets throughout international
capital markets. Lower interest rates, disinflationary pressures,
and slowed outlays all have the effect of freeing cash for global
stock markets.

The second cycle observed by Kondratieff began its upswing
in the 1840s and hit the fall season in the early 1870s. After the
fall, it began its decline to the bottom of the long-wave winter
trough in 1896. The 1880s and early 1890s experienced a global
deflationary depression.

The third cycle began its spring season in 1896 and reached
the peak of its summer season in 1920. Kondratieff's research
covered this period. The cycle appears to have experienced its fall
season through the 1920s and shifted from fall to winter in the
early 1930s as international capital markets crashed, right on
schedule. Kondratieff (1951) acknowledged that the dates of turning and peaks are flexible, give or take a few years, and are not
intended to be dogmatically and rigidly interpreted.

After reviewing all the data and information he had collected,
Kondratieff (1951, 30–33) made the following observations,
which I quote from his interpreted article, "The Long Waves in
Economic Life," that was republished in Readings in Business
Cycle Theory. The original article in Russian was translated by
W.F. Stolper of Harvard.

(1) The movements of the series which we have examined
     running from the end of the 18th century to the present
     time show long cycles. Although the statistical-mathe-
     matical treatment of the series selected is rather compli-
     cated, the cycles discovered cannot be regarded as the
     accidental result of the methods employed. Against such
     an interpretation is to be set the fact that these waves have
     been shown with about the same timing in all the more
     important of the series examined.

(2) The cycles accelerate or retard the rate of growth in series that don't show a trend.

(3) There is a very close correspondence in the timing of the wave movements of the series in the individual countries, in spite of the difficulties present in the treatment of these data. Deviations from the general rule that prevail in the sequence of the cycles are very rare.

(4) Although for the time being we consider it to be impossible to fix exactly upon the years that marked the turning points of the long cycles, and although the method according to which the statistical data have been analyzed permits an error of five to seven years in the determination of the years of such turnings, the following limits of these cycles can nevertheless be presented as being those most probable:

First long wave   1. The rise lasted from the end of the 1780's or beginning of the 1790's until 1810–1817.

    2. The decline lasted from 1810–1817 until 1844–1851.

Second long wave   1. The rise lasted from 1844–1851 until 1870–1875.

    2. The decline lasted from 1870–1875 until 1890–1896.

Third long wave   1. The rise lasted from 1890–1896 until 1914–1920.

    2. The decline probably begins in the years 1914–1920.

(5) Naturally, the fact that the movement of the series examined runs in long cycles does not yet prove that such cycles also dominate the movement of all other series. Our investigation has also extended to series in which no waves were evident. On the other hand, it is by no means essential that the long waves embrace all series.

(6)   The long waves we have established relative to the series most important in economic life are international; and the timing of these cycles corresponds fairly well for European capitalistic countries. On the basis of the data that we have adduced, we can venture the statement that the same timing holds also for the United States.

Based on the series Kondratieff used, such as interest rates, government bond prices, and commodity prices, and his own conclusions, the evidence clearly suggests that the end of the third long-wave advance came around 1920. The fall season of the decline phase lasted from 1921 until 1930. The winter season lasted into the mid- to late-1940s.

World War II came within the long-wave winter season and helped to alleviate the economic stress of the downturn by cranking up the military industrial complex. The force and effect of war on the global economy must be recognized as an all-important element in the cycle.

The end of the third long-wave decline, based on interest rates and prices, appears to have come between 1945 and 1949. The latest long-wave spring season really didn't begin until the late 1940s. The fourth long-wave cycle advance, based on the evidence emphasized by Kondratieff's earlier work, began by 1949. Spring ended, and the summer season began in the mid-1960s and heated up with inflation in the 1970s. The global economy peaked its long-wave expansion growth in the 1980–1981 recession with a blowoff in prices and interest rates.

Evidence indicates we entered the long-wave fall season in the early 1980s. The 1980s and early 1990s were once again the disinflationary plateau of which Kondratieff wrote that is best understood as the fall season of the long wave. The plateau fall season appears to have lasted from 1981 to approximately 1995, although Japan appears to have already left the fall season and entered the winter season of the decline. Japan began the shift from the fall to the winter season when the Tokyo stock market

Table 2.1
The K Wave and Its Four Seasons
of Development

Important phases, dates and general trends

All dates are approximations; give or take two to three years

[Each K Wave season averages 12 to 16 years]

[Each K Wave season has four regular Kitchin Cycles that fluctuate from three to four years each in length from trough to trough or peak to peak]

The K Wave Spring Seasons

1789–1802
1845–1858
1896–1907
1949–1966
2006–2018?

- Trends During Spring: Stocks Up, Bonds Down, Commodities Up
- New Optimism Arises in General Population
- Economy Grows Solidly
- Stock Prices Rising Consistently
- Very Low Inflation But Steady Advance
- Raw Material and Commodity Prices Rise Very Slowly
- Real Estate Prices Rise Very Slowly
- Interest Rates Begin to Rise
- New Technologies and Inventions Creating Whole New Industries
- New Banking System Healthy with No Failures
- Recessions Shallow and Brief and Recoveries Strong & Long

The K Wave Summer Seasons

1803–1816
1859–1871
1908–1920
1966–1980
2018–2030?

- Trends During Summer: Stocks Down, Bonds Down, Commodities Up
- Inflation Heats Up
- Military Conflicts Arise
- Debt Levels Increasing
- Stocks Stagnate Nominally and Crash in Real Terms
- Rising Expectations
- Rising Prices Coax Industry into Overshooting World Demand
- Runaway Inflation In Late Summer
- Raw Materials and Commodity Prices Spike Up at End of Summer
- Farm Land Prices Peak
- Interest Rates Peak
- Rate of Long-Wave Economic Growth and Expansion Peaks
- Primary Recession at End of K Wave Summer

The K Wave Fall Seasons

1817–1829
1872–1884
1921–1932
1981–1995?
2030–2042?

- Trends During Fall: Stocks Up, Bonds Up, Commodities Down
- Fall Comes After Primary Long-Wave Recession
- Worldwide Overproduction/Overcapacity

- High Debt Levels Continue to Grow Throughout
- Global System Awash in Cash
- Financial Speculation
- Economic Growth Pace Slows Significantly from Long-Wave Advance
- Interest Rates Decline
- Global Stock Markets Boom
- Laissez-Faire Political Posture and Deregulation
- Early Deflation and Disinflation
- Falling Raw Material, Commodity and Farm Land Prices
- Commercial and Residential Real Estate Prices Peak in Late Fall
- Expansion by Acquisition/Takeover
- Slower Capital Investment Pace
- Banking System Weakens and Failures Begin
- Trade Protection Pressures Build
- Psychological Optimism for Society (Roaring '20s and '80s)
- Economic Growth Slower than Spring and Summer
- Greed Runs Wild
- Individual Investors Follow the Herd into Stocks
- Final Speculative Stock Blowoff at End of Fall
- Record New Stock Offerings

The K Wave Winter Seasons

1830–1844
1885–1896
1932–1948
1995–2007?
2042–2054?

- Trends During Winter: Stocks Down, Bonds Up, Commodities Down
- Global Stock Markets Enter Extended Bear Markets

- Interest Rates Spike In Early Winter Then Decline Throughout
- New Stock Offerings End
- Economic Growth Slow or Negative During Much of Winter
- Some Runaway Deflation and Falling Prices
- Commercial and Residential Real Estate Prices Fall
- Trade Conflicts Worsen
- Social Upheaval and Society Becomes Negative
- Bankruptcies Accelerate and High Debt Eliminated by Bankruptcy
- Stock Markets Reach Bottom and Begin New Bulls in Winter
- Overcapacity/Overproduction Purged by Obsolescence and Failure
- Greed is Purged From System
- Recessions Long and Recoveries Brief
- Free Market System Blamed and Socialist Solutions Offered
- Banking System Shakey New One Introduced
- New Technology and Inventions Developed and Implemented
- Real Estate Prices Find Bottom
- National Fascist Political Tendencies
- New Work Ethics Develop Since Jobs are Scarce
- Interest Rates and Prices Bottom
- Debt Levels Very Low After Defaults and Bankruptcy
- View of Future at Low Ebb
- Bright Spots Appear and Social Mood Improves
- There is a Clean Economic Slate to Build On
- Investors are Very Conservative and Risk Averse
- A New Economy Begins to Emerge

2.1 Idealized K Wave

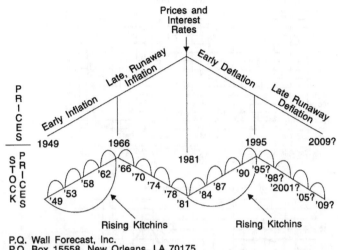

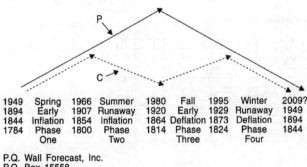

P.Q. Wall Forecast, Inc.
P.O. Box 15558, New Orleans, LA 70175
1-800-259-0088

2.2 K Wave Seasons

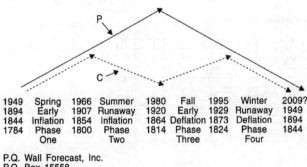

1949	Spring	1966	Summer	1980	Fall	1995	Winter	2009?
1894	Early	1907	Runaway	1920	Early	1929	Runaway	1949
1844	Inflation	1854	Inflation	1864	Deflation	1873	Deflation	1894
1784	Phase	1800	Phase	1814	Phase	1824	Phase	1844
	One		Two		Three		Four	

P.Q. Wall Forecast, Inc.
P.O. Box 15558
New Orleans, LA 70175
1-800-259-0088

"P" is essentially price, the true price of everything including interest rates (the price of renting money) and real wages (the true price of labor.) "C" is corporate efficiency (and hence the price of stocks,) and just like physical efficiency it is greatest in spring and fall when it is neither too hot (runaway inflation) nor too cold (runaway deflation.)

2.3 Kondratieff's Original Charts

Index Numbers of Commodity Prices

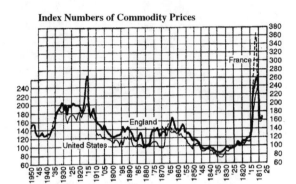

Quotations of Interest Bearing Securities

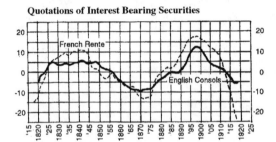

Wages in England

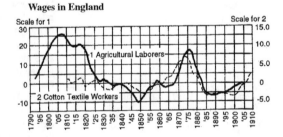

French Foreign Trade

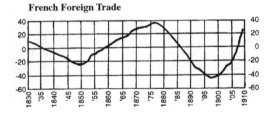

cracked and began to tumble in December of 1989. Sometimes it can get exceptionally cold in late fall.

Remember that all nations do not yet move in perfect unison within the K Wave. One day they may. The free-market economy is increasingly tightly bound together by the ever-growing strength of the global marketplace. Global financial markets and the debt-ridden economy are therefore able to reach higher levels of excess than in the past before their collapse. The emerging global marketplace allows the global economy to expand further and reach far greater heights than nations reached independently during past cycles. However, the global economy and close association of nations cannot stop the inevitable.

The latest winter season can be expected to last from approximately 1995 to around 2005. Many countries and markets will bottom and be pulling into the next advance long before the end of winter, even as early as the year 2000.

Kondratieff expressed the belief that the dynamics of free-market economics are not linear (moving in a straight line) and continually progressing upward. Kondratieff clearly saw the world economy as cyclical (advancing in cycles). He (Kondratieff 1951) acknowledged that each cycle advanced and developed the economy further and brought it to new heights, but clearly taught that this advance was a cyclical advance and not a linear advance.

He taught and believed in the intermediate 7–11-year cycle that many economists believe in today. However, Kondratieff taught that reducing the system to this cycle only was simplistic and that a broader long-wave scope should be superimposed onto the development of the system. He (Kondratieff 1951, 35) recognized and was open to the necessity of flexibility in the system and said, "the long cycle fluctuates between 45 and 60 years."

Here he also pointed out the flexibility of the intermediate 7–11-year cycle, relative to its length, is far greater than the K Wave. Another cycle accepted today and recognized by Kondratieff is based on the work of Joseph Kitchin who showed a cycle that fluctuates between three and four and one-half years. Relative to its length, the K Wave is more precise than smaller cycles.

There is evidence that there are four Kitchin cycles in each of the four seasons of the long-wave cycle. This means there are sixteen Kitchin cycles in each Kondratieff cycle.

The foundation to Kondratieff's theory, and the element considered to be one of the most important aspects of his research, is the cycle's impact on the rise and fall of prices. The movement of prices is key to understanding the K Wave and the effect the K Wave has on investments. Raw material and commodity prices in recent decades have closely followed the outline Kondratieff laid out for the rise and fall of the cycle. Raw material and commodities include wheat, oil, iron, coal, beef, cotton, soybeans, lumber, and pork bellies.

National Affairs (1988, 58), a former prominent Soviet publication, reported that Kondratieff

> like few economists of the time—perceived that the market was irreplaceable as a meeting place for demand and supply, as a procedure for comparing consumers' desires with production's potential. Kondratieff—again like few people in both our country and the West—realized the importance of prices as a most reliable and irreplaceable information system telling producers what consumers want from them.

Prices reflect the nature of the cycle. Raw materials and commodities, especially agricultural commodities, constantly rise during the long-wave advance and peak in price during the primary recession and the shift from the summer to the fall season. Clearly, this was evidenced in the 1920 recession and the 1980–1981 recession. The collapse of raw material and commodity prices usher in the fall period of early deflation and disinflation in the economy. When this occurs, the agricultural and raw materials industries are thrown into deep recession and depression.

Remember what happened in the oil and agricultural industries globally in the 1980s. They were also in a depression in the 1920s, long before the rest of the economy took the plunge into depression in the 1930s.

The deflation doesn't hit retail prices and wholesale prices until the end of the fall plateau and the beginning of winter when the secondary recession pushes the economy over the edge and into the long-wave decline. Then prices decline until the long-wave winter reaches bottom—sooner or later. It is also important to note that deflation or falling prices hit agricultural land during the primary recession and the beginning of the fall season. Deflation and falling prices in commercial and residential real estate prices come at the end of the fall season and accelerate as the long-wave winter sets in and as the speculative bubbles around the globe begin to burst.

Falling prices of raw materials and commodities are an important point because they lend energy to the financial speculation and booming stock markets that take place during the fall season. The wholesalers who sell to the retailers and the retailers who sell to the final consumer experience increased efficiency during the fall season. This is because the costs to produce the goods they sell are going down. Remember raw materials prices are falling; therefore, the costs of production for everything from a loaf of bread to a car is going down. Did gas prices at the pump ever fall as fast as the price of oil? No way. The middlemen and retailers were making a killing while the companies that pulled the raw material out of the ground were in deep trouble.

During the fall season, the long-wave consumer spending and demand has yet to peak and keeps wholesale and retail prices rising slightly during the fall. The raw materials industry is getting hammered while the wholesalers and retailers are watching their profit margins explode as consumer optimism surges with the debt binge. Improving margins for most companies along with a global economic system awash in cash after a long-wave advance creates the financial boom of the long-wave fall season. Society is coaxed into a natural speculative frenzy that ends in a bust. Eventually, the collapse of prices hits the wholesale and retail level. All the debt that must be paid off with high retail revenues begins to unravel and default in the long-wave winter, just as it happened to the raw-material producers when the prices they received fell during the fall season.

An example of this is when oil began a rapid decline in the early 1980s. It collapsed in 1986 and threatened the stability of the global banking system. Major drops in the price of oil may be the force that ushers in the next international banking crisis in this long-wave decline. Governments will try and prop up the price of oil to avoid this from happening—even if it means war.

The price of oil affects the price of almost everything else. Lower prices sound good for consumers, but eventually it is lower prices that bring a leveraged global economy to its knees. Global assets are financed based on inflated values and anticipated future rising prices during the good times of the long-wave advance. When the long-wave decline sets in and asset values fall, the international banking system that financed these assets faces potential collapse.

We are all aware that a price collapse in every sector of the world economy will bring the stock markets crashing and almost all global economic expansion to a halt. The incredible amount of debt throughout every area of the economy only magnifies the collapse.

Kondratieff (1951) was quick to bring wages and the amount of global trade into the long wave. Kondratieff analyzed the weekly levels of wages in the English cotton and textile industry as well as the number of agricultural workers. To observe the relationship of trade to the long wave, Kondratieff looked at the sum of French exports and imports. True to form, the levels of trade rose as the cycle rose and declined as the cycle declined.

Kondratieff (1951) got very brave in his analysis of the capitalist system and took a look into production. His analysis of prices, interest rates, and wages he considered to be value based characteristics and felt the true test would come in a purely physical (production) series (year-to-year studies of the same group).

For his (Kondratieff 1951) analysis, he picked coal production and consumption, and the production of pig iron and lead in England. The physical series held true. Although sections of the data were missing, there appeared to be an obvious long-wave trend.

Kondratieff (1951) mentioned other series in which the long wave appeared evident. A number of such series were as follows: the deposits and the portfolio of the bank of France; deposits at the French banks, English imports, and total English foreign trade; coal production in the United States and Germany, as well as the whole world; lead production in the United States; the number of spindles in the cotton industry in the United States; cotton acreage in the United States; and oat acreage in France.

A major reason for Kondratieff's (1951) conclusions on the long wave come from the historical rise and fall of interest rates. He believed analysis of interest rates should be based on yields from government bonds because of their stability relative to other instruments, so he looked at yields and prices from the French *rente* and the English *consol* (both are government bonds). True to form, the price of bonds follow a long-wave cycle.

Although Kondratieff did not use the United States's yields and prices, they closely follow the French and English model. Interest rates reach their peak as the long-wave summer season peaks before the primary recession and beginning of the fall. Bond prices reach their lows as rates reach their peak with the beginning of fall, and bond prices reach highs close to the end of the winter season of the long wave.

Of course interest rates have a direct impact on economic activity and the expansion of all sectors of the economy. The highest interest rates in the cycle indicate the long-wave advance. Summer has ended, and the fall has begun; interest rates collapse. Remember the high interest rates in the early 1980s before the collapse? The same thing occurred in the early 1920s. This was a sure sign we had entered the fall season of the cycle and were headed for global financial speculation. Fall is the only season when stocks and bonds boom together.

In observing the fluctuation of interest rates, Kondratieff (1951, 26) remarked, "The periods of these cycles agree rather closely with the corresponding periods in the movements of wholesale commodity prices."

After Kondratieff had exhausted his statistical studies of the long-wave cycle, he began to look at the empirical (practical, non-scientific) characteristics of the rise and fall in free-market capitalist countries.

He (Kondratieff 1951, 33–34) introduced this area of his study with the following statement:

> From another point of view, the historical material relating to the development of economic and social life as a whole confirms the hypothesis of long waves. Several general propositions which we have arrived at concerning the existence and importance of long waves are as follows.
>
> (1)   The long waves belong really to the same complex dynamic process in which the intermediate cycles of the capitalistic economy with their principal phases of upswing and depression run their course. These intermediate cycles, however, secure a certain stamp from the very existence of the long waves. Our investigation demonstrates that during the rise of the long waves, years of prosperity are more numerous, whereas years of depression predominate during the downswing.
> (2)   During the recession of the long waves, agriculture, as a rule, suffers especially pronounced and long depression. This was what happened after the Napoleonic Wars; it happened again from the beginning of the 1870s onward; and the same can be observed in the years after World War I.

(3) During the recession of the long waves, an especially large number of important discoveries and inventions in the technique of production and communication are made, which, however, are usually applied on a large scale only at the beginning of the next long upswing.

(4) At the beginning of a long upswing, gold production increases as a rule and the world market for goods is generally enlarged.

(5) It is during the period of the rise of the long waves, i.e., during the period of high tension in the expansion of economic forces, that, as a rule, the most disastrous and extensive wars and revolutions occur.

Kondratieff (1951, 34) concluded, "It is to be emphasized that we attribute to these recurring relationships an empirical character only, and that we do not by any means hold that they contain the explanation of the long waves."

In Kondratieff's discussions on the nature of long waves, he emphasized the relationship of gold to the cycle. He realized that gold is a commodity and has a cost of production. Once the economy has moved into the decline, the cost of production is at a low point. There is naturally going to be more gold production because gold will have its greatest purchasing power at the time it's cheapest to produce.

Because of the complexity of gold and its pricing in a volatile economy, I will spend Chapter 18 discussing gold's relation to the cycle—especially the present winter season.

Kondratieff's (1951, 41–42) conclusions in his presentation on the long wave emphasize his increasing conviction of its existence while at the same time hinting of the question as to its origin:

> The objections to the regular cyclical character of the long waves, therefore, seem to be unconvincing. We believe ourselves justified in saying that the long waves, if existent at all, are a very important and essential factor in economic devel-

opment, a factor the effects of which can be found in all the principal fields of social and economic life. Even granting the existence of long waves, one is, of course, not justified in believing that economic dynamics consist only in fluctuations around a certain lever. The course of economic activity represents beyond doubt a process of development, but this development obviously proceeds not only through intermediate waves but also through long ones. In alerting the existence of long waves and in denying that they arise out of random causes, we are also of the opinion that the long waves arise out of causes which are inherent in the essence of the capitalistic economy. This naturally leads to the question as to the nature of these causes.

In 1988, *National Affairs* (1988, 55) finally reported that the day in 1926 when Kondratieff read his paper on long waves became, "renowned in the history of world economic thinking." His work did not record the cycle's entire fall plateau season through the decade of the 1920s; however, the drastic global economic contraction and market crashes in the early 1930s were projected by his research.

In the late 1920s, Kondratieff had become one of the most well-known Soviet economist in the world. He was editor of a prominent economic journal and was an elected member of several scientific societies abroad. *National Affairs* reported that he was a member of the American Economic Association, the American Academy of Social Sciences, the Association for Agricultural Questions, various Russian sociological and statistical societies, and London's economic and statistical societies.

History has shown that most prophets are rejected in their native land. Nikolai Kondratieff proved to be no exception to this rule. Stalin enjoyed the idea of the eventual collapse of the free-world's economy. However, there was much more to Kondratieff's theory. Quite obviously the results of Kondratieff's research did not sit well with the Stalin regime, nor did his struggle for the introduction of market mechanisms and more independence in the Soviet agricultural system. Stalin was outraged with Kondratieff's prediction that the free market would come back stronger than ever after being purged of its inefficiencies, debt, and excesses. Kondratieff was rewarded in the usual Stalin style with arrest and imprisonment in 1930. His work and research was banned in the Soviet Union.

After his arrest and imprisonment, Kondratieff became a persona non grata in the Soviet Union. For all practical purposes, he vanished from the world scene, but his long-wave theory remained. Much of his work was lost or destroyed. One of his books, which was written while he was in prison, has yet to be published.

Alexander Solzhenitsyn, in his book, *The Gulag Archipelago,* wrote of Kondratieff's death, which came in 1938, while Kondratieff was in solitary confinement. Kondratieff's death came only after the fulfillment of his prophecy of the inevitable downturn of Western economies, which took the disturbing form of the Great Depression.

It was only in the late 1980s that Kondratieff's name, work, and ideas began to circulate again in Soviet literature. A *Forbes* article (Fuhrman 1988, 34) on Kondratieff also reported that, "Banned since 1930, Kondratieff's writings have begun to circulate freely again in the Soviet Union since this summer . . . the Soviet Government has published, for the first time, a book of Kondratieff's essays. Kondratieff's prison writings are being sorted through. The economist's daughter, Elena, has been making public appearances in Moscow."

Most shocking are the fundamental changes the writings of Kondratieff have made in Russian economic thinking. Andrey Poletayev is the Russian economist leading the effort in the resurrection of Kondratieff's work. Poletayev told *Forbes* (Fuhrman 1988, 34), "Marx' theory of the inevitable decline of capitalism isn't accepted by any of the influential economists in the Soviet

Union now ... There is also a transition in the highest levels ... toward accepting that the capitalist economies are self-regulating, not self-destructive."

The *Forbes* (Fuhrman, 35) article noted, as the Soviet Union was rapidly unraveling:

> In abandoning a bankrupt socialism, the Soviet rulers need a native prophet to justify new policies. They have found him in the long-dead Nikolai Kondratieff." The story went on to say, "Nikolai Dimitriyevich Kondratieff is respectable again in the Soviet Union. Thanks to perestroika, the reputation of the famed originator of the Kondratieff long-wave theory of economics has been rehabilitated.

Kondratieff clearly believed that the causes of the long wave are inherent within the capitalist free-market system. The long wave appears to be an integral part of the capitalist system and is the market's way of cleaning out the impurities that will always build up. The buildup of debt and the overly speculative spirit as well as overproduction and inflation have to be purged from the system for it to get a fresh start.

Someone will invariably say, "Kondratieff wrote this theory in 1925; this is another time, the age of the microchip and fine tuned monetary control. Surely you don't think we will see the full extent of the decline of the fourth Kondratieff long-wave cycle in the global economy?"

The cycle Kondratieff wrote about—that hard evidence suggests exists—is beyond the reach of innovation and monetary control. No more than a meteorologist can control the path of a hurricane, can the Federal Reserve, the World Bank, or anyone else control the inevitable ebb and flow of the Kondratieff long wave.

Weather satellites are the highest technology in the prediction of hurricanes, but do they prevent the coast from being smashed by high winds and waves? The answer is, of course, no, but there is a lesson to be learned here. The satellite, if heeded, can save valuable property and possessions and prevent needless pain.

Likewise, the Federal Reserve can lessen the impact of a decline with intelligent decision making, but they cannot change the inevitable. We all tend to shun bad news, acting as though it does not exist, especially during times of plenty. Anyone who speaks of bad times to come is avoided and ignored. However, these are the ones who could smile in the 1930s, watching their lot increase, while those who had been enjoying the good life a few years earlier were scrambling to save the devalued remains of their lifelong investments. This will also be the case during the latest long-wave decline.

Who in the mainstream of business in recent years can remember the pain of the Great Depression? Very few. A new generation of optimists and risk-takers fueled the economy, having no recollection of the last decline or understanding of the dangers of excessive debt.

One is accurate in saying that the present is extremely different from when Kondratieff formulated his theory. But, are the differences truly deep in terms of the fundamental structure of the global economy, or are they only surface differences that cover the same old long-wave face?

Works Cited and Additional Sources

Fuhrman, Peter. 1988. "Another Stake Through Stalin's Heart." *Forbes.* December 26.

Kondratieff, Nikolai D. 1951. "The Long Waves In Economic Life." *Readings in Business Cycle Theory.* Translated by W. F. Stolper. Homewood: Richard D. Irwin.

1988. "Purged Economist Kondratyev Market Ideas Hailed." *National Affairs.* Reprinted from Sotsialisticheskaya Industriya (in Russian.) Moscow.

Sterman, John D. "The Economic Long Wave: Theory and Evidence." Working Paper 1656–85 at M.I.T. Cambridge, Massachusetts. 1985.

Forrester, Jay W. "Managing the Next Decade in the Economy." Address to the Joint Economic Committee of Congress in Washington, D.C. Germeshausen Professor of Management, Sloan School of Management, M.I.T.

3

MODERN TIMES

"When business embarks on a rampage which does not help humanity to live and GROW—when it pushes beyond this range of usefulness and overproduces human needs—or when it falls behind and outlives its usefulness—it runs into trouble of some kind. And when the business tree is crowded with these dead or dying branches, the tree as a whole begins to suffer. We run into a business depression or plunge into industrial war to shake the rotten branches down."

V.C. Kitchin

To fully appreciate Kondratieff's observations and the foundations of K Wave theory, it is useful to briefly review highlights of the economic and financial history of the period to which K Wave theory is applied. This exercise will provide solid K Wave guideposts for the reader. Here we will examine chronologically some of the key events and developments in the four long-wave cycles that have emerged from 1789 to the present and that were presented in the last chapter.

This review is skewed toward U.S. history, although close examination of other capitalist nations will reveal developments with a similar seasonal K Wave resonance in the same time frames.

Before examining the advance of the first long-wave, which began in 1789, it is enlightening to examine some of the facts that indicate a K Wave winter was in force and ending just prior. Following on the heels of the Revolutionary War, there was a brief time of prosperity and improving economic conditions. The relief of the end of conflict often brings spurts of economic activity. During the three years 1782, 1783, and 1784, after the war, conditions were prosperous. The jubilant feeling of victory brought optimism. There was also a great deal of money left in the country by the British and French armies. This post-war prosperity did not last long, however, ending with the depression of 1785–1789. Money quickly left the United States to pay for imported goods from Europe.

Remember that the primary force of the K Wave is prices. After the surge in post-war economic activity, which peaked in 1785, a sharp decline came in virtually all prices. America was a nation hardly three years old when its people were introduced to the hard reality of the international power play of nation against nation in international commerce. Scarcely weaned, the United States was banned from trade in the British West Indies in 1784. Our young nation was elated by its newfound freedom. But it was short-lived; soon the bills had to be paid in international markets.

American merchants found themselves embarrassed when they had no money to cover credit purchases from overseas. The government was forced to beg for loans from foreign governments. Perhaps in its scope and scale, this crisis was greater than the Great Depression, relatively speaking. Benjamin Franklin couldn't get the money he asked for from France because they were having problems as well. It appears as though a K Wave cycle winter was in force and fortunately coming to an end.

A clue that this was an ending K Wave winter was that during this time the first protective tariffs against foreign competition were established by the new U.S. government. This legacy haunts us today and plays an extremely important role in the long-wave cycle. It is important to point out that these tariffs came from the support of none other than the manufacturers, without concern for the consumer—a tradition still kept today.

An interesting side note for our protectionist warlords of today is that America ran a trade deficit for 59 years after its freedom from England. The year 1840 was the first year we showed a surplus; the figures were $113,896,000 in exports and $107,142,000 in imports. We were insightful enough to see that profits made on the goods sold here were reloaned and reinvested in America. Maybe we could learn more than a few political lessons from our founding fathers.

These were trying times. As European manufacturers, while selling their goods in America, were attempting to stifle start-up manufacturing in America. The historian Lightner (1922, 94) recorded a humorous account of the ends to which the British were willing to go to secure their markets:

> In 1787 a Philadelphia man came into possession of two carding and spinning machines which were supposed to save the labor of 120 men a day. These machines were purchased by an agent of a British manufacturer and shipped back to Liverpool, the object being to nip American manufacturing in the bud.

No doubt this is a comical story when considering the awesome force and world power the United States manufacturing sector grew to be in subsequent years. We hear rumors today of Exxon supposedly buying up 200 mpg engines. Will we one day look back in comical relief from the 21st century as we scoot along at 200 mph in our electric cars, seeing the humor only Father Time possesses?

The depression of 1785 brought on conditions that spawned the first American insurrection in the form of Shay's Rebellion. This rebellion had 15,000 supporters. Being blessed with far more zeal than leadership, they were soon dispersed. Times were hard for our new nation, to say the least, but we were a nation with a vision. A K Wave winter was ending.

It is interesting to see that major financial changes come at the bottom of long-wave declines when nations are in crisis. In the works for a few years, in 1791 the U.S. government chartered the first bank of the United States. There was solid evidence in prices and interest rates of the beginning advance of the first long-wave cycle. It would be safe to say that the world was entering a new era of international relations and economic development late in the 18th century.

The constitutions had gone into effect in 1789, which had granted government the right to coin money. Before long, the United States was back in business with an inflationary money system and growing economy. A K Wave spring had begun.

This time marks the beginning rise in international prices that peaked in 1814. This period represents the spring and summer advance of the first recorded K Wave cycle in the global economy. A growing economy without inflation and a free banking gold-based money system would have been more attractive and better for the people in the long run, but government was learning quickly that it could buy power and votes with money using a banking system the people don't understand.

Trade for the United States exploded in the early 1790s due to the war that broke out between France and England, which the rest of Europe was soon drawn into. During this period, America was master of the seas. Trade flourished for the new country. A large and steady demand of our agricultural produce by nations at war kept the shipping lanes busy from the states to the old world. Foreign trade was multiplied four times in the decade.

During the advance, the United States experienced a recession in 1808 and 1809 due to a well-intended embargo by Jefferson. This embargo was created in response to Napoleon's decrees against neutral trade. Recessions are brief during K Wave advances. As an illustration of what trade wars can do to an economy, it is important to note that U.S. exports fell from $108,300,000 to $22,400,000 annually during this embargo. This was far greater proportionately and took place much more abruptly than any business decline in American history. Jefferson gave in to pressure and lifted the embargo, and business soon returned during this K Wave advance.

The year 1812 found us once again at war with England. Washington was captured by the British on August 24, 1814, sending shock waves through global financial markets. We rebounded quickly after the war, which had been a humiliating draw at best even with our excellent showing led by future president Jackson at the Battle of New Orleans.

An economic rebound in Europe did not last very long after the Napoleonic Wars had ended. Soon after the relief of the end of the war had passed, Europe was in the midst of a severe depression. Led by France, Europe entered the disinflationary fall season of the decline of the first long-wave cycle between 1813 and 1815. The United States followed suit in the year 1818. It should be noted that the United States didn't enter the decline until a few years after most of Europe. There is often a number of years between nations moving into a new K Wave season.

It is important to note that this period represents the beginning of the fall season of the K Wave decline. This particular fall season was more severe than more recent fall seasons because the economy was almost entirely agriculturally based at the time. Agriculture suffers most during the K Wave fall, ahead of the rest of the economy, which suffers most in the K Wave winter season. When an economy is less dependent on its agriculture, it is reasonable to expect that the fall season will be more mild and winter will be more severe.

There had been a general expansion of business for the decades leading up to this period of decline. In light of long-wave theory, the reasons for this decline, as presented by Lightner

(1922, 117–118), are fascinating: "A depression had to come for several reasons: first, as a reflection of European troubles; second, a stoppage of overproduction; and third, to get money on a better basis." The comparison of the global conditions of this K Wave declining period with the situation in recent years are all too obvious. Even with a clear understanding of the long-wave cycle theory and its predictable outcome, the similarities still provide troubling insight.

News spread across the American states in 1818 that the banks were in critical condition. It seems that the central bank of the United States, which had been the pet project of Alexander Hamilton before being silenced by Aaron Burr, had created serious trouble in the economy. The inflationary tendencies of the bank had run full course. Banks couldn't return the gold that had been deposited for the simple reason that they had loaned out far more money than there was gold to back up. Attempts to shore up the system failed, and the banks greatly restricted their loans. Credits and loans to business and agriculture were curtailed.

This period marks the first widespread financial panic in American history. In 1819, a depression was well underway. Banks began to fail and shut their doors. Globally the picture was much the same, as Europe had led the way into the depression and economic downturn a few years earlier.

After rising since 1789, "the four years between 1817 and 1821 the holders of property in the United States were supposed to have suffered a depreciation of nearly $800 million." K Wave decline deflation. "General bankruptcy spread its darkness over the land; many of the wealthiest families in America were reduced to poverty." In Europe, the story was the same. Average working men and their families suffered for want of bread, let alone meat. Development was abandoned. Scenes of national distress ensued.

We see a number of recessions on the way to the bottom of the first long-wave decline. The year 1825 saw the collapse of cotton prices in England and subsequently the collapse of banks in New Orleans. Note that the long-wave decline doesn't come all at one time or hit one location. It was spread out over a number of years and started at different times in different countries. The New Orleans crisis lasted only a few months and order was soon restored. A recession from 1837 to 1839 was due almost entirely to banking speculation and crop failures. There was a brief period of inflation before U.S. wholesale prices dropped to their lowest points of the cycle in the late 1830s to mid-1840s.

The bottom of the first long-wave decline of Kondratieff's research came during the early- to mid-1840s. The economy began to expand after this bottom as the next long-wave advance got underway. There was a recession in 1847 that was short-lived due to the discovery of gold in California, which restored enthusiasm to all financial markets and confidence in general. The period between 1837 and 1857 is considered the "Golden Age" in U.S. history due to the great gold discoveries. Gold has always taken on new importance at the bottom of the long-wave decline.

Observing history, we see that recessions during long-wave advances are short, whereas recessions or depressions during long-wave declines are longer. The United States suffered another brief recession in 1857. The amount of money in circulation during this period had risen greatly, including both gold and bank notes. Speculation both in land and industrial development increased drastically.

The Golden Age had seen enormous advances in the accumulation of wealth in this country and was accompanied by an increase in many prices. Records show that during the period 1850–1857 President Buchanan calculated the production of gold in the United States at $400 million. This same period had seen a doubling of banks in the country and an explosion of railroad construction. The United States had seven-ninths of the world's railroad mileage. Clearly, the second long-wave advance identified by Kondratieff was in full swing.

Investors and the public were investing in inflated future expectations. Excessive optimism ruled the minds of investors. There are incredible stories about banking conditions during this time.

One account tells of a bank examiner as he traveled through the Midwest. The banks knew his travel plans and had the same gold coin follow him around to be whisked in the back door of the banks he visited and quickly deposited in the vault. There was a vast amount of fraud and circulation of bad bank notes. It makes you think of many of the crisis shenanigans that went on in the 1980s in the U.S. banking system—only with a few high-tech twists.

The *Nichols' Bank Note Reporter* carried 5,400 descriptions of false money in 1858. This crisis and panic was due to speculation and overexpansion of credit in a K Wave summer season. Prices were rising due to the enormous output of gold from California and Australia. However, it is generally accepted that a single incident pricked the bubble.

The Ohio Life Insurance Company had $5 million tied up in railroad loans. Their New York agent defaulted, causing the failure of the company with large liabilities. The dominos were set in motion, and one institution after another followed suit. Many eastern railroads failed. In 1857, the United States witnessed almost 5,000 corporate failures. It was one of the more severe recessions during a long-wave summer advance and is comparable to the 1973–1974 recession and banking crisis.

The resilience of the U.S. economy and the long-wave advance helped the United States make a quick comeback from the recession in 1857. By 1860, things were back to normal with business as well as prices on the rise, in tune with the long-wave pattern of an advance.

The first half of the year 1860 saw business running as usual, but as the election drew near, the storm clouds began to form on the horizon. Business began to slow as a result of heightened tension in both the North and South. November saw the election of Abraham Lincoln, and business came to near standstill awaiting the action he would take.

December 20, 1860, saw the secession of South Carolina from the Union, which proved the beginning of wild confusion in financial markets. "Bankers and financiers the country over perceived the gravity of the situation. They feared that the nation's trade would collapse and the whole framework of our political and financial system would be in danger," according to Lightner (1922, 149–150).

The lines were soon drawn in the economic heat of a K Wave summer. In 1861, the South stopped payment on all financial obligations to the North. It is estimated that the amount of southern indebtedness to the North was $2 billion. The war was filled with economic and financial uncertainty. When peace came in 1865, the nation was relieved of the stress of war. Business in the North revived very quickly, but the South was held responsible for repaying many debts it had assumed to finance the war. The South was in deep depression for a number of years. In time, the wheels of commerce began to roll as the preserved union reentered the world market.

The United States saw a peak in prices in 1864 due to war demands, while European prices climbed until 1873. The K Wave summer in the United States had ended, and fall had begun. In Europe, a K Wave summer lingered. This marks the period of the shift in the second long-wave from summer to fall.

The United States faced a small recession in 1869 due mainly to speculation in gold. September 24, 1869, was known as "Black Friday" due to the crash in the gold market (This crash is comparable to the gold price crash in the early 1980s as the early global disinflation and deflation gets started). European prices held up longer. There were a number of failures during this time, but the panic soon passed and business was back to normal.

There had been a steady global advance in the long wave since the mid-1840s. We see this advance beginning to peak internationally in the early- to mid-1870s, with world prices at their highest levels since the early 1800s. The mid-1870s to the mid-1880s represent the global fall season plateau of the second long-wave cycle that Kondratieff's discovered.

Economic expansion and contraction were increasingly being seen on an international basis at this point. A global economy was emerging. The effects were sobering.

Lightner (1922, 160) observed that internationally:

> Every line of industry had been stimulated beyond its needs in anticipation of still greater profits. Borrowers went heavily into debt, paying high rates of interest, to develop new industrial enterprises with the inevitable consequences of overproduction. The depression of 1873 was marked by failures and bankruptcy of many banks and business houses all over the country. This was a worldwide depression. It began in Vienna in May, 1873, spreading through Europe, particularly to London, England, Germany, Italy, Russia and South America. Although it was said to begin in Vienna, London was the real leader in terms of this period representing the peak of the British Empire.

The global recession/depression of 1873–1878 (the equivalent of the global 1980–1981 recession) marked the beginning of the fall plateau phase of the second long-wave cycle decline. In the United States, there were over 20,000 business failures and money loss of a billion dollars. Over three million people lost their jobs. Internationally, prices began to slide at this time and did not reach their bottom until the end of the K Wave winter season in 1896.

During the fall and winter season decline of this second K Wave decline, there were recessions in 1873, 1878, 1884, and 1889. The years 1893 to 1895 brought an acute recession/depression that proved to be the force that bottomed the great long-wave cycle.

The industrialization of the world made this recession in the 1890s unusually difficult, with large amounts of people being thrown out of work in industrialized regions. This brought on severely depressed conditions that would not have had as severe effects on a population that wasn't centralized for industrial output. During this time, great industrial centers were emerging in the Northeast of the United States that were extremely vulnerable to recessions. However, coming out of this setback, America and the world were in an advancing upswing of the long wave that would see the international marketplace reach such levels as were never before dreamed possible.

A new K Wave advance and spring season, the third revealed in Kondratieff's research, began in the late 1890s. International finance witnessed the dawn of a new era of growth and prosperity. Even World War I proved to slow the advance of the new world economy for only a short season. Of course the war had drastic effects on European industry, but they revived fairly quickly.

The upswing of the third long wave was noted by a number of brief recessions. A recession in 1903 was attributed to the U.S. monetary policy initiated in 1896. There was a large drop in stocks on all the exchanges, but the industrial machinery of the Western world soon pulled us through and had us on the move again in a long-wave advance.

The United States suffered a slight financial panic in 1907 that was used as the impetus to bring about the passage of the Federal Reserve Act. With the outbreak of World War I in 1914, international financial markets were in confusion, and every stock exchange in the world was closed. Financial markets soon regained stability, but business was hampered by the war.

Large amounts of gold were recalled from the United States that were owed to Europe; but as we began to export war materiel, the gold flowed back. The panic brought by the war caused a recession in the United States. This recession was brief for America as orders began pouring in from Europe in 1915.

You will note that war tends to come during the advance of the long wave.

In 1920–1921 we had the fall recession that kicked off the fall season of the third K Wave, and the resulting disinflation it caused. Commodity prices dropped significantly in the first few years of the decade and then held up until 1929 when the bottom fell out of world prices. The United States had 50 percent of the world's gold in it vaults in 1920. This gave us the feeling of security. The recession of 1920–1921 was marked by no runs on banks or major failures in the U.S. corporate community. Business slowed but was soon back to normal and was building steam as the United States moved with speculative vengeance into the roaring 1920s and another fall season of the long wave.

The 1920s was a classic K Wave fall season. Interest rates were falling during the 1920s. Deregulation of financial markets and other industries was a great theme during the 1920s (a tune played again in the 1980s). The 1920s created the illusion of a prospering global economy, while fundamental problems were beginning to develop. There was virtually no inflation and in many areas there was actually deflation—just as in fall seasons in the 19th century. The stock market was surging as overexpansion of industry left nowhere else for money to go but into financial markets and speculation.

Agriculture was in a severe depression in the 1920s, as in the other long-wave fall season plateaus. Virtually every industry was fighting for protection in a world economy that was overproducing everything. The close observer saw many disturbing signs as the roaring 1920s approached the close of a decade of disinflationary good times.

It was now time for one of the most severe K Wave winter seasons on record. Many theories surround the worldwide depression that began in the early 1930s and threw the world into more than a decade of industrial decline and stagnation. There are, however, a few facts accepted by everyone, such as prices had begun to decline in 1920, which undermined bank loans backing industrial outlays and expansion. Other facts were that the entire economy was clearly overproducing most goods in the late 1920s. Companies that hadn't already realized they were pouring money into a bottomless hole by expanding in a deflating economy began to slow or end expansion in 1928. In June of 1929, industrial expansion, production, and output peaked and began to decline. Corporate and personal debt had built up just as it had by the 1810s and 1870s.

There was only one place for prices to go with no buying power behind industry or the individual. Stock markets had such momentum and speculative force that it was late October before the markets came to the realization that there was no economy underneath them to match the price level of stocks.

I can't help but think of the roadrunner cartoon in which the coyote runs off the road and keeps running in midair for some time before he finally stops, looks down, and realizes he left solid ground some time back. At this point, he proceeds to fall into a deep canyon.

The free fall that inevitably came in stocks and economic activity during the K Wave winter brought destruction to the world economy that could never have been imagined. Details of the stock market crash are fascinating. Many have the tendency to equate the depression with the crash, but the crash was only a symptom of the underlying problem. The market crash and the depression would be comparable to an uncontrollable sneeze at the outset of pneumonia. The economy had taken its long-wave course and was to see a slowing of activity, not thinking to ask the permission of equity markets.

As the K Wave winter continued its downward momentum, the global banking order collapsed in 1933. Unemployment reached as high as 25 percent of the working population in the United States as the industrial complex continued its demise. World trade was cut in half during the early 1930s due to the foolish protectionism of the nations of the world who failed to see their interdependence with one another. The Smoot-Hawley tariffs almost single-handedly wiped out world trade as nations turned inward to solve their growing problems. World trade dropped sharply, exacerbating the global problems of overproduction.

The growing strength of the world economy and the power wielded by bodies such as the Federal Reserve Board appears to have lengthened the advance of the long wave. This more lengthy advance creates more volatile global markets in the last few years of the fall season leading to the beginning of winter. This phenomenon may lead to an accelerated decline because of the height that debt and prices are able to reach.

The seriousness and depth of the third long-wave decline has come to be known as the Great Depression. The Great Depression is attributed to isolationism in world markets and a hesitancy of the business community in the fear and memory of what we had just been through. It should be noted that the United States suffered a serious setback in 1937–1938. The K Wave winter season completed its decline around the time WWII was coming to an end.

The latest K Wave advance didn't begin until the mid- to late-1940s. Interest rates and prices bottomed in this time frame. The spring season of a new K Wave advance was beginning. Following the war, there was a slight decline in output beginning in March 1945, but by November things picked up and the economy was on the rebound. We saw another slight setback in 1948.

We saw slight recessions in 1958 and 1961, but these were soon forgotten as the economy continued to expand in the long-wave upswing. The global economy moved from the spring season to the summer season of the advance around 1966. The height of U.S. involvement in Vietnam brought recession in 1968 because of the large drain on national resources—as well as the time being one of national worry and frustration.

The inflationary heat of the K Wave summer gave us the energy crisis in 1973, as well as a business recession, but this recession was followed by exploding prices and high inflation. Many wholesale prices fell in the 1973–1974 recession, and many observers argue that this marked the end of the long-wave advance and the beginning of the fall season. The bulk of the evidence, however, indicates this was not the case. Prices continued to rise and the economy continued to expand at a good clip after the 1973–1974 recession. Prices and, importantly, interest rates, the price of money, didn't peak until the 1980–1981 recession when gold and silver prices spiked up before a free fall.

The recession of 1980–1981, which broke the back of inflation, marked the end of the long-wave cycle advance and summer season and the beginning of the speculative disinflationary fall season. We saw a peak and the beginning of a massive decline in commodity prices in the early 1980s, just as we had in 1920. The fall season is a time of a declining rate in capital outlays. The keen observer sees an erosion of real prices under the surface and the potential for a crash in world prices.

It is clear that prices for raw materials and commodities in the fourth cycle peaked from 1980 to 1981, as summer turned to fall, just as the third cycle peaked in 1920 to 1921. The Japanese stock market peak in December 1989 appears to have once again marked the beginning of the global shift from the fall to the long-wave winter season, as disinflation turns to deflation. In time, the entire global economy and all stock markets should join in as the long-wave decline runs full cycle. It now appears that the fall season, apart from Japan, lasted from 1981 to the mid-1990s. Evidence suggest a K Wave winter lies ahead.

The heights of debt and prices of the latest fall season are unprecedented and could lead to a sharp purifying global economic winter. Some estimates put total debt in the U.S. economy in the early 1990s at close to 20 trillion dollars. The Japanese economy was burdened with over 10 trillion dollars in debt in the 1990s. Much of this debt will likely be purged from the system in the dawning K Wave winter.

Participants and leadership in the global economy once again do not recognize the familiar trends and the inevitable passing of the long-wave economic seasons. The die is cast. As a result, the world will suffer. Intermediate planning is not enough for long-term forces. If history is our teacher, it is highly probable that the wrong moves will be made in the years ahead, and like its predecessor, the Great Depression, the latest long-wave winter will be far worse than it has to be.

For the investor, just as appropriate clothing protects from the winter, so certain investment instruments protect from the cycle. Long-range planning is not for the near-sighted. Long-range planning is for the investor with patience and a sincere belief in the reality that history has a nasty habit of repeating itself.

The depth of the Great Depression was the result of government and business leadership attempting to force the economy in the opposite direction the long wave was headed. A long-wave cycle decline may be inevitable, while a severe depression is the work of misguided politicians. The long wave can be distorted for a time; but in the long run, the cycle always wins. We can either learn from our mistakes and use them to our advantage, or we can forget the pain felt by previous generations.

Works Cited and Additional Sources

Lightner, Otto C. 1922. *The History of Business Depressions*. New York: Burt Franklin.

Schumpeter, Joseph A. 1954. *Business Cycles*. New York: Oxford University Press.

4

SYSTEM DYNAMICS
AT M.I.T.

"Very much of what we call the progress of today consists in getting rid of false ideas, false conceptions of things, and in taking a point of view that enables us to see the principles, ideas and things in right relation to each other."

William D. Hoard

The research of a young Russian leaves many observers questioning the validity of K Wave theory and wanting to see more evidence. Doubts are certainly reasonable, and a desire for more hard evidence should be expected.

In this chapter, you will find that some of the best evidence of the existence of the long-wave cycle comes from a most fascinating source. The work of a man who has literally revolutionized the world with his inventions in the computer field and established a research program at one of the most prestigious schools in the world, gives the K Wave its greatest credibility.

Some of the most powerful and convincing evidence for the Kondratieff long-wave cycle comes from the work of Dr. Jay W. Forrester and others at the Massachusetts Institute of Technology.

His research has silenced many skeptics and raised the discussion of the K Wave theory to a new level internationally.

Holding the patent for computer random access memory (RAM), the brain of all modern computers, is only one of many of Dr. Forrester's contributions to the world. But when the history books are written, his contribution in the creation of the system dynamics program at MIT may well be seen as his greatest accomplishment. Forrester's development of the computer-simulated model known as the National Model, and the research it has initiated in the long wave, is one of his most fascinating achievements.

When Kondratieff discovered long waves in the economy in the 1920s, he was looking at historical data. From the reams of data he collected, he observed the emergence of the long-wave cycle. The system dynamics program at MIT does research using the structure of complex systems, such as ongoing economic, political, and financial relationships that make up economic activity. The program seeks to project characteristic behavior and development of complex systems. After great success with his earlier smaller-scale models of urban development, Dr. Forrester created the National Model in the early 1970s.

Forrester expanded the use of powerful computers to create simulated models. The object of the National Model was to project the future direction of the national economy due to a myriad of complex relationships and processes.

The National Model (NM) is a computer simulation of our entire national economy. The NM utilizes over 2,200 equations to project the future based on the outcome of current economic, financial, business, and political decision-making processes. It is important to note that old data are not used in the model. The National Model is based on current decision making and relationships that produce spontaneous events. Forrester was looking for the future trends that relationships create by their interaction with each other.

When Dr. Forrester first fired up his computer-generated National Model, it naturally created and projected an approximate 50-year cycle of boom and bust in the economy. He was not expecting this. The model did not look at the past. It projected that the economy will naturally have a K Wave cycle due to "current" complex relationships and decisions being made.

When Dr. Forrester looked closer at the disturbing future projected by the National Model he found that production, prices, and debt got out of control and created K Wave periods of prosperity and depression. The long-wave cycle was created due to the every day decision-making processes in the highest circles of business, government, and finance. The elements that generated the boom and bust in Dr. Forrester's National Model were the same ones Kondratieff had discovered. They were the same forces outlined and to be controlled in the Levitical law passage of the Jubilee.

Addressing the Joint Economic Committee of Congress in the 1980s, Dr. Forrester tried to convince the politicians in Washington of the consequences of his research and the dangers faced by the global economy. He (Forrester 1984, 1) introduced the idea of K Waves with the following statement:

> The long-wave consists of rising economic activity for two or three decades, then a broad peak some ten years wide, and then a rapid drop into a major depression that can persist for a decade. After the depression, another long-term recovery starts.

The National Model at the system dynamics program is a groundbreaking approach to studying the economy. Forrester's (1984, 1) research using the National Model caused him to make the following observations about his work and the K Wave cycle to the members of the joint committee:

> Some of us at M.I.T. have been drawn into considering the economic long-wave through our work on the System Dynamics National Model. The National Model differs substantially from the more familiar econometric models. The

National Model is built up from the operating policies within corporations and government, rather than from macroeconomic theory. It is derived from management policies as observed in the practical working world, rather than from a statistical time series representing aggregate economic behavior.

It is clear that Forrester's (1984, 1–2) research was coming at the subject matter from a totally different angle than Kondratieff's research. Forrester continued his address to the committee with the following evidence:

The National Model generates, from interactions within its internal policies, the same patterns of change that have been observed in real life. The Model exhibits short-term business cycles of three-to-seven years' duration. Under the appropriate circumstances, it manifests stagflation and reveals the cause of simultaneously rising unemployment and inflation. Also, from the interactions within the private sector and government, the National Model produces an economic long-wave, or Kondratieff cycle, of 45 to 60 years between peaks. The National Model provides for the first time a coherent theory to explain how a major rising and falling economic pattern spanning half a century can be systematically and internally created within an economy.

Forrester (1984, 2) went on the explain to the joint committee some of the basic characteristics of this remarkable cycle:

The long-wave is an alternating over- and underaccumulation of capital plants. In Western industrial economies, capital investment has been concentrated in periods of economic excitement lasting about three decades. Such periods of aggressive new construction have been interrupted by major depressions occurring in the 1820s, 1890s, and 1930s. Now, after the expansion of the last several decades, we are probably entering another such economic downturn. Along with the overbuilding of capital plants go rising prices, leveling out of productivity, speculation in physical assets, rising unemployment, and accumulating debts. Debts, which were taken on during expansion with the expectation of rising prices and profits, become burdensome when profits decline and interest rates remain high. Banks must write off uncollectible loans. Speculatively elevated land prices must re-adjust downward to come into balance with salaries and wages."

In considering Forrester's observations, it is obvious that the latest K Wave spring advance began in the mid- to late-1940s. The spring and summer advance lasted during the 1950s, 1960s, and 1970s. The 1980s were the fall season after the real economic peak in growth in the late 1970s. The 1990s are witnessing the accelerating global decline predicted by Kondratieff and projected by the simulation of the National Model. Washington fiddles with whom to tax the most between elections, while our national economy enters a K Wave decline.

John D. Sterman (1985, 6) in the system dynamics program at MIT in a working paper entitled "The Long Wave: Theory and Evidence," put forward the following thoughts on the origin of the K Wave:

> The long wave is characterized by successive waves of over-expansion and collapse of the economy, particularly the capital-producing sector. Overexpansion means an increase in the capacity to produce and in the production of plant, equipment, and goods relative to the amount needed to replace worn-out units and provide for growth over the long run. Overexpansion is undesirable because, eventually, production and employment must be cut back below normal to reduce the excess.

I encourage you to reread this paragraph and consider how it applies to global automobile, computer, and commercial real estate markets in the 1990s. There is only one solution to the excessive production in virtually all areas of the global economy: A severe economic decline is inevitable. The cutbacks, bankruptcies, and mergers in these three industries alone will tell the K Wave story of decline all too well in the 1990s. How many new makes of cars were introduced in the 1980s and new production plants opened?

Sterman's (1985, 1) observations of the National Model and the K Wave show just how extensively it affects our lives:

> Though the model focuses primarily on economic forces, the theory emerging from the NM is not monocausal; it relates capital investment; employment, wages, and workforce participation; inflation and interest rates; aggregate demand; monetary and fiscal policy; innovation and productivity; and even political values. The NM is unique among recent theories of the long wave in that it views the long wave as a syndrome consisting of interrelated symptoms and springing from the interactions of many factors. The NM integrates diverse hypotheses about the genesis of the long wave. The NM also provides an analytical framework in which alternative theories can be tested in a rigorous and reproducible manner.

The most insightful and practical research and analysis of the K Wave and what can be done to curtail its effects on business takes place at MIT in the System Dynamics program. When the global economy has suffered enough K Wave booms and busts, we may see the program at MIT called upon to play a role in the corporate and government decision-making process to avoid the extremes of the K Wave. We can always hope that our national leaders and those from other nations will realize the value of the work done by Forrester, Sterman, and many others and will call upon the program and its experts for advice.

Forrester (1984, 8) ended his address to the Joint Economic Committee of Congress with the following observations:

> Social, political and economic innovations are needed to reduce the hazards that lie ahead and to accentuate the strengths we now have. But can we be sure of choosing policies that will make the best of the situation? Too often, laws passed at times of crisis are either ineffective, counter-productive, or too late.

The National Model seems to say that the old ways of doing things in the private sector and in Washington will perpetuate the severe boom and bust of the K Wave. Forrester (1984, 8) touched on this when he said:

> Intuition and political compromise are not an adequate basis for dealing with the complexity of our economic system. New approaches that can explain more realistically how private-sector policies and governmental laws interact are needed. One such approach is the System Dynamics National Model from which I have been drawing insights. If we are to cope in the best possible way with growing economic stresses, there should be a national priority for quickly achieving a much better understanding of economic behavior.

Long before the cold war was pronounced over, the Soviet Union dissolved and the global economy hit the skids, Dr. Forrester (1984, 8) made these observations in his address before the joint committee:

> We should reexamine our national priorities. The internal economic threat to the country is now far greater than the external military threat. Even so, the country does not strive for economic understanding with the forcefulness and adequate funding that are established patterns for military research. It is time that seeking a better understanding of economic behavior should receive attention in keeping with its importance. Several major projects should be established, each with the goals of reaching within three years an improved understanding of how to avoid those policies that would make matters worse and of finding the few high-leveraged policies that will take advantage of existing national economic strengths.

Dr. Forrester's advice has yet to be followed as our domestic economy, along with the global economy, heads into the latest K Wave decline. The year of Jubilee, like Forrester's idea of finding a new ways of dealing with K Wave economic forces, was to protect the economy from the natural internal tendencies of a free-market economy.

I agree with Forrester that we can find ways and take steps that would greatly reduce the pain of the long-wave cycle, but I believe it will always exist in some form in a free-market economy. The long-wave cycle runs deeper than economic and political statistics and decision making. It is part of the psychological learning curve in the arrival and passing of new generations of individuals that make up our society. Each new generation is destined to learn its own lessons.

The year of Jubilee was a time of celebration for the new economy that would begin after a year of economic corrections and adjustments. My own optimism for the future is reinforced by Forrester's (1984, 9) views:

> A bright new economy lies ahead, but it begins about a decade from now. There is a swamp of economic difficulties to cross before reaching the rising ground on the other side. Many choices can be made in moving from here to there. Those choices will affect how smoothly we make the transition from the old economy to the new economy. If we simply react to pressures as they arise, we will continue to be dominated by forces for which we are unprepared. On the other hand, by coming to a better understanding of how economic forces are being created, we can begin to shape policies for a more desirable transition into the new economy.

If we are ever as a nation or global economy going to learn to deal with the causes and consequences of the K Wave cycle, it is very likely that such breakthroughs will come from research on the National Model within the system dynamics program at MIT. If you believe that, your company, foundation or government could benefit from the work and research done at MIT in system dynamics, I encourage you to arrange to support the program. A number of individuals, international companies, foundations, and governments are sponsors of the National Model research program. Allegheny Corporation, Citicorp Investment Management, Kollmorgen, Digital Equipment, Merrill Lynch, and Polaroid are just a few of the corporate supporters of the program. Intelligent corporate leaders are using the National Model to consider their own plans for the future.

Sponsors' tax deductible contributions range from a yearly $10,000 for participation in research to $100,000 for firms who wish deep involvement in the various aspects of the program. You can receive additional information on the National Model program by writing: System Dynamics Group, Sloan School of Management, Massachusetts Institute of Technology, Cambridge, Massachusetts 02139.

Works Cited and Additional Sources

Forrester, Jay W. 1984. "Managing the Next Decade in the Economy." Address to the Joint Economic Committee of Congress in Washington, D.C. Germeshausen Professor of Management, Sloan School of Management, M.I.T.

Hendrick, Bill. 1992. "M.I.T. Scholar Sees Historical Pattern in Downturns." *The Atlanta Journal and Constitution,* February.

Sterman, John D. 1985. "The Economic Long Wave: Theory and Evidence." Working Paper 1656–85 at M.I.T. Cambridge, Massachusetts.

5

FIELD THEORY: THE NEW ECONOMICS?

". . . he conceived and developed the nature of the field and established the reality of the field as the underlying reality of all spatio-temporal phenomena."

T.F. Torrance
On James Clerk Maxwell

"Maxwell's equations are laws representing the structure of the field. . . . All space is the scene of these laws and not, as for mechanical laws, only points in which matter or charges are present."

Albert Einstein

Examining 20th-century developments in the hard sciences from a cyclical perspective is an important exercise for any study of K Wave theory. A possible scientific explanation of K Waves in both the U.S. economy and the global economy comes from a fascinating and fairly advanced scientific perspective. The concept of business cycles, K Waves in particular, being the manifestation of interconnected "fields" of financial, economic, and political activity must be briefly explored.

The term fields as used here can be defined as a specific range in space and time of interconnected phenomenon. This definition of fields is analogous to the concept of business cycles. Economic activity is certainly interconnected phenomenon, as demonstrated by the National Model at M.I.T. But naturally occurring fields of interconnected activity are far more accepted as the explanation for observable phenomenon in the hard sciences. This is particularly true in the area of electromagnetic and quantum fields in physics and morphic fields in the most advanced theories in microbiology.

The bridge between the application of field theory that is accepted in the hard sciences to K Waves or economic cycles in the social sciences has yet to be fully constructed. It is important to note at the outset that economic cycles are at their heart social cycles. Economic activity is a manifestation of social action, or, as the case may sometimes be, social inaction. Arguments presented in this book should be seen as a rough stab or draft for one possible bridge between the social sciences and the hard sciences.

Field theory warrants detailed consideration as the debate on K Waves and their origins continue. The advanced work of financial analyst P.Q. Wall, and what may prove to be some of his breakthrough applications of the principle of fields in the hard sciences to fields of disequilibrium in political/economy phenomenon, was my first introduction to the relationship between hard-science fields and the K Wave or what could be seen as a social cycle. Credit for the ideas presented here belong to the remarkable and ever-active mind of P.Q. Wall (1993). Others invariably have and will make significant contributions to the eventual acceptance or rejection of such an application.

Introduced here is the proposition that the field theory accepted in the hard sciences, such as physics and biology, is important to the study of K Waves in the social sciences. Certainly a complete presentation of field theory is beyond the scope of this book. However, an introduction to some of its basic premises is a reasonable goal. Here I merely present the argument that there appears to be a relationship between the innerconnected nature of the K Wave and field theory.

A review of field theory along with K Waves is in line with the injunction of Paul Samuelson (1947) in his book *Foundations of Economic Analysis*. He asserted that physics is the science for economics to imitate. However, Samuelson appears to have had in mind physics based on objective-oriented Newtonian mechanical physics, which were actually displaced before his observations were written. Samuelson believed in the Keynesian approach of objectively determining macroeconomic values and imbalances in the system and controlling them with government's institutional intervention. Samuelson believed Keynes's perpetual boom was achievable through the mechanical intervention efforts of government institutions.

Samuelson was evidently not aware that Newtonian theory had been displaced by electromagnetic field theory and then quantum field theory, which pushed physics out of the realm of objective mechanical laws or points of action and into the realm of subjective fields of influence.

This same displacement of mechanical physical concepts of cell development by field theory has occurred in advanced microbiology. James Lovelock and Rupert Sheldrake have postulated a radical change in how we view the development of living biological life forms. They have discovered what they call morphic fields that work alongside DNA codes, which P.Q. Wall noted (1993, 2), are "shaping both development and behavior of living things."

The cyclical development of interconnected activity over what appear to be the predictable spans of the regular trade cycle and the K Wave resembles the notion of observable fields of interdependent development in the flows or movements of energy and matter and the development of living organisms. The implications of field theory for the social science of international political economy, if applicable, are no less radical than they were for the hard sciences of electromagnetics, physics, and biology.

The possibilities, as further evidence will indicate, appear to be the opposite of the mechanical understanding and intervention Samuelson intended to endorse. It is, of course, conceivable that there is no link between fields discovered in the hard sciences and those that appear to be evident in the K Wave, but such remarkable coincidences are doubtful. Certainly, drawing such parallels could be a misguided premature proposition, but the possibilities should at least be open for discussion. They should be explored and debated in light of the evidence for what appear to be naturally occurring K Waves displaying interconnected field-like characteristics.

A mechanical approach to economic intervention could have been implemented with scientific authority when mechanical Newtonian foundations ruled the science of physics. The world was believed to be mechanical. Mechanical analysis and solutions to social ills were therefore logical. However, electromagnetic field theory and quantum field-theory have removed much of the objective measurability of physical phenomenon. This is due to the logical consequences of basic field theory characteristics.

In electromagnetic field theory, Newtonian mechanics were undermined as the complete explanation for physical action. In quantum theory, the notion of discontinuous as opposed to continuous release and absorption of energy that manifests itself in fields made the causes of physical phenomena unmeasurable in many respects. Sure the size of the fields produced in terms of time and space can be measured, but what cannot be measured is precisely how and why the deviations of the fields occur based on intrinsic actions and facts or a measured breakdown of component parts. Institutional economics have yet to catch up with modern physics in terms of what makes or doesn't make things happen in the physical universe.

In his book on James Clerk Maxwell's formulation of the theory of the electromagnetic field, T.F. Torrance (Maxwell 1982, 23–24) writes:

> Clerk Maxwell 'created for the first time a field theory which was independently testable against Newtonian force theories.' He created a situation in which the dominance of Newtonian mechanics over the whole spectrum of physical science was called into question and decisive steps were taken in the direction of a non-mechanical thoroughly relational understanding of the intelligible connections immanent in the universe ... Clerk Maxwell's work was of profound conceptual importance ... he conceived and developed the nature of the field and established the reality of the field as the underlying reality of all spatio-temporal phenomena. At this point we cannot do better than let Einstein himself speak. 'The formulation of these equations is the most important event in physics since Newton's time, not only because of their wealth of content, but also because they form a pattern for a new type of law. ... Maxwell's equations are laws representing the structure of the field. ... All space is the scene of these laws and not, as for mechanical laws, only points in which matter or charges are present.'

Fields are here suggested to be interconnected activity in space and time—a sort of ebb and flow discovered in the physical universe. The parameters of these fields can be observed, but the field itself is inherently dynamic. The fields appear to be guided by external degrees of freedom that are somehow separate from the internal forces at work. The proposition put forward here is that K Waves in the global economy, as observed by Kondratieff in historical data and projected by the National Model at M.I.T., and all that they entail, are indeed a spatio-temporal phenomenon. That is to say they exist in space and time.

The clear implication, if the global economy is categorized as a spatio-temporal phenomenon, as it surely must be in numerous if not all respects, is that the underlying reality of our global economic system is that of a field of interconnected human activity. It cannot be logically argued that social activity, both economic and political, is not a spatio-temporal phenomenon. The formation of the global economy resembles the development of a living organism. What a number of theorists in the hard sciences have observed is that the development of life appears to resemble more of a mind than a machine. Economic and political activity, indeed all social activity, occurs in space and time. Maxwell and Einstein's work would appear to suggest that this activity, due to its spatio-temporal characteristics, must be part of a field of one form or another. The obvious implication here is that the K Wave is the representation of one such social field.

The further implication is that Maxwell's work on the electromagnetic field and its impact on light was the foundation of that part of Einstein's work that lead to relativity theory. Relativity in turn led to the formulation of quantum field theory. These discoveries produce a major problem for the institutional mechanical tools of government interventionism. One observation concerning the problem of objective measurement in quantum physics relative to fields was expressed by Aharonov and Petersen (1971, 138) in *Quantum Theory and Beyond*; they concluded:

> . . . it is not surprising that the relativistic constraint on interactions imposes limitations on measurements in the quantum domain. For example, to measure the momentum of a field according to the canonical method one would need an interaction proportional to the momentum and to some external degree of freedom belonging to the apparatus.

Remember that free-market thinker Friedrick August von Hayek noted that the expected deviations for calculations in the international economic structure cannot be known; in the same way, there are limits on measurements of the field in the quantum domain. The bottom line of the new physics for the policy makers is that this suggests that any measurement of an economic phenomenon that occurs in space and time in terms of determining value for wages or prices appears to be truly relational or subjective, in the deepest scientific sense. It is truly a relative exercise, relative to the ever-changing structure of the global economy, as literally trillions of decisions by billions of individuals are perpetually changing the allocation and use of their material, physical, and mental resources in the international system. Bottom line, the social system is interconnected and dynamic just like the quantum field.

What this logic suggests is that Hayek was correct about the danger of a scientific approach to economics when all the data is not, and apparently cannot, be known. Following this argument to its completion, a statistical and objective calculation of what the minimum wage, prices, or the interest rate should be presents a serious problem, unless one ignores the fact that Newtonian mechanics no longer represents the complete equation for measurement of spatio-temporal phenomenon. If so, one bases decisions on simplistic and potentially incorrect assumptions of value regardless of the consequences. The result is the distortion of the global economy or the field of interconnected activity in the national or international system.

A.S. Eddington (Dewey and Dakin, 8) presents the argument for a subjective approach to the world and therefore policy in *The Nature of the Physical World*:

> The quantum physicist does not fill the atom with gadgets for directing its future behavior, as the classical physicist would have done; he fills it with gadgets determining the odds on its future behavior. He studies the art of the bookmaker, not the trainer.

Government interventionists believe that economic problems and social ills just need institutional gadgets for correction. Field theory says such programmable gadgets cannot be accurate, and therefore cannot be effective. The action and impact of the gadgets that make up the global economy can be observed, as seen in K Waves, but not controlled and directed since their values within the dynamic field cannot be measured. The suggestion is that the entire field itself can be observed but not measured and directed internally, at least not successfully over time.

Newton's view of the universe was mechanical. The arguments in support of government intervention and central banking were based on this concept of mechanical monetary tools for redressing imbalances. The more fully-developed "scientific" arsenal of economic statistics emerged with Mitchell's institutionalism in the 1920s and 1930s. It was presumed that objective scientific data reinforced arguments for central bank manipulation of the monetary system for desired economic and therefore social results.

Scientifically based economic institutionalism received a theoretical boost with the publication of Paul Samuelson's arguments in 1947 and many other Keynesians who believed in what they called the new economics. This was just a few years after Bretton Woods launched the international institutions that could be used for the intervention and application of the new economics of Keynesianism. The monetary and bureaucratic mechanics could go to work.

Government institutional activity clearly represents what are asserted to be objective rather than subjective perspectives of value in the international system. The approach was clearly appealing to anyone with Newtonian scientific leanings. But if Samuelson is to be taken at his word, then the study of political economy must consider the relevance of quantum field theory.

Government institutionalism believes it can objectively and scientifically figure out, regulate, and know both economic causes of events and the economic values that should exist in the system. This includes minimum wage, car gas mileage, prescription-drug regulation, and tariffs. The idea that economic events and solutions to problems are mechanical and can be known objectively clearly leads to mechanical solutions. Keynesians believe that solutions to social problems can be applied objectively with solid planning through institutional frameworks of analysis and intervention. They use limited knowledge and call it objective fact to dictate policy they claim is scientifically grounded.

With the disequilibrium that emerged with economic crisis in the overheated K Wave summer of the 1970s and the crisis as the K Wave fall began in the early 1980s, it became increasingly clear that Keynesian-based decisions had not been as scientifically grounded as presumed. All the data had not been considered in the government's equations. The economic projectiles did not fly according to even the best laid mechanical plans. Other forces must have been at work—forces significant enough to produce severe crisis and uncoordinated economic activity. The idea of social development occurring in an interconnected field, in which the optimum level of values cannot be known objectively and therefore manipulated effectively by government, appears to be more relevant than ever, and field theory may well offer some insights. The fact may be—and this is the first K Wave in which it will be put to the test on a grand scale—that government intervention actually exacerbates the extremes of the field.

If the application of field theory is a valid concept, there appears to be interrelationships in the fields that are incalculable and so complex as to be unknowable. The give-and-take within the fields of the global economy produce recognizable K Wave patterns of international system development. Adam Smith clearly stated that the natural price prevailed at a specific time and place. By implication, the next moment, in the same or a different place, natural price or value could change. This dynamic characteristic of price-imputed value is due to the continual emergence of new product and service uses, substitutions, discoveries, and technologies, which must be incorporated into values. What's more, the information that informs the market as to these changes may be late, biased, or simply bad. Disequilibrium is to be expected in prices.

Smith never addresses the matter of price in terms of definitive equilibrium, but in terms of what more closely resembles disequilibrium. Smith's arguments suggest that market prices and thus the market is dynamic.

Field theory suggest that even in a pure unencumbered market system there would be a natural cyclical expansion and contraction tendency in all interconnected fields, which defines the parameters of the field. This is a reflection of the disequilibrium forces of market price in search of natural price; in other words, the search for value. The search appears to be lead the system into regular recurring patterns of not only 3- to 5-year trade cycles, but 50- to 60-year K Wave cycles.

The case that K Wave theory makes is certainly relevant to the general observations of field theory. The international system appears to have a natural, even predictable, tendency for perpetual, although regular, disequilibrium. From another perspective, this could certainly be seen as a very broad equilibrium.

Price is always searching but never finding a static level of value. This process of perpetual disequilibrium appears to produce interconnected, field-like characteristics. This is clearly opposed to the classical notion of a system that does, or could if given a chance, tend toward equilibrium.

The final answer to the question of whether the field theory accepted in the hard sciences is related to what appears to be regularly recurring K Waves in the social sciences may still be some time away. However, the question certainly deserves to be asked and discussed. Long-wave cycles, if they exist—and the evidence is impressive—are certainly interconnected social phenomenon taking place in a specific range of space and time.

Works Cited and Additional Sources

Aharonov, Yakir and Aage Petersen. 1971. "Definability and Measurability in Quantum Theory." *Quantum Theory and Beyond.* Ted Bastin ed. Cambridge: Cambridge University Press.

Dewey, Edward R. and Edwin F. Dakin. 1947. *Cycles; The Science of Prediction.* New York: Henry Holt and Company.

Maxwell, James Clerk. 1982. *A Dynamical Theory of The Electromagnetic Field.* T. F. Torrance, ed. Edinburgh: Scottish Academic Press.

Samuelson, Paul. 1947. *Foundations of Economic Analysis.* Harvard University Press: Cambridge.

Wall, P.Q. 1993. *P.Q. Wall Forecasts.* New Orleans: P.Q. Wall Forecasts, Inc. Volume 5, Number 2,. February.

Destiny is Real. New Orleans: P.Q. Wall, P.O. Box 15558.

6

THE GLOBAL
ECONOMY

"The future of nations cannot be frozen . . . cannot be foreseen. History is a story of growth, decay and change. If no provisions, no allowance is made for change by peaceful means, it will come anyway—and with violence."

Herbert Hoover

We are now living in an interconnected global economy. K Wave theory therefore has immediate and drastic global ramifications. Before the 19th century, what happened in one country or region typically didn't have a very large impact on what went on in neighboring states. There was a time when one region or country could have been in economic turmoil and its neighbors might not even have known of its plight.

The tulip fiasco in Holland in 1635 didn't have much of an effect on market conditions in London. Portugal's loss of a major trade expedition to hurricanes wouldn't have affected the markets in Frankfurt, Germany, in 1675. China's large, public investments in the Great Wall had no repercussions on barbarian trade in Europe. Particular areas and regions in the world were independent economic entities or economic organisms that could get sick or die off without a large impact on other parts of the world. In the late 1700s this independence began to change.

The close of the 18th century saw the distinct beginnings of the emergence of an interdependent global economy. The trend toward a truly global economy gathered momentum over the past 200 years. Over the past few years we have seen international ownership, foreign investment, financial exchange activity, and therefore global interdependence exploding to record heights.

An all-important piece in the world economic puzzle was the rise of the international bankers beginning late in the 18th century. The study of the rise of the banking families is fascinating. Before this new era, nations were as a rule financed from within for their various governmental and business activities, whether public works or military conquests.

The international banking community emerged as a sovereign, able to make or break leaders and guide the destinies of whole peoples by a simple yes or no to requests for financing. Trade and commerce were financed through the network of the international private bankers, which were intertwined with increasingly powerful central bankers. Growth and stability, to a significant degree, could be controlled by financing decisions and by the bankers' manipulation or influence on rates over the short run. Though divine right as a political institution faded during this time, we can still trace lineage of a few of the current prominent banking families back to families of the international money changers of the 18th century. In the long run, though, the market and the K Wave still rules over the bankers.

Observing the global economic organism, we must label the flow of funds controlled by the international private and central bankers of the world as the blood that flows through the veins of the global system. When banking is run on false premises the entire system is threatened. The expansion and contraction of global banking practices and money supplies are a major component in the K Wave. However, regardless of the power of the bankers, the supply and demand of money is largely driven by the prevailing psychology of the marketplace. The K Wave would exist even if the banker's power to create and control money were restricted, although the K Wave very likely wouldn't be as extreme when subject to the whims of monetary manipulators.

We have no choice in the realm of international trade but to pay our bills, secure a line of credit in the international banking system, or dip into the till at the International Monetary Fund. Global relationships, which benefit all of us, also come with strains and new tensions that are not always easily resolved. This is evidenced by the fact that armed conflict among nations has increased rather than decreased since the K Wave emerged. The K Wave appears to be superimposed on our international economic relationships.

The global economy operates with accounting standards, although the standards occasionally have been bent and twisted. Governments may rise and fall, but the business records are still being kept. To play in the international economic arena as a sovereign state, you must play according to the wishes of the financial rulers.

Kondratieff observed that the long-wave cycle was a global capitalist phenomenon. The cycle passes through all capitalist economies of the globe simultaneously, although evidence indicates there may have been long-wave cycles before the advent of capitalism.

A number of obvious forces have shaped the emergence of a global economy over the past 200 years; but as mentioned, there are two major ones. This first is innovation in transportation, the second is advances in communications.

Shipping evolved from limited, often unseaworthy, sailing ships to vessels carrying vast amounts of goods to virtually anyplace in the world. Canals from the Suez to Panama opened up trade lanes for enhanced efficiencies in international commerce. Railroads, on the cutting edge of world industrialization brought

the trade of the continents to the major world ports. Water transportation became more dependable and affordable for tourist and
official travelers alike. From Hong Kong to New York, from
Bombay to Rotterdam, and from Rio de Janeiro to Cape Town, the
states and continents of the world became dependent on each
other for the flow of goods.

During the 1920s, the stage was set for global interdependence to accelerate a great deal. Charles A. Lindbergh made history by flying across the Atlantic from New York to Paris in 1927.
This marked the beginning of a great explosion in the already
growing business alliances between Europe and America. Air
travel began to take off early in the 20th century and made the
world even more susceptible to international economic dealings
and financial relationships. The consequences of the global interdependence in the 1930s are remembered by everyone who experienced or studied the period.

The second major force of this new global economy could be
placed on a pedestal. It is the advance by leaps and bounds that has
come in communications. In scarcely a century, the economic centers of the world went from communication by pigeons, when
they flew where they were supposed too, to instantaneous communication and information by satellite. The impact and consequences at times is almost overpowering and unimaginable.

In more recent years, the advent of computers and satellite
communications systems, along with sweeping transportation
innovations, have precipitated the new economic reality. What is
the new reality? It is simply that all nations play a role and are an
integral part of an interdependent global economy.

President Reagan takes a bullet from a would-be assassin's
gun in 1981, and within minutes we see the dollar fall to long-time
lows on the major money exchanges from New York to London to
Tokyo. Half a millennium earlier, America was not even known to
exist and England was still looking over its shoulder for an invasion from Nordic barbarians.

One example of this new global economy is that there is a great deal of serious talk today about 24-hour trading on both stock and money markets. Many stocks and currencies are traded on a 24-hour basis already. When the trend is taken to its limit, our financial world will be even smaller. Imagine going to bed at 10 P.M. and getting up at 6 A.M. to find the value of your portfolio has dropped by 25 percent. Talk about nightmares!

Major brokerage companies are developing the plans and skills necessary for a global market on which the sun never sets. There is no doubt that many will fight such innovations, but with terminals and phones at home, the office, and in the car, the world will soon adjust. Hopefully weekend trading will never be introduced!

News that affects markets is known immediately throughout the world due to our advances in communications. These advances have done a great deal to increase the number of banking transactions on an international basis, which does a great deal to stimulate world trade. International orders are being processed in a fraction of the time it took a few years ago because of the financial links through new communications technologies. Electronic transfer allows for same-day order execution from virtually any location on the globe.

Every day, over one trillion dollars zips around the globe within the high-tech financial system that has developed over the past few decades. It is estimated that over $30 trillion in derivative contracts are linking global financial institutions and markets today. No one knows what will happen when these new global financial links are forced to unravel in an international crisis. The outcome is unpredictable. Advanced communications have gone far to build our global economy. The full consequences of the latest K Wave winter will be unparalleled in history.

Another key element in the emergence of the global economic organism is the multinational corporation. Many of these giants have a gross national product larger than that of dozens of smaller nations totalled together. They command vast empires on which, like the emerging global stock market, the sun never sets. For years, we tended to think that the control of a company resided in one nation. Not so for the multinational. These companies are owned by residents of almost every nation in the world. No longer is GM held strictly by Americans nor does GM produce only cars and trucks in America. Owners and management of the company no longer necessarily consider that what is good for GM is good for America.

The same goes for the biggest companies, such as IBM, Exxon, and Archer Daniels Midland. Foreign-based multinationals are in the same situation. Virtually all major European and Japanese car builders now have plants in America that hire Americans and sell to Americans as well as build cars for export out of America back to their own countries. Virtually all other industries have experienced the same expansion of global relationships. Most basic products, such as cars and computers, are made with parts and materials from dozens of different countries. These trends are causing the people and economies of the world to be tied together more closely than ever.

National companies that have chosen not to join the international trend will eventually be put out of business if they haven't already failed. In a general sense, there is no longer such a thing as a domestic economy. You would be hard-pressed to find any company that is not in some way affected by the global economy. The multinational has, perhaps more than any other element, forced national government into the global economic organism.

Having a formidable interest in every corner of the world, the large multinational must have a vehicle to express and/or guarantee its interest. This job has often been taken up by governments. It has even been rumored that governments have been toppled in line with the desires of the multinationals. They form a network in global commerce that tightens the bonds of the global economy.

Energy needs came hand in hand with industrialization, so treaties and pacts between and among nations began to emerge based on access to energy markets. Alliances and trading partnerships were formed from every corner of the world due to the demand for black gold—oil. Certain regions had an abundance of energy but no climate for agriculture, so marriages were made and strategic interests were solidified by the fate of nature.

In recent years, there has been an enormous increase in foreign investment and ownership. Taking a close look at the U.S. model, we see total assets in the United States owned by foreigners rising from just over $100 billion in 1970 to several trillion in the 1990s. The three major components of this investment are in treasury securities, direct investment, and corporate stocks.

Agriculture is an all-important element in the rise of the global economy. The superfarm is changing the way the world feeds itself and is making many nations vulnerable to major difficulties in the event of an unhealthy climate of world trade.

Energy is another case in point. Japan and much of Western Europe are slaves to the oil fields of the volatile Middle East. Another example of interdependence in the world community is South Africa. Because South Africa is the major producer of a number of strategic metals used in the U.S. defense complex, the Pentagon and the CIA closely watch developments on the southern tip of Africa, thousands of miles away from American shores.

The last few decades of this latest advance and especially the latest K Wave fall season saw more extensive links in the global economy than ever before. More so than at any time in history, every nation of the globe is a player in one form or another in the global K Wave cycle. Anyone who says that what happens in Japan, Germany, Russia, Mexico, China, or England will not affect America is only kidding himself.

The reality of our current present predicament in a truly global economy brings us to a number of sobering conclusions. There is no such creature as an independent economic nation. We are all bound by the global economy; thus, our fate is linked by the global system.

A small, developing nation can send shock waves throughout the world financial markets by defaulting on its obligation to pay its creditors. An oil tanker struck in the Persian Gulf in regional hostilities or an explosion at an Indonesian refinery can send oil prices up on world markets. Above all, the downturn in a few key capitalist nations can bring the global economy to its knees—as we saw in the 1930s.

Of course, this works both ways. We enjoyed a K Wave expansion and advancing global economy from the 1940s to the 1980s. We are now facing a K Wave winter that brings falling prices, an international increase in bankruptcy, a global real-estate depression, a global banking crisis, and a worldwide business contraction. Even though the K Wave winter tends to begin in one leading speculative nation of the advance, such as Japan, the K Wave is still a global phenomenon.

The fact that the ties in the global economy are stronger than ever means that during this K Wave winter solution to the crisis may well take on global dimensions never before dreamed possible.

There is the possibility of a global New Deal being the solution offered by a consortium of leading governments such as the G–7 financial powers, including the United States, Great Britain, France, Germany, Japan, Canada, and Italy; or the Group of Ten that would add Belgium, the Netherlands, and Sweden to the list. There is also a great chance that governments will not be able to work together due to internal pressures caused by a K Wave winter crisis.

In the new era of the global economy, there is increasingly an interlinking regular rythym to the booms and busts in the international system. The next step for the system dynamics research program at M.I.T. may well be the global model. In evaluating the present situation, we have to come to a simple yet telling conclusion; as participants in the global economy, we are all riding the K Wave together!

Part II:
Signs of the Cycle

7

THE CYCLE AND PSYCHOLOGY

"I can calculate the motions of the heavenly bodies, but not the madness of people."

Isaac Newton

Laissez-faire economics, the supremacy of individual capitalism and entrepreneurism, was the rage of the 1980s. The quest for acquiring the almighty dollar was at levels not reached since the 1920s. There was a mood in the air that said, "Give me an ounce of opportunity and the will to succeed and nothing in the world can keep me from cutting out my piece of the pie." Social and psychological forces similar to those prevalent in the United States were also evident in Europe and Asia. Basically, global society was in a historically upbeat mood in the 1980s. Recent years, like the 1930s, are seeing a society that is far more subdued and introspective. The trend seems to be accelerating.

In this chapter, we will observe that public mood may well be a primary force in driving the cycle. It may be a leading K Wave indicator. The 1980s were amazingly similar in social mood and political policy to the 1920s. Therefore, the years immediately ahead of us may be similar to the prevalent depressing mood of the 1930s and early 1940s. The acid test of the psychological and social aspects of K Wave theory will be the personal experiences of the coming years. True critics of popular psychology will be able to remove themselves from the drama as it is unfolding in the years ahead and see how the popular mood is leading the action.

Competition was king in the 1980s. From airlines to banking to trucking, government was cutting the strings and letting the capitalist nature take its course. Conservative politics have long been the ticket of the free market and have endorsed the belief that the private sector can do far more to make society and the economy reach new heights of return and personal reward than can government intervention and meddling. Indeed they are right, but what is the other side of the coin? For each action there is an equal and opposite reaction.

Does the success of a free market push human psychology to an extreme that takes a good thing beyond its healthy bounds? Does the inevitable reaction usher in a new era of regulation and more government intervention? Could it be possible that human psychology plays an important role in the rise and fall of the long-wave cycle? The evidence leans towards just such a hypothesis.

Due to the amount of data available and the fact that the decline known as the Great Depression occurred in the 20th century, it is weighed heavily in analysis of psychological implications of the K Wave.

Though we can trace liberal and conservative political and social movements running in conjuncture with the K Wave for the past 200 years, the Great Depression tells us far more about what to expect in the latest K Wave decline because of its closer approximation and resemblance to current times.

The yuppie generation that was the driving force in the 1980s had no memory of the pain of the depression in the 1930s. They, instead, had the idea stuck in their heads of a fairly pain-free, risk-less society. They were the engine driving a new breed of speculators and risk takers in global markets. Their only experience was with rising global stock markets and real-estate values. I have long enjoyed the political philosophy of Englishman Jeremy Bentham, who is quoted by Dick Stoken in an article on the Kondratieff Cycle and its effects on social psychology in the February 1980 issue of *The Futurist*.

Bentham (Stoken 1980) said, "Nature has placed man under the governance of two sovereign masters, pain and pleasure. It is for them alone to point out what we shall do." This thought conjures up the vision of humanity as a great pendulum swinging back and forth within the economic K Wave. Individuals first find their economic freedom and after taking it to a painful extreme, swing back to a stifling protectionist stance, turning control back to government as a force beyond themselves. Few are able to rise above the mood of the masses and remove themselves from the spirit of the times.

In the 1980s, the most respected person on the block was the one with the newest, most expensive car and the fanciest clothes. In the early 1990s, the mood change of a K Wave decline was already becoming obvious. Now the person with the used, functional car and moderate lifestyle is the more respected. The expensive shopping malls have been replaced in popularity by price-cutting Wal-Mart type stores.

In the 1980s, living "beyond our means" was in. Living frugally, working hard, and saving for the future is a trend accelerating today. When this decline reaches its worst years, frugality will practically become a religion. Will the capital formation of such an attitude of thrift and hard work help the economy move forward in the next advance? You can bet it will!

When one individual finds him- or herself a few rungs higher on the ladder of financial success and more economically independent, as happens at the end of a K Wave advance, he or she tends to become a freewheeler, willing to try something new, willing to step a little closer to the edge of uncertainty for just a little more financial gain. This individual can have little effect on the direction of the global economy and history of the world as a lone actor, but when whole nations are experiencing this phenomenon in unison, as happened in the 1920s and the 1980s, the history of humanity is hanging in the balance.

Fifty years is sufficient time to drain pessimistic and cautious blood out of the mainstream of economic activity. We tend to forget the stories our parents and grandparents told us about food and unemployment lines. Visions of the Great Depression had no place in the consciousness of those in a position to potentially see it coming again in recent decades—therefore, they took no action to lessen the impact of dangerous trends.

In his article, Stoken (1980, 14–17) said:

> When people perceive less risk they put more trust in their own powers. They become more adventurous and more willing to take chances. Because they are now being directed by a different set of underlying assumptions than during a downswing, they do things they would not have done during hard times. Economic success leads people to believe they now have control over their own destiny, with the power to solve their own and society's problems. They idealize existence and become less tolerant of injustice.

When the trend of optimism and its manifestation in speculation have run full course, the cycle peaks and begins its decline. The psyche of society takes on a new character, and humanity is not so confident in its ability and power to overcome obstacles. Unbridled capitalism loses its luster and falls from its pedestal. The dreams and aspirations of the proponents of a poorly executed laissez-faire system are shattered, providing the pain necessary to begin the swing of the pendulum back to a sedated view of the system.

Quoting Stoken (1980, 14–17) again:

> On the one hand, a long period of prosperity and affluence produces increases in assets, wages, social mobility and the standard of living that exceed people's expectations, causing them to be pleasantly surprised. A depression on the other hand, has an unforward effect on jobs, wages and asset val-

ues. People unexpectedly see their goals frustrated and this serves as a lesson of pain. Pain produces a definite psychological change in most people. They become motivated to avoid pain and to seek security. In a risky world people feel helpless, lose faith in their own powers and become very cautious and unwilling to take chances. To protect themselves and ward off danger, they bond together into groups. To modify behavior in the direction of group unity, there must be rules and social restraints as well as the acceptance of some kind of authority. Naturally the mood at such a time runs against individualistic capitalism, with its free markets and emphasis on competition.

We can see this clearly in the growth of the unions in the 1940s and the 1950s as the pain of the Depression was fresh on the minds of people all over the world, yet now as this generation has grown old and the economy is in good shape, we see unions struggling for survival. If history holds true, unions will once again be on the rise and membership will be booming soon after the world economy enters its next advance and a more sober society gets back to work in a new economy.

As a cautious and risk-averse generation becomes the rule in the decline, a slow change occurs: A few individuals step out from the group and buck the trend. These new leaders come from within industry and companies as well as in the form of lone rangers. They are the inventors and the innovators that are, through their bold and aggressive natures, going to lead the world out of its mesmerized risk-averse state of decline and into the next advance of the long-wave cycle.

During the last years of the K Wave advance, you tend to find everyone and his brother jumping on the entrepreneurial bandwagon, as everything is looking up and everyone is prospering in an advancing economy. A large majority are parasites looking for a quick buck at the expense of someone else. The true entrepreneur emerges when the chips are down and the economy is in a decline. These are the entrepreneurs who have the "right stuff;" the impostors will be flushed out with the downturn.

In the upswing, moral and ethical restraints are replaced by more permissive and rebellious attitudes. Discipline and authority are lost concepts, and the younger generation grows up with a carefree, easy-come, easy-go attitude, to the frustration of parents who worked hard for their place in society.

Perhaps herein lies one of the clues to the imminent demise of the economy at the end of the advance. For this generation has a misconception of hard work and the value of a hard-earned dollar, yen, pound, mark, and so on. Good economic instincts are learned—not hereditary. While the parents of this new generation were working to provide their children with something more of the good life, the children's value systems lost touch with notions of hard work, thrift, and sacrifice. Yet these children have grown up to be the managers of today. Their way of looking at the world, as if it owes them a living, is most popular after a long advance of the K Wave.

As the world economy begins to decline, conservative politics take a back seat to sweeping liberal political plans and government's reinvolvement in the private sector. The Great Depression saw government taking the driver's seat in business, trying to steer the economy clear of the carnage created and left by what was thought to be mistakes of the free market of the 1920s. In fact, it was only a natural shakeout, separating the sheep from the goats, and government should have stayed out of business. But the new psychology of the decline pleads for big brother's help. Since government was already in charge this time around, we may see a revolt against government.

The psychology that moves the K Wave is affected enormously by the broad-based move toward a more spiritual worldview as the decline deepens. Religion becomes more important. We are told in Christian scripture that Christ came to save the meek, the poor, and the humble; all three categories have exploding populations during an economic downturn.

When things are looking good and the economy is on the upswing, individuals look within for their strength. We see positive thinking and get-rich quick seminars on the increase. We witnessed this in the 1970s and 1980s. These seminars are very similar to the self-help programs of the 1920s. But as the tide turns and the chips are down, the average person, although introspective, doesn't look within for strength, but looks to secure institutions such as government and church.

The 1920s had its own version of the sexual revolution. Stoken (1980, 14–17) speaks of how women just after receiving the vote did away with the conventions of the Victorian period. Women began drinking and smoking in public, and skirt lengths rose to the knee. Other changes were taking place:

> There was a proliferation of sex magazines, which were gobbled up by a public obsessed with the subject. People liberated themselves from the restraints of puritanism. There was a vast increase in the divorce rate which rose from 8.8 for every 100 marriages in 1920 to 16.5 for every 100 marriages in 1928.

All these psychological changes took years to penetrate the mainstream of society and emerge as the current social norms. Like a great wave moving through history, the K Wave cycle is the innerconnected sum of a broad array of social forces.

Again, I must quote Stoken (1980, 14–17) with his gifted perception into the psychology of the wave as he follows the social revolution into the downturn:

> Initially, few people expect that a depression is going to last a long time. Most people think it is a cyclical contraction rather than a major change in the economy. The first sign that people no longer see the world in risk-free rose-colored terms often occurs with a subtle change in the relationship between the sexes. At the outset of the Great Depression, women lowered

their skirts, dressed more conservatively, began to wear white gloves and became more respectful of a meal ticket. The sexual code was no longer flaunted so flagrantly. There was less ado about sex, while glamour and romance came into their own. The deepening depression shattered the assumptions of a relatively risk-free world that had dominated the mood of the 1920s. People became more cautious. Hedonistic behavior subsided and there was less tolerance of deviant social behavior. The younger generation became more respectful of their parents and less scornful of the old traditional values. The music slowed down. Marriage and the family became more highly prized as social institutions and the divorce rate fell. People stayed home and spent more time with their families.

Taking a broad view we see that the K Wave is driven by political trends, morality, religion, and social mores. It is a staggering thought that a cycle that has run its course only three times since the freedom of America can be seen in the divorce rate.

This chapter has emphasized America and how psychology has driven K Wave developments and been reflected in the theory. But human nature is the same around the world, and this chapter was not meant to limit its scope to America only. The reactions here apply to any peoples being pulled in one direction or the other by the K Wave, as can be observed in Japan with the major psychological changes going on presently in that society. Japanese psychology is leading the global K Wave, and the Japanese are increasingly sober in their views and expectations.

We cannot take too lightly the history of the wave and the potential force it has been shown to generate. This force could have an enormous impact on social and political change during the present decline—an impact relevant to national safety and international stability. We can have at our disposal all the statistical data in the world, but if we cannot understand and perceive human nature and what human response will be in situations beyond our immediate control, our data will be of no use.

National and local elections are guided by the mood of the people and what they are looking for as a result of their psychological disposition at election time; thus, a knowledge and understanding of the K Wave could be of enormous importance to would-be candidates. The platform necessary for election or reelection during the most critical time of the cycle would be closely related to the psychological impulses of the K Wave and their influences on constituents. One could almost design a rough platform years in advance by the known impact of an economic decline.

So the K Wave does not stand alone, but measures and is guided by the psychological impulses of the population of the globe. It is a sobering thought that psychological tendencies reflected by the K Wave guide the destiny of nations. Many of the latest trends are already evident as the global economy has weakened and nations begin to enter the decline. A more sober view of the world and the economy began emerging in recent years. The full psychological effects on the economic binge of the latest K Wave advance and speculative fall season will not be realized until the cycle reaches bottom in the years ahead. The effect of fear and frustration will be magnified tenfold before the cycle has completed its purifying and painful decline.

After looking at the ups and downs of human psychology in the expansion and contraction of the K Wave cycle, we gain a new respect for Jeremy Bentham and his view of humans being guided by the two masters of pain and pleasure. There is no doubt that society swung far in the direction of pleasure in the most recent K Wave advance and speculative fall season. If one were wise, one would begin bracing for the full effect of the pain yet to come as the pendulum completes its full swing.

Works Cited

Stoken, Dick. 1980. "The Kondratieff Cycle and its Effects on Social Psychology." *The Futurist.* February.

8

THE CYCLE AND WAR

"A wise prince should never remain idle in peaceful times, but industriously make good use of them, so that when fortune changes she may find him prepared to resist her blows, and to prevail in adversity."

Machiavelli

This review of war is not an attempt to make the case that war guides the K Wave, but just the opposite. War is guided by the same social forces that produce other K Wave manifestations. War, like the K Wave itself, appears to most often be the result of fundamental shifts in the economic structure of the international system. Evidence indicates that military conflict is far more likely during the economic expansion phases of the K Wave advance. This chapter will examine wars as they fit into and provide evidence of the four long-wave cycles from 1789 to the present.

Since records have been kept, men have been in conflict and at war with their fellow men. There are several periods during which the conflict has not been as widespread and destructive, but basically all of history has seen war. However, an interesting pattern begins to emerge as we take a closer look, especially over the past 200 years of K Wave history.

As the economies of individual nations begin expanding and growing they tend to become competition for each other for raw materials. Interaction between national economies is similar to individual action. When an individual begins to get established economically and to reach certain levels of success, he or she begins looking about to see what the next venture might be. In time a country needs more raw materials, capital and markets. Thus, as times are good, output is increasing, internally the economic outlook is stable and the domestic population is comfortable, national leaders begin to get restless and look beyond their borders to see where and how they may expand their economy and influence.

The nation, just as the individual, will invariably step on someone's foot; and that nation, just as the individual, will retaliate. It may be a dispute over scarce resources and raw materials or conflict over markets. It may just be a restless leader seeking to expand his influence or use his military arsenal and new weaponry.

We will take a look only at the history of armed conflict since 1789—the beginning of the upswing of the first K Wave. A telling fact is that almost the only time great powers were at war in modern times was during spring and summer upswings in the long-wave cycle. Great powers typically do not do battle during K Wave fall and winter seasons. World War II was an exception, clearly a very big exception. We must consider what a great power is in order to draw such a conclusion.

The book, *War in the Modern Great Power System*, by Jack Levy (1983, 16) assisted me a great deal in considering the relationship between the K Wave cycle and war. Some of my material in the review of war as well as the following quote is taken from that work:

> A Great Power is defined here as a state that plays a major role in international politics with respect to security-related issues. The Great Powers can be differentiated from other states by their military power, their interests, their behavior in general and interactions with other Powers, other Powers' perception

of them and some formal criteria . . . Most important, a Great Power possesses a high level of military capabilities relative to other states. At a minimum, it has relative self-sufficiency with respect to military security. Great Powers are basically invulnerable to military threats by non-Powers and need only fear other Great Powers.

The first of the long-wave cycles began its advance around 1789 and peaked around 1815. Our first major conflicts of this period were the French Revolutionary Wars from 1792 until 1802. The storming of the Bastille on July 14, 1789, marked the beginning of France's transition from a monarchy to a democratic nation. The coalition had its difficult moments as it went through its reconstruction period from 1789 to 1791. The new constitution collapsed in 1792, and the new legislative assembly declared war on Austria on April 20, 1792, accusing them of counterrevolutionary agitation. This marked the beginning of 10 years of war fought from the Caribbean to the Indian Ocean, though most of the conflict was in the low countries, the Rhineland and Lombardy.

During this first upswing of the K Wave, Western nations were emerging and beginning to lay the groundwork for the capitalist nations that would dominate the world to the present day. Early conflicts in the first advance set the stage in France for Napoleon. The internal French Revolutionary Wars saw the death of some 700,000 in battle, while the expansionary Napoleonic Wars can be attributed close to two million deaths.

Napoleon Bonaparte proclaimed himself emperor of France in 1804 and waged war throughout Europe until 1815. The object of the allies of the nations of Europe was to stop French expansion. Napoleon was finally defeated by the Duke of Wellington at the Battle of Waterloo on June 18, 1815. The Napoleonic Wars were by far the most costly conflicts during the first upswing.

Other wars that deserve mention during this period are the Russo-Turkish War and the War of 1812. In the latter, America settled its independence from Britain once and for all, though not as quickly and decisively as it would have liked. The war lasted until January 1815 when General Andrew Jackson won a decisive victory at New Orleans. A surging nationalism swept America after that victory, in which the British lost over 2,000 men and the Americans lost only 100.

Around the year 1815, the first K Wave began its decline, continued until the 1840s. This close to 30-year period was virtually war free, with the exception of the Franco-Spanish War, which lasted from April to August 1823 and was the result of France trying to interfere with the liberal revolution going on in Spain.

Another conflict was the 1827 defeat of a Russian-British-French fleet at Navarino Bay by a Turkish-Egyptian fleet. This embarrassing defeat caused Russia to declare war in 1827 and came to be known as the Russo-Turkish War. During this conflict, Russia launched an invasion of Bulgaria. Turkey was forced to sign the treaty of Adrianople in 1829, which recognized Greek independence. The treaty also gave Russia a majority of the Black Sea's Caucasian coast.

The remainder of this first K Wave downturn seemed to scarcely produce a fist fight, so reserved were nations during this time of economic contraction. There appears to be a clear pattern of more conflict during the period Kondratieff labeled as the long-wave advance and far less during the decline in the first K Wave.

The second K Wave began in the 1840s. As we enter the upswing of the second K Wave cycle and the economics of the nations of the world begin to expand, we again see an enormous increase in both the number of wars and their severity. The first incident of this period was the Austro-Sardinian War in 1849, which cost close to 6,000 lives. This same year saw the First Schleswig-Holstein War as well as the Roman Republic War; both were no more than brief skirmishes.

The next battle of this second upswing came in 1852 and was the first major confrontation since Napoleon's defeat: the Crimean

War. Russia's desire to see the Ottoman Empire destroyed was the chief cause of this war. France, England, Prussia, and Austria joined to fend off the aggression of Russia in the Crimean region. They were successful but at the expense of 500,000 lives. The Treaty of Paris on March 30, 1856, guaranteed independence to the Ottoman Empire. One of the good things that came out of the Crimean War was the work and leadership of Florence Nightingale, by whose work army hospitals and nurses came into existence.

The year 1856 also saw the Anglo-Persian War, which lasted only four months and cost fewer than 1,000 lives. In 1859, the region that is now Italy began struggling for its economic independence. This led to the War of Italian Unification. All the major powers of Europe had interest to one degree or another in this area. But under the leadership of Garibaldi, the Italians fought for their freedom and established Rome as the capital of their new nation. The first national Italian Parliament met on February 18, 1861, and Victor Emmanuel II became king.

By far the bloodiest war of the upswing in the second K Wave cycle was the American Civil War, 1861–1865. The death toll by many estimates exceeded 500,000. The war was, in many respects, over conflicting economic interests of the North and South during this time of rapid economic expansion. Not only was the slavery issue settled, but so was the issue of where the industrial strength of the United States would lie for a hundred years to come.

Napoleon III was responsible for a number of French ventures during this period, one of which was the Franco-Mexican War, lasting from 1862 until 1867, in which some 8,000 died. The French army had put Maximilian on the Mexican throne, but his troops and the native Mexican forces were able to overthrow him.

The unification of Italy caused developments to the north that were settled by the Austro-Prussian War. Italy was defeated at Sadowa, July 3, 1800. Venetia was ceded to Italy as a result.

The final major confrontation of this second upswing in the K Wave came in the Franco-Prussian War, 1870–1871, in which

200,000 died. France lost and its government was left in shambles for attempting to avert the unification of Germany.

The second K Wave began to peak and turn down in 1873, and for almost 30 years the world economy slipped into an economic decline of previously unknown proportion. During this period, the world was in a state of peace it had not known since the days of the Roman Empire. Two brief conflicts marked this period. One was the Russo-Turkish War, 1877–1878, which culminated with the treaty of Berlin (July 13, 1878). This conflict saw 120,000 men lose their lives. The other conflict during this time was the Sino-French War which took place from 1884 to 1885 and cost 2,100 lives.

The year 1896 saw the bottom of the second decline of the long-wave cycle. The pattern was once again clear, with more war during the advance than during the decline.

The beginning of the third advance of the K Wave came in the mid-1890s. When nations began expanding their economies, war was not long in coming. The first war of the period came in 1904: the Russo-Japanese War. Apparently Russia was exerting too much control and influence in Manchuria and Korea, causing the Japanese to get restless. Negotiations failed, and Japan attacked the Russians in Port Arthur, Manchuria, on February 8, 1904, without a declaration of war. Japan had far superior organization and leadership as well as shorter supply lines and was able to deliver a final blow by destroying the Russian Baltic fleet at Tsushima (May 27–28, 1905). President Roosevelt arranged a peace conference at Portsmouth, New Hampshire, on August 5, 1905. Japan was granted its wishes in the region, but only after 45,000 men lost their lives.

The next conflict during this third upswing was the Italo-Turkish War (1911–1912). During this campaign the Italians were able to annex Libya at the price of some 6,000 lives. And of course the next war was "the war to end all wars," World War I (1914–1918). For the first time in history, the entire world—or so it seemed—was at war. The death and destruction were unimaginable. Close to 30 million lives were lost, and the total cost of the war was over $180 billion. Did you ever stop to consider the real reason for the war? It really stemmed from a conflict of economic interests between the nations involved. This war came during a surge in the industrialization of the world, and nations were still securing colonies for the supply of raw materials and cheap labor.

The last confrontation of this third upswing came in the form of the Russian Revolution. Nicholas II abdicated the throne on March 15, 1917, and for a brief time Russia was a democracy. But on October 23, 1917, the Bolsheviks, who were the most extreme of revolutionaries, seized power. Thus we had the emergence of the Union of Soviet Socialist Republics. Surprisingly, there was not a great deal of bloodshed in the initial revolution; the bloodshed came in the form of internal purging later on.

The K Wave peaked shortly after the close of the first world war, plateaued throughout the 1920s, and then fell dramatically in 1929 and the early 1930s. This period, from the early 1920s into the 1940s, was the third decline in the K Wave cycle. The world was once again fairly peaceful most of this time of economic decline. The only wars to speak of during this time were the Manchurian War and the Italy-Ethiopian War in which a combined total of some 14,000 lives were lost.

The Sino-Japanese War began on July 7, 1937. Its causes were deeply rooted, but it broke out over a minor clash of Chinese and Japanese soldiers on Marco Polo Bridge near Peking. What followed was a bloody Far East war that was to merge four years later with World War II.

Typically, wars among major powers do not occur during K Wave winter seasons. But World War II has shown that one madman, in this case Adolf Hitler, can have an impact on the long-wave cycle. His ruthless aggression once again brought the entire world into war. It is estimated that some 20 million lives were lost, and the cost in property and monetary damages would be futile to estimate.

The Russo-Finnish War fought in 1939 and 1940 could be listed with World War II, but was somewhat of a separate conflict and cost some 16,000 lives. The Communist Revolution in China came to a close during this period. While no one can be sure of the death toll, it was certainly in the millions.

The pattern in this third K Wave appears to follow the trend established for the cycle except for the big problem of World War II. Clearly it is a problem.

From soon after the end of World War II until 1980, we were in the fourth advance of the long-wave cycle. Let's consider the wars that occurred during this period.

The Korean War, 1950–1953, was the first military stance taken by the united Nations as it joined against Communist aggression at a price of over one million lives.

The Russo-Hungarian War of 1956 cost some 7,000 lives and Hungarian hopes of more political and economic freedom.

The Vietnam War, 1962–1973, which cost 56,000 American lives, and the Iran-Iraq War which started in 1979 and cost 500,000 plus lives are both wars that can be attributed to the fourth advance of the K Wave. Of course, the fourth decline of the K Wave, or the beginning of the fall season, began with the 1981 recession. The advance of the fourth K Wave, which lasted from the late 1940s to 1981, appears to have been a less severe period for wars than were other K Wave advances.

The Gulf War, during the decline, was not a war among great powers. Iraq could not produce its own weaponry, although the evidence says that they were trying and getting close. Virtually all of Iraq's weapons were bought and imported from great powers such as the former Soviet Union, France, and the United States. America still had an impressive showing of military might, technology, and ability, even if Iraq cannot be labeled as a great power. It should be noted once again WWII was the only instance of a war between great powers during a plateau or decline.

In review of this chapter, a startling fact emerges, one which goes a long way to enforce the argument in favor of the existence of a K Wave cycle. This fact concerns the totals in the loss of life in the wars that have ravaged the world during the period from 1789 to the present. During K Wave downswings, except for WWII, which I readily concede is a massive exception, we have seen only several hundred thousand deaths from armed conflict, while during K Wave upswings there have been in excess of 30 million deaths due to war.

The evidence speaks for itself. The world is far more likely to see war during advances of the K Wave than during declines. In recent years all the great powers have been too concerned with their internal problems to get involved with foreign entanglements. Britain, Russia, France, Germany, Japan, China, Canada, Italy and others are spending their time and energy dealing with problems in their national economies. China is in better shape than most. Unemployment, slow or negative economic growth, financial crisis, banking problems, and real-estate collapses are all keeping governments busy within their own borders.

Once the problems—recessions and depression—are worked through and internal conflicts are straightened out, things will be different. When the nations and economies of the globe move into a new K Wave economic advance, internal tensions will subside and will not be so critical and all-consuming. Nations will once again begin to look with lust beyond their borders at raw materials, labor, and markets. China may be a potential leading aggressor during the next advance due to its growing economic strength. Japan is another likely candidate once again.

The Japanese stock collapse that began in December of 1989 appears to have marked the ending of fall and the beginning of the latest global winter of the K Wave in many respects. Therefore, we should have a fairly peaceful world until early in the 21st century, at which time we can expect to see a rise in armed conflict among nations—even between great powers. Although if we suffer a sharp global economic decline that flushes most of the excesses out of the global system in a short time, global hostilities could come a bit sooner than would normally be anticipated.

We will not enjoy total peace during a K Wave winter. There will inevitably be a few clashes and conflicts; however, there should be no major conflict between great powers. There will always be small wars and eruptions on hostile borders during the K Wave decline. We can only hope World War II was a major aberration and that war is far less likely between great powers during a declining phase of the K Wave, since we now appear to be in such a phase.

There is always the danger of a madman like Hitler rising to power. The most likely spot for such a leader this time around will be Russia. Just as Germany lost World War I, Russia lost the cold war and will have major internal problems that could breed despotic leadership.

All in all, the willingness or lack thereof of nations to wage war sheds a revealing light on the K Wave and vice versa. The relationship of war to the cycle should be studied closely to understand and gain insight into the nature of the K Wave and how it expresses itself in international affairs.

Works Cited and Additional Sources

Levy, Jack S. 1983. *War in the Modern Great Power System, 1495–1975.* Lexington: University Press of Kentucky.

Martino, Joseph P. 1985. "Does the Kondratieff Wave Really Exist?" *The Futurist.* February.

9

THE K WAVE AND CRISIS IN THE GLOBAL BANKING SYSTEM

"The ultimate effect of shielding men from the effects of folly, is to fill the world with fools."

Herbert Spencer

Unbeknown to most, the global banking system is in a precarious position as this K Wave cycle enters the winter season—particularly in Japan. In the United States, with creative bookkeeping encouraged by Uncle Sam, a good spread in interest rates, and financing for massive bailouts extorted from taxpayers, we managed to keep the banking system afloat. But major problems still lie under the surface. Many of the loans made during K Wave advances and the boom years of a speculative fall season go bad during the K Wave winter. Projected growth patterns and price trends calculated during a K Wave advance and speculative fall season just don't hold, and the banking system is destabilized.

Banks must make solid loans to private industry and individuals to be viable for the long term. A beneficial interest-rate spread can create only a temporary bailout for banks. In recent years banks borrowed from the public at low rates with CDs and savings accounts and loaned to governments at higher rates by buying government debt and funding the incredible deficits. This created temporary bank profits and the illusion that the fundamental banking problems of the 1980s had gone away. But the improvement will not last as the K Wave decline fundamentals finally come to bear on the banking system. Even a temporary rise in interest rates would derail the banks' strategy.

In Japan and many other nations, the banking system is teetering on the edge. Japan now has some of the largest banks in the world. Real estate values have dropped as much as 40 percent, undermining bank loans. The Japanese banks have also taken major losses on stock market investments. When the banking system in one country collapses as the K Wave decline accelerates in the winter season, the entire global system could be thrown into crisis because of the incredible global financial interdependence today.

Japan will likely be the banking crisis trigger this time around. Entrenched deflation is eroding the value of the loans and therefore assets of the biggest banks in the world. One of them is bound to fail and act as a shot heard around the world for the global banking system. Many U.S. municipal bonds are insured by Japanese banks. Japanese funds that are loaned around the world will be repatriated to Japan in an accelerating Japanese depression.

There are many reasons for the banking crisis, but when they are boiled down to the basics, we see the fundamental forces of the economic long-wave cycle at work, chipping away at the foundations of the system. The solid K Wave expansion provided healthy loans for the banking system. But there is a group mentality that expects trends to last forever. When major trends reverse with the K Wave, most banks and business people are taken by surprise. When the K Wave is combined with government trying to protect the people from the consequences of bad business ventures, instead of letting the market and justice system purge the guilty, the result is disaster.

The days of banking as we know it are numbered. Every K Wave decline has seen major changes and restructuring take place in the international banking system. The 1930s saw major changes and the removal of gold as the basis to the dollar. The K Wave decline of the 1870s and 1880s saw constant restructuring of the banking system and was marked by persistent banking failures. Banking failures and restructuring in the K Wave decline of the 1820s and 1830s were commonplace. These major changes don't come due to great new ideas springing spontaneously from government and the banking industry. The banking system eventually comes to the end of its rope. Changes come because crisis, failure, and chaos demand them—the bankers and the bureaucrats have no choice. The latest K Wave decline will be no different.

Bad loans that accumulated during the latest K Wave advance and fall season in the form of real-estate debt, consumer debt, corporate debt, and Third World debt are being reshuffled faster, and with more slight of hand, than a deck of cards in a back-room poker game. The safer money may be in the poker game, however, because poker players at least know the risks. Most depositors go blindly about their business, expecting the government to baby-sit the bankers and their deposits. Taxpayers don't understand that the baby-sitter can charge trillions of dollars for the job. Would you pay your sitter with a blank check, a sitter with a reputation for paying $2000 for a toilet seat? The latest K Wave fall and winter decline with rising bank instability and failures is typical. The next K Wave advance will also be typical, with very few bank failures.

When you reach the end of the speculative fall season and plateau of the K Wave cycle, all types of debts are at unprecedented levels. This includes personal, corporate, and government debt. In early 1993, Japan had $10 trillion in interest-bearing debt and another $8 trillion in derivatives. Tracy Herrick in *The Money Analyst*, pointed out that this amounts to $6 for every $1 of gross domestic product. It doesn't take a great deal of thought to realize that the game being played, as in past K Wave cycles, has got to come to an end. But before coming to grips with the day of reckoning, let's evaluate the banking situation in some hope of gaining an understanding of how we could have gotten ourselves into such a predicament.

Bankers came out of the Great Depression very conservative in nature—as did everyone else. Interest rates were low, and the industrial corporate world was expanding, providing safe havens for the banker's abundance of free cash. And free cash it was, as the humble public would never ask for such a thing as interest on demand deposits. So the bankers found themselves in a position that was hard to beat. Asset values were rising, so few loans went bad; borrowers were conservative; and investors were scared of stocks and other financial instruments, so they kept their money in the banks and accepted low returns.

In the latter years of the K Wave expansion, the public became more demanding. The generation that had experienced the Depression were growing older, and a new generation was taking over. They began putting money in liquid investments that appreciated the value of the dollar and that were willing to pay customers handsomely for their considerable deposits. The bankers, on the other hand, figured they were doing the public a favor by opening their doors from 10 A.M. until 2 P.M. and were under a false illusion as to their worth and service to humanity.

Banks were slow in understanding the gravity of the shift in consumer demand—a shift in K Wave psychology. The thrifts and savings and loans had cut deeply into the banks' bottom line before bankers began seeking solutions to the growing problem. This newfound competition, coupled with rising interest rates and inflation on an upward trend, as it always is in the upswing of the K Wave, forced bankers to evaluate their situation closely and use a bit more creativity in their financial dealings. They became more aggressive.

One of the ways of increasing business came when a number of big banks struck on the idea of making high-yielding loans to the developing Third World. Bankers have an acute tendency towards the herding instinct, so when the giants such as Chase and Chemical began loaning to the Third World, the entire world banking community figured it was a good idea. The loans were good for a while, and interest payments were made. However, Third World debts were the first of the loans made in the last K Wave advance to begin plaguing the system. Billions in loans have been rolled over or converted into equity in recent years. Banks are beginning to realize the equity they received isn't worth what they assumed. Billions more were packaged and dumped on the World Bank so the world's taxpayers could pay for the banker's mistakes. Many loans still on the books will soon be rolled over one time too many, helping to roll the global banking system itself out of bed—and with it the global economy as we know it.

A nation is sovereign and lives a perpetual existence, its citizens hope, not like a corporation, which can turn bottom up and vanish when times get bad. This misconception seemed to play a major role in the thinking of the world bankers during the late 1960s and 1970s, as they somehow could not perceive a nation or state becoming insolvent. But, sovereignty cannot be expected to take the place of solvency.

With a bunch of Western bankers in pin-striped suits waving billions of dollars in their faces, the leaders of the Third World were more than happy to oblige and take the money. This is not to say that the leaders of the Third World were forced to take the loans and are thus not responsible for the current crisis situation. They are very much responsible and should be held so. They were well aware of the amount of debt they were taking on and what the limits were of the countries they ruled. What they were not aware of was the shifting tide of the world economy and the havoc played by depressed economic conditions on a nation that must sell its raw materials on the world market to pay its massive loans. The fact of the matter is that billions of dollars lent to the Third

World are uncollectible and have to be written off the books of banks. This process began in the 1980s and will likely be finished by the late 1990s.

Three body punches will bring the international banking system into submission during the latest K Wave decline. These have occurred and are continuing to occur over the fall and winter season of the K Wave. The Third World debt crisis was the first punch to be landed on the international banking system, a powerful punch that weakened the entire system. The second punch is proving to be even more devastating: the collapse of commercial and residential real-estate prices, with Japan the global leader. The big money-center banks were primarily affected by the Third World debt crisis. Real-estate deflation is affecting almost all banks globally. The third punch, which will most likely be the knockout punch for the banking system as we know it, will be default and failure of consumer and corporate loans. When the full force of the third punch has landed, a soft breeze will be sufficient to send the global banking system to the mat.

Like all other components of the economy in the K Wave cycle the banking system overestimated the future. This overestimation of business expansion and future growth and the belief in ever-rising prices coaxed banks into overexpansion of loans to segments of the economy that were peaking and headed for decline. You can't blame the bankers. Not everyone looks at the economy from a K Wave perspective. The bankers didn't know that agriculture, oil, real estate, and eventually consumer spending were going to enter a K Wave cycle decline. The overexpansion that brings falling prices is the key to understand the problems faced by the banks.

The impact of bad real-estate loans and the effect on banks was just coming to the forefront in the late 1980s and early 1990s. Commercial and residential real estate has fallen by 30 to 40 percent in many areas. Loans are still carried on the books at the old valuations as prices fall lower and lower. Tokyo real estate has been in a free fall, declining 25 percent in value in 1993 alone. As real-estate failures and defaults accelerate, banks will have to record the losses, and balance sheets will be weakened further.

Corporations are currently in debt-to-equity situations and debt-to-working-capital and debt-to-available cash positions that have not been seen since the Great Depression. If that's not bad enough, the individual consumer is in far worse financial condition than prior to or during the Great Depression.

There invariably comes a time when the corporation and the individual have borrowed beyond their limit. This tends to happen at the end of the fall season of the K Wave cycle—the late 1920s and now in the 1990s—causing spending to come to a screeching halt. Since government makes the rules, it can be more flexible in its spending habits as the K Wave runs its course. The U.S. government was actually in good shape when the Great Depression began. But presently, the U.S. government is in terrible financial shape; and this time around Uncle Sam will not have the borrowing power available to ease the pain.

When individuals, corporations, and governments have borrowed beyond their ability to pay and cannot borrow more to pay off interest and loans, the game is over. The assets they have borrowed to buy fall in value. The credit binge begins to contract and unravel. This accelerates the deflation of the K Wave decline—pulling the rug out from under the real market value of the loans made by the banks. As the assets backing the loans fall in price and become worthless, the banking system plunges over the edge. The financial house of cards created during the upswing comes tumbling down. These forces are at work to varying degrees throughout the global economy. The system has been purged of the imbalances when it reaches the bottom of the K Wave decline.

An important point the public should be aware of for the present decline of the K Wave is that the FDIC insurance for banking institutions is really not supported by law. That is to say that if enough banks go under in the coming collapse, the federal government has no responsibility by law to refund depositors' money if the insurance agency runs dry of funds. The belief that government banking insurance will survive a K Wave downturn is only wishful thinking.

James Grant, (Feinberg 1987, 184) who is a former *Barron's* bond reporter and is now editor of *Grant's Interest Rate Observer*, gives us these not-so-encouraging words in relation to a banking failure:

> Anyone who assumes that 'they' are not going to let this happen is making a profound miscalculation . . . so much credit has been created outside the banking system that the Federal Reserve Board now regulates a less and less significant sector.

Robert Prechter (Feinberg 1987, 184), editor of the *Elliott Wave Theorist*, has some fascinating insights into the banking problems:

> The idea that government can insure the banks has made them more unsafe, not less, because it has encouraged them to take imprudent risks. Many are technically bankrupt right now. During the crash, so many bank loans will go sour that the government will have to declare a national bank moratorium. They won't call it a default. They'll say, 'You still have your money but you can't touch it until next year.' Of course, that year will stretch into many.

Falling prices are very destructive to a bank's loan portfolio. There are those who believe the power vested in the Federal Reserve Board by the Monetary Control Act of 1980 will eliminate destructive deflationary pressures. This is an understandable mistake, but I must disagree. The Fed was given power to buy foreign bonds and loans and reduce the reserve requirements of our banks to zero. The theory that creating money in this manner will stop disinflation (slowing increases in prices) and deflation (falling prices) has proven to not hold water.

In the past, we have seen a great deal of loosening of the money supply with rising figures of M1 and M2 (figures for the amount of money in the economy), yet we have had disinflation and deflation of prices during this same period.

Today, there is so much slack in the economy, with industry operating far below capacity, that large increases in the money supply still don't inflate prices. Industry scrambles to fill increases in demand and is forced to keep prices low to attract new business. Prices are incapable of moving up any sustainable extent when the economy is operating at far below capacity.

What is clearly happening to the money created by the Fed during the fall season is that it went pouring into the stock markets where it encouraged and fueled financial market inflation and bull markets throughout the world. The Fed was creating paper millionaires in the stock market with financial inflation, not real-asset inflation. The Fed is at a loss to understand why their loose money policies have not ignited inflation to any substantial degree. The fact is that the only way one can come to a clear understanding of the situation we are facing is by taking the all-encompassing view revealed by the K Wave theory.

Deflationary pressures build as the K Wave takes its course in the fall and winter season. No monetary manipulation is able to stop the inevitable. As the amount of world debt in all sectors continues to mount and the sliding real values of commodities, capital outlays, and capital expansion become evident, the market value of bank assets fall. This puts banks in a squeeze. The underlying values of the loan portfolios of banks collapse with the falling asset prices during the K Wave decline. If you loaned $1 million dollars on a building that is now worth $500,000, you have a problem. You can apply this concept to almost all bank loans. Falling asset values are undermining and will continue to undermine the foundation of the entire banking structure. If you understand this basic principal of the K Wave, you understand why banks are in deep trouble during the K Wave fall and winter seasons.

Where are the nations, corporations, and individuals who can afford to take on the money the Fed intends to create? The idea that the Monetary Act of 1980 can stop deflation is simply invalid. In time, the Fed has to realize that the money it creates is only fueling the raging stock markets of the world. Falling prices that undermine bank loans are inevitable. The Fed will prove to be impotent in trying to avoid the inevitable flow of the K Wave cycle.

The over-production in all industries creates price competition to capture markets. When the world is over producing and prices are falling, there eventually emerges a lack of borrowing. The world is producing more than it needs. It doesn't matter how low interest rates go. Demand of loans drys up and banks can't make any more solid loans. World prices slide in this competitive market. The loans that backed the production, based on higher prices, go bad as prices fall. Banks are squeezed.

Nations, companies, and individuals will eventually simply not be able to afford any more spending on borrowed money. Eventually, there is not enough spending to support bank loans that finance production. Because of the continued and increasing weakness in demand across the board, prices will tumble further. It is a vicious downward spiral. The slowdown will force layoffs and firings, thus ending buying strength and demand even further. Bank loans become weaker and weaker. As the K Wave declines, the prices of raw materials, wholesale goods, commodities, consumer goods, and real estate collapse.

We have seen radical drops in raw material and commodities prices since 1981. The forces generating these drops will soon be seen throughout all industries and the entire global economy. Falling prices spread to real estate, wholesale prices, and consumer prices in the early 1990s. The effect of falling prices will snowball into the decline. First it is disinflation, but as the decline accelerates, we see deflation across the board. Deflation means only one thing for the banking community: trouble.

The natural turning in the K Wave will be fueled by an important component in our global economy and the chief means by which much debt owed to the banks is being repaid: the price of oil. Mexico, Argentina, Indonesia, and Nigeria pay bank loans with oil export revenues. If prices fall low enough, oil-exporting Third World nations will not even be able to pay interest.

Many of the oil-producing countries also have debts that must be repaid with oil revenues, Russia, for example. Repayment of foreign loans are only a small part of the picture when it comes to the effect of oil on the economy and the banking system. All goods are shipped by some means: rail, ship, truck, or air. If oil prices plunge, the prices of delivering goods also drops significantly. A drop in the price of oil will also force down the price of other competing energy sources, including coal and natural gas. Oil byproducts are used in the production of many products, such as cars, tires, computers, televisions, plastics; the list could go on and on. Oil and its byproducts of gasoline and diesel fuel affect the price of almost every economic and business activity you can think of.

Falling oil prices accelerate price declines of virtually every other product and industry. Falling prices, i.e., falling oil prices, undermine bank loans. The Gulf War was fought because Saddam Hussein wanted to stop Kuwait from cutting prices on oil and undermining Iraq's markets. Far from keeping oil prices low, the Gulf War boosted prices for several years by taking Kuwaiti's production out of the market along with Iraq's. The deflationary acceleration of the latest K Wave decline would probably have come sooner if it hadn't been for the Gulf War.

In the years before the war, oil prices had already fallen far below their peaks of over $30 a barrel in the 1980s. By some estimates, if oil drops below $12 a barrel for any extended period of time, the international banking system will not survive. The banks can only write down so many loans. The amounts of default will be so great that no juggling act by the IMF, World

Bank, or Washington, or a concerted effort by the G–7 nations will help the situation.

The global banking-system support level is more likely in the neighborhood of $10 a barrel for oil, before the deflationary impact creates defaults across the board. The natural K Wave forces of supply and demand will eventually drive oil prices down sharply. War, which destroys wellheads and production facilities, is the only option to keep market oil prices at higher levels and hold in check the deflationary consequences of lower oil prices on every area of the entire economy. These forces make another Mideast war in the years ahead highly likely. But war would only be a temporary setback for the deflation that threatens the global economy.

Soon, the Russian oil fields will be coming on-line as Western technology and capital go to work for our new capitalist comrades. A Middle East war will hopefully not be the option taken to keep oil prices at levels that keep the banking system from collapsing. However, politicians do remarkable things to stay in power and keep from being blamed for hard times.

Even an oil import tax imposed by Washington will only prop up prices for a limited length of time before oversupply pushes them down again. Though oil prices are a crucial factor, they don't hold the only key to the coming collapse. As the entire world economy slows, other forces will eventually and of necessity force all prices down. Oil prices cannot be given total credit for the coming banking crisis and K Wave winter season, but should be looked upon as a major force that has taken the economy into deflation. Virtually every sector of the economy will be placing pressure on the banking system. The straw that finally breaks the camel's back could come from any number of places, but it will most likely be Japan.

A major banking collapse has come with the decline of every K Wave since 1789, and each collapse has been followed by major changes in the financial system of the world. The Great Depression and the banking collapse of 1933 saw the world come off the gold standard, and we saw fiat money (money not backed up by anything but faith) enter as the new standard for international transactions. The 1930s crisis also prompted more power to be granted to the Federal Reserve system and an overall centralization of banking in the United States and the world. Government banking insurance was introduced in the Great Depression. It is an illusion that may be dashed during the latest winter season of the K Wave.

If government had only gotten out of the way in the 1930s, the banking system would have taken care of itself. The bad banks would have been purged from the system, and depositors would have been wiser and more cautious next time. The Depression would have been far shorter, and it wouldn't have taken World War II to get the economy and people back to work. Our economy would likely be far more advanced and developed than it is today had the market been allowed to clean the slate. Instead, we got a promise from government that they would protect us from foolish banking practices by guaranteeing everyone's deposits.

Sure, there would still be bank failures occasionally in a genuine free-market banking system. But the culprits would be run out of town or jailed. Instead, the entire banking system is corrupted and pushed to the edge of insolvency and failure.

The greatest crisis years of this latest K Wave decline will be reached sometime before the early 2000s. When the crisis hits, depositors will demand action by government. The fact is that the government created the crisis with its intervention and meddling in the market. It will be interesting to see what sort of banking system and reforms the government puts forward as the solution to the latest K Wave crisis.

In recent years, there has been a push to put more financial power into the hands of the United Nations. It is likely that some sort of banking scheme and emergency powers will be introduced that give enormous authority to the World Bank, which is under the authority of the United Nations. An international currency unit may well be introduced as the savior of a global banking system in crisis. It is likely this new currency, if it is introduced, will be modeled after the ECU (European Currency Unit) and backed fractionally in gold.

A banking system run from the top down on a global scale will not work. It would only create another level of government bureaucracy to choke the life out of the economic system. In time, such a system would fail more miserably than any system to date.

The greatest possible change we could make in the crisis of this K Wave decline would be to go to a high-tech, gold-based free-market banking system. Most people think a gold-based system is archaic and outdated. The fact is that a very efficient gold-based money system could be created easily today. A modern gold system would combine the solid principles of gold money with the efficiency of advanced information technology. You wouldn't have to lug around gold coins. Electronic money could be backed in gold. For thousands of years gold has returned faith to economies in times of crisis.

The chances of our all-powerful government allowing such free system outside the controls and watchful eye of Big Brother are slim to none. However, if the decline ends with severe economic/political collapse, the free market might just take over without consulting the politicians, who made the situation far worse than it ever had to be in the first place.

In a true market banking system based in gold, there would still be occasional banking failures. However the system would be so productive that failures would be short-lived and cause little pain to the whole system. Depositors would learn to find out if their bank was safe or not by checking with reputable rating agencies. A true free-market system would self-regulate instead of self-destruct.

Necessary but painful innovations often must be implemented due to unavoidable catastrophe. Only when the economy is in a state of disarray and confusion are the changes made. What changes will come with the coming crisis in the international monetary system during this high-tech age of the computer and microprocessor? What effect will our shrinking world community and a true global economy have on the new system that will emerge from the financial carnage created by the latest K Wave winter? An all-powerful centralized global banking system and a single world currency is certainly possible. But there is a good chance that true free-market reform could take place. This would be the best possible outcome—even if its chances don't look that great at present.

There are plenty of banks in great shape that will survive the crisis and do fine. They will fully participate in the banking system that emerges in the years ahead. Only time will tell us what system will lead us into the next K Wave advance. We can only hope that the global economy moves toward more freedom for individuals, business and financial markets—and not headlong into the arms of financial tyranny.

Meanwhile, you would be smart to check the safety of your bank with a respectable bank rating agency. My estimate is that between 25 percent and 35 percent of the banks that were in existence in the 1990s will no longer exist by the time this Kondratieff winter is over. Make sure your bank is not one of the K Wave casualties. [See rating agencies listed in the Appendix.]

Works Cited and Additional Sources

Clausen, A.W. 1983. "Third World Debt and Global Recovery." *Vital Speeches,* April.

Feinberg, Andrew. 1987. "The Crash of 1989." *Gentlemens Quarterly,* February.

Herrick, Tracy. 1993. *The Money Analyst.* Jeffries and Company: Los Angeles.

Hindle, Tim. 1982. "Banking's House of Cards." *World Press Review,* May.

Kennedy, Susan Estabrook. 1973. *The Banking Crisis of 1933.* Lexington: University Press of Kentucky.

Malabre, Alfred L. 1987. "Debt Keeps Growing, With Major Risk in the Private Sector." *The Wall Street Journal,* 2 February.

Simmons. 1983. "Washington Memo: Worst-Case Scenario." *Financial World,* 15 October.

Snyder, Julian M. 1983. "An Economic Theory for the Real World." *Vital Speeches.* Southold N.Y.: City News Publishing Co., August.

Woche, Wutschafts, 1982. "Banking Crisis Ahead?" *World Press Review.* N.Y.: The Stanley Foundation, November.

Yamani, Ahmed Zaki. 1983. "Control and Decontrol in the Oil Market." *Vital Speeches,* June.

10

A TIME FOR
TRADE WARS

"A self-contained nation is a backward nation, with large numbers of people either permanently out of work, or very poorly paid in purchasing power. A nation which trades freely with all the world, selling to others those commodities which it can best produce, and buying from others those commodities which others can best produce, is by far the best conditioned nation for all practical purposes."

Walter Parker

The global market system works best when the consumer is granted freedom to choose. Free access is crucial if consumer decision making is expected to produce smooth operating markets. The consumer must be the central force and pivotal element of the market system. The consumer, free of constraints, creates the economic phenomenon of demand. Industry, free of restraints or props, responds with the economic phenomenon of supply. Protectionist sentiment injected into the system is a poison. It eventually produces trade conflict and, in time, trade wars. Trade wars distort both supply and demand, creating inefficiency, waste, and stagnation in the system.

Unfortunately, protectionism is a distinct characteristic of K Wave declines. History has shown that during the K Wave decline, there are always periods of abrupt decline in the volume of global trade. This has proven to be the case in all three K Wave declines of the past 200 years. The latest K Wave decline will likely prove to be no different.

Trade deserves close attention in relation to the K Wave so that we may gain an understanding of the nature of this disturbing interruption in commerce among nations.

Since the peak of the K Wave advance in the early 1980s, calls for protectionism and demands for trade barriers have been a part of the regular political discourse and popular debate. This is typical in a K Wave decline, although there have been what appear to be breakthroughs in global trade in recent years: the North American Free Trade Agreement (NAFTA) and the General Agreement on Tariffs and Trade (GATT). But just under the surface, protectionist sentiment has continued to stew. These aggreements will come under a great deal of pressure and criticism before this K Wave decline and winter season is over and may very well collapse due to the long-wave forces at work. Protectionist pressure that builds in a K Wave fall season (1981–1995), invariably erupts into crisis in a K Wave winter season (1995–200?).

Domestic economic problems exacerbate international trade relationships. The 1920s were experiencing many of the same protectionist pressures of recent years. This was also the case during the fall season of the 1870s, not to mention the conditions in the years just before and following Napoleon's defeat in 1815 in Europe. The old country was being swamped by goods from America, and protectionism produced trade conflict.

For a better understanding of what is in store for global trade in the years ahead, we need to review what occurs throughout the stages of a complete K Wave cycle in relation to trade. Just what are the forces that lead to protectionist sentiment, trade conflict, and global trade wars?

When the global economy comes out of a K Wave decline and winter season into a new advance, interest rates are low, and the world economy has been flushed of its burdensome debt. Global overcapacity of industry has been removed by corporate failures and bankruptcy.

Labor is cheap in the spring season of the K Wave, and laborers are willing to put in a hard day's work. They have learned to appreciate holding a job after long periods of unemployment and worry. Employees are willing to sacrifice to get their company and the economy rolling after experiencing the pain of the hard times during the decline.

A key to understanding why global markets tend to open up in the K Wave advance is that there are new industries driving the economy. New inventions and technology are being introduced to global markets. These breakthroughs create new young industries in communications, transportation, and other areas. As these new industries are too young to be overproducing or stepping on each other's feet, there is plenty of room in the market for eveyone.

Producers have been streamlined and made more efficient during the decline and are willing to support the tearing down of tariffs and barriers prohibiting international trade. Interest rates and wages are low. As prices begin to pick up in the spring season advance, profits are on the rise. Global tensions in the K Wave advance come from the need for access to raw materials rather than from overcapacity and overproduction in every industry.

Demand for new and old goods is on the rise as economies pick up in anticipation of better days to come. But the world is still cautious during the spring phase of the new advance. Companies are still risk averse. In the spring season of the advance, companies will not take the chance of expanding production of their goods beyond what they know for sure the markets will sustain. Managers and owners still remember the damage done in the decline to companies that overshot the needs of the marketplace.

At this point of the cycle, the world is slowly moving into a state of recovery and renewed optimism about the future. World prices begin to rise more rapidly, and the economy picks up steam. Prices begin to rise slowly as the demand for products is on the rise.

During the spring season, there is no reason to seek protection because business is cautious enough that goods are not overproduced, and there is plenty of demand. The 1950s and early 1960s were such a spring season of the K Wave. Competition was not intense. In a K Wave advance, companies are eager to peddle their wares in foreign markets and give others the right to do the same. Protectionist sentiment is almost nonexistent.

As the spring season becomes a K Wave summer, the global marketplace is once again demanding an ever-increasing amount of products. However, the global economy is not yet producing more goods than markets can comfortably absorb. In fact, in the summer season there tend to be shortages, which produces inflation and coaxes existing producers to expand production and new producers to enter markets.

Producers in many industries, such as electronics and computers, didn't exist in the 1920s and 1930s when other industries were overproducing. When these new industries began during the latest spring and summer seasons, there were more than enough markets for their products. In the 1980s and 1990s, they reached maturity, and the competition affected the bottom line. They then began screaming for protection from the competition.

The system is pushed too far when the global K Wave advance has experienced several decades of growth with only a few, small recessions. Industry owners and managers believe a new era of eternal growth has emerged. There has been a turnover in leadership in the global economy, and the new blood does not remember the last major decline and depression. Time and general prosperity has the effect of draining most of the caution out of the system. Corporations, individuals, and governments become willing to pay more for the right to borrow money, not to mention borrow far greater amounts. Growth and profits are projected many years into the future based on the previous year's trends in growth and prices. This was happening in the 1970s.

A classic example of the effect of the K Wave advance on industry is the global oil industry. The industry geared up for the expansion of the 1950s, 1960s, and 1970s, and production capacity eventually far exceeded the world's need for oil. Production was based on rising expectations and not real economic needs of the global economy. A great deal of money was borrowed and used to expand refinery and production facilities in developing countries. Those facilities eventually aided in the overproduction of oil, thus forcing prices down and making those developing countries incapable of paying their loans. Domestic oil producers wanted protection from foreign producers and increased tariffs and taxes on oil imports.

When prices were rising and markets were growing, this protectionist pressure didn't develop. Eventually, supply outstripped demand. This same series of events occurred in numerous markets from textiles to agriculture to microchips. There was overcapitalization and too much production capacity created in virtually every industry during the upswing.

Interest rates climb throughout the upswing of the K Wave, increasing the costs of capital. This drives all prices higher. Sales increase and business booms. The decision makers driving business and future expansion plans overestimate the future due to innate optimism and the overall economic expansion. These forces build to a climax or final blowoff for economic expansion. This is what occurred in the late 1970s.

Interest rates peak and then fall as the economy enters into the fall season where overproduction becomes the rule. Investment shifts in the fall season away from real expansion and into the financial markets.

Obviously, one of the most important aspects of the more competitive global marketplace of the K Wave decline is the effect on trade among nations. Industry, fighting to survive its overexpansion which was financed with expensive debt, begins pressuring government for more protectionist legislation. Since the peak in the economic expansion in the early 1980s, the introduction of legislation for trade barriers and tariffs has been on the rise. This has not been confined to Washington, D.C. Every capital in the world has begun to feel the pressure.

The push for protection explodes in the winter season of the decline as demand, for goods by consumers in global markets, shrink as economic activity collapses. Unfortunately, in a K Wave winter someone has to go out of business to bring the global system back into balance. No company owner wants it to be her company, and no politician wants it to be a company from his area, employing his constituents. No national leaders want it to be the companies from their country. But the inevitable trend is unstoppable.

The K Wave would take its course with or without the element of trade barriers and trade wars emerging in the fall and winter season. However, it is still important to take a brief look at the forces and outcome of protectionist sentiment.

In a speech delivered to the America Society in New York City during the 1980s fall season, David Peterson (1987, 230–231), the premier of Ontario, presented some startling thoughts on the tides of international trade. Here are a few highlights:

> We are all aware of the consequences incurred when the international trading system collapsed after the adoption of such measures as the Smoot-Hawley Tariff of 1930 and the British Tariff of 1932.
>
> The sudden surge of protectionism snapped a golden age of trade, cutting down assembly lines and creating soup lines, closing banks and foreclosing farms.
>
> The foundations of those protectionist trade walls bear a remarkable resemblance to trends we see today, more than a half-century later.

The trade wars of the 20s and 30s were sparked by slow growth in demand for traditional goods and services; a sudden spread of technological knowledge which narrowed competitive gaps between nations; an abrupt decline in the need for raw materials; and rapid shifts in the balance of market power.

The similarities to today's conditions remind me of the words of a great philosopher, Yogi Berra: "It's deja vu all over again."

You can't really blame industry for wanting protection from foreign competition in a K Wave decline. Profits drop as the economy enters the mature K Wave phase of overproduction. Without looking at the K Wave or the National Model at M.I.T., you could not have predicted the new era of disinflation/deflation and overproduction. Farmers, carmakers, shoe producers, computer makers, and dozens of others have legitimate complaints. They do face stiff competition and loss, but they are the ones overproducing. Why should consumers pay more for everything to cover up producers' mistakes and miscalculations.

A market economy has to decide whether it will side with the producer, who overcalculated and has his or her neck on the financial cutting block, or the consumer, who just wants the best product at the best price. In a true market system, there would be no choice. The consumer would be king, and producers would be told to sink or swim on their own and not beg for legislated protection.

Companies fighting for protectionism believe consumers should be forced to pay the bill for their inefficiencies and lack of responsibility. They took on more debt than they could handle and expanded beyond the needs of the global economy. In a free market, there must be punishment for economic mistakes. Otherwise, the economy gets confused and miscalculates even more dramatically. Much of the time, producers want consumers to pay more for goods to protect industries that actually belong in other countries. Japan wants to protect its rice farmers even though rice can be grown far more cheaply elsewhere in Asia and even in the bayous of Louisiana.

The fact is that the domestic economies are hurt by protectionism, not helped; but, more importantly, the brunt of this inefficiency falls on the consumer. The lifeblood of the economy is the discretionary income of the consumer and is the economic factor most threatened by protectionist policy. If decisions are based on what is best for the consumer, the economy always comes back faster from a decline. The only bright spot in the entire affair is that the new economy that emerges from the carnage of a K Wave decline promises to be better for both consumers and industry.

The storm clouds of trade wars are forming on the horizon as they have in the past when we have moved into the advanced stages of a K Wave decline. If trade wars are allowed to get under way, this decline will be far deeper and darker than necessary, just as the Great Depression was far deeper and lengthier than it should have been due to growing international trade isolationism. There are enormous hidden costs in protectionism, which stifle the economy. The Center for the Study of American Business at Washington University released a study in the 1980s that should have deterred the protectionist warlords, but that has not yet ended their special-interest financed blindness (Andres 1985). Adjusting for inflation, the American consumer in one year in the 1980s paid foreign governments and foreign manufacturers conservatively more than $4 billion for textile and apparel quotas alone. Tack on another $19 billion for the tariffs, a tax we pay our government on the value of apparel entering this country, and the total comes to $23 billion, money that could have gone to revitalizing and spurring growth in our economy.

In remembering that for every action there is an equal and opposite reaction, we must consider what protectionism in Washington will bring in retaliation from Tokyo, Seoul, London, Peking, and Taipei. In looking at the past, it would appear the reaction is often stronger than the action. For example, in the

1980s, when we restricted $55 million worth of cotton blouses from China, China retaliated by canceling $500 million worth of orders for American grain. A brilliant move by our farsighted Congress. This is an excellent example of how protection of one industry shifts the burden onto another. As one nation blocks trade, the nation that is hurt will surely retaliate, and the entire world will suffer.

John Oliver Wilson (1985, 517–519), chief economist at Bank of America, has spoken of a repeat in history in the area of protectionism:

> This is not the first time in our history that the threat of trade war has erupted. And it is useful to briefly recall this history, for the lessons from the past can serve us well in the present. In 1930, the United States passed the Smoot-Hawley Act which broadened tariff coverage to 25,000 products and provided for substantial increases in over 800 tariff rates. The reaction of the rest of the world was immediate. Widespread protests erupted. Tariffs were raised in a dozen major countries and they were targeted against American products. The League of Nations, which was working hard to halt the upward trend in tariffs, was powerless. The seeds of economic isolation had been deeply planted.

The trade wars ahead will likely be conducted by the three major trade blocks of Asia, Europe, and North America. We may see free trade within these blocks while the three blocks themselves engage in trade wars and protectionism.

A major trade conflict between the United States and Japan or the United States and China appears inevitable. At some point in this K Wave winter, a U.S. administration will be forced, due to political pressure, to enact the Super 301, which gives the president power to erect trade barriers and sanction imports. These sanctions will likely progress into a full-scale trade war. Other nations will invariably be drawn into this conflict. Throughout history, trade wars have often become shooting wars. Hopefully, this will not be the case in the inevitable conflict between the United States and our trading partners.

When the world plunges deeper into the K Wave decline and barriers are thrown up everywhere to protect ailing industries that have expanded beyond world demand with expensive capital, the situation will get so bad as to force major changes. It is possible that a trade crisis during this K Wave winter will produce sweeping changes in our global trading system in the direction of real free trade for the next K Wave advance.

There is no doubt that the economic conditions and forces that brought about the protectionism and trade wars of the last three long-wave cycle declines exist just under the surface of the global economy today. Unfortunately, the more severe the global trade conflicts become in the years ahead, the deeper the K Wave decline is likely to be.

Works Cited and Additional Sources

Andres, William A. 1985. "The Case for Open Trade" *Vital Speeches,* August.

Eckes, Alfred E. 1985. "International Trade in Turbulent Times" *Vital Speeches,* July.

Henske, John M. 1982. "The Changing World Environment for International Trade." *Vital Speeches*, October.

Porter, Roger B. 1983. "International Economic Challenges of the 1980s" *Vital Speeches,* January.

Peterson, David. 1987. "Neo-Conservatism." *Vital Speeches,* February.

Whalley, John. 1985. *Trade Liberalization among Major World Trading Areas.* Cambridge: MIT Press.

Wilson, John Oliver. 1985. "Trade Wars." *Vital Speeches,* June.

11

THE FAILING FARM

"I'm going to see the handwriting on the wall, and I'm not going to be here to read the last sentence."

American Farmer

In every recorded K Wave decline, there has first been a sharp deflationary and debt-liquidating decline in agriculture during the fall season. A fall season decline also strikes other raw material and commodity industries. The rest of the economy suffers the worst years of decline and debt liquidation in the winter season.

Falling land prices, high interest-rates, sliding commodity prices, and enormous amounts of debt are a few of the problems farmers have faced in recent years, the same problems they faced periodically every 50 to 60 years in the past.

This history of long-wave cycles in agriculture and their connection to other forces at work on a society is a rather extensive and disturbing history. Some of the evidence predates Kondratieff's own work. In his book on economic cycles, Jake Bernstein (1991, 58–59) observed:

> Lord William Beveridge in 1922 isolated and studied extensively an approximate 54-year cycle in European wheat prices. Using historically reconstructed data, Beveridge tracked the cycles in wheat as far back as the 1200s . . . In addition, there is evidence that 50–60 year cycles are present

in other phenomena as well. Records of the Mayan civilization suggest that its economy fluctuated in approximately 50-year cycles. The Aztec Indian calendar was, in fact, based on an approximate 50-year cycle . . . In reporting his validation of the 50–60 year Beveridge wheat cycle, Dewey observed that the wheat cycle appeared to be closely correlated to the 54-year cycle in Arizona tree-ring widths.

Our primary concern in this book is with more recent and tangible history. American and European agriculture was suffering fearfully around the time of the defeat of Napoleon in 1815 during the first K Wave fall season. Prices were plunging, and the agricultural industry was in deep trouble. This was the case again in the late 1860s and 1870s, as the global economy entered the second K Wave downturn phase. In the fall season of the third decline of the K Wave, the 1920s, falling prices and overproduction was once again plaguing the industry.

Is the repeat of the farming crisis in the 1980s, which is still being felt in many respects, just a coincidence? Is it a fluke with no real significance? Or is a periodic decline in agriculture another manifestation of the global forces at work, the sum total of which is the K Wave? It seems a bit far-fetched that these agricultural depressions—all in the fall season time-frame of recorded K Waves—are isolated incidents unrelated in their causes and timing. K Wave theory suggests that they are not.

As Kondratieff emphasized so effectively, as the fall season begins, prices peak and begin to drop due to overexpansion, which brings even more overproduction and extreme competition. This erosion of prices does not happen automatically, across the board, but begins slowly, first in farmland and agricultural prices, commodities, and raw materials. This occurs early in the fall season. Then the process works its way along until it finally reaches wholesale and consumer goods in the winter season of the K Wave.

Farmers are caught in a squeeze. They are paying high prices, which are still rising for machinery and production products, while the price they are getting for their produced goods is falling. Caught in the middle during a period of rising costs and falling prices on world markets for their products, farmers are the first to feel the pain of the decline. The K Wave forces that hurt farmers are actually making many industries more efficient and productive by lowering their raw material costs.

The value of U.S. farmland fell 49 percent from 1981 to 1992. A cut in value of almost one-half is no small drop. Anyone who questions the deflationary principles of the K Wave need look no further than the price of agricultural land. Many farmers were going into debt in the late 1970s, buying more land for expansion and increased production. It is not too difficult to realize where the problems have come from in the industry. Crop prices have fallen almost as much as land in most cases.

Financing of farmland and the desire to borrow was based on bankers' and farmers' expectation that production would rise at the rates of previous years. The reason farmers fail when prices actually decline in a deflationary fall season should be obvious. The same phenomenon occurs in almost all other industries as the K Wave decline progresses. Residential home owners and commercial real-estate owners, such as Donald Trump, who have seen the price they paid for real estate drop by 20 to 50 percent are now coming to understand the plight of the farmer. The computer industry is the latest consumer industry to realize the impact of K Wave deflation due to excesses in the system. What happened to agriculture in the 1980s is the first act of the Kondratieff play being acted out on the stage of the global economy.

One would tend to ask at this point why it is that prices first begin to fall on farmland and in agricultural, raw material, and commodity products. The answer most likely lies in technology developed during the decline and implemented during the upswing. This new technology helps to pull agriculture out of its slump and make it more productive. Through innovation, the farm becomes more efficient and competitive on world markets. The improved technology and productivity pushes agriculture into a period of overproduction first as the K Wave advance comes to an end.

We are all aware that food is the most basic of human needs. This need will be met before the world delves into other projects as the new upswing is getting under way. There is a change in priorities during a decline. Things that seemed to be important as the economy moved into the peak of the K Wave, such as sports cars and mink coats, are given a back seat to agriculture in the new advance. However, just as the world economy peaks again, agriculture, as it enters its phase of overproduction, takes a back seat to the luxuries of life.

Food is a priority that will be met before humanity endeavors to meet other less basic needs. Herein lies one of the reasons for agriculture being the first to begin the upswing of the K Wave cycle and why it is the first area to implement the new technology developed during the decline. It could also be said that because agricultural products are the most basic and practical of all products, they give a better reflection of true value, so they dictate to the rest of the market what prices should be doing and are thus a leader as the economy goes into a deflationary period. This is to say that agricultural prices clearly make the statement that enough is enough and that it is time for world prices to come back to earth.

The agricultural decline is in no way independent of the rest of the K Wave cycle. As we reach the top of the cycle, we see agriculture put in a triple squeeze. Agriculture is first caught in the situation of rising operating costs and falling land and commodity prices. These price shifts come during a period of high interest rates. To top it off, agriculture is asked to do business in a world of growing international protectionism. This is especially difficult since agriculture is the United States' largest export. The pressure is just too much, and the farming community is thrown into depression 10 years earlier than the rest of the global economy.

A visit to any Midwest farming town in the 1980s would have convinced you that no one in these areas was under the illusion that an expanding, growing economy existed, unlike people in the rest of the world. The farming community is a reflection of what the rest of the world invariably experiences in a K Wave decline.

An article in *The Wall Street Journal* (Wall 1986, 1) gave exceptional insight into the situation on the farm during a K Wave fall season when early price deflation had already begun.

> The farm economy, still burdened by tremendous overcapacity, is merely pausing before another long bleed, many economists say . . .
>
> Capital will be slowly wrung out of the sector, as lenders eventually push billions of dollars of land onto the market at lower and lower prices. As the farm depression drags on, a swelling number of farmers and farm suppliers will lose the war of attrition and some analysts see the exodus of the next four years exceeding that of the last four . . .
>
> Certainly, for some farmers and suppliers, the worst is over. Land prices, having plunged more than 50 percent in some areas, won't fall as far or as fast in the future . . . .
>
> Excess capacity will plague U.S. agriculture for the next decade, a study by the Food and Agriculture Policy Research Institute suggests. It predicts that enough land will come out of production as the result of federal policy or economic pressures to restore equilibrium by the mid-1990s. But idled land is still there and if farmers again planted all available acres, they would still produce about 30 percent too much wheat and 35 percent too much cotton, the study calculates . . .

The financial situation darkened severely in the latest K Wave fall season as a number of statistics show. Debts climbed from $60 billion in 1973 to $212 billion in the mid-1980s. These debts have now slowed because farmers are running out of borrowing power just as the rest of the world's industry will soon be doing as the global K Wave decline accelerates.

Farmers were going broke in the 1980s at rates not seen since the Great Depression, due to the many debt and price pressures we have been discussing. The farms that survive the difficult times of this K Wave decline will take on many new characteristics. These changes will be the result of financial necessities brought on by the pressures created by K Wave forces. The farm will likely be forced to do without many of the price subsidies, government purchases, and other supports. Government will simply not be able to afford the support programs.

Price supports and government props do nothing more than increase the inefficiencies in agriculture. There will be great pressure for more government in agriculture as things get worse, but these pressures should be resisted as the free market is the best regulator in any industry. The worsening of the decline will be an excellent opportunity to remove Washington from the farm by purging inefficiencies through failure. Unfortunately, we may see Washington become even more involved in the farm economy in the years ahead, as it did in the Great Depression, and therefore do more damage to the system.

It was interesting to hear the public and those in other industries in the 1980s say, "The farmer got himself in this situation; let him get himself out." These people are now caught in the same situation of falling prices in their industries and too much debt service to cover their expenses. They are now seeing the value of their collateral eroded so that their pleas for working capital at the local bank are falling on deaf ears.

The farmer is now at least given more sympathy since the rest of the economy is also suffering.

The trouble that began first on the farm in no way left the rest of the economy unscathed, especially in areas directly affected by the farm economy. One such area is the banking industry, which has suffered greatly over the past few years and will no doubt suffer far more in the coming years due to the uncollectible loans lent to farmers during the good old days of the 1970s.

The government-backed Farm Credit System has gotten itself into deep trouble, and there is still no light at the end of the tunnel. Rural banks are dropping like flies in the Midwest, and the number of failures is still on the increase. The Farmers Home Administration is deteriorating at a rapid pace, with delinquent loans reaching astronomical proportion. The Federal Deposit Insurance Corporation is in the red because of the enormous number of insured bank failures due to the farming crisis. The question arises, How much more pressure can the banking system take given the pressures from developing countries, energy-loan troubles, the farming crisis, and the real-estate debacle? What is going to happen when the decline in the rest of the economy accelerates?

The banks are not the only business being affected by the farm crisis. The stores on Main Street in farming communities all across America share the pain of the farmer. As farmers are pinched for cash, so is every store that depends on their business. The U.S. farm-equipment industry is operating at less than 50 percent of capacity, and grain exporters are operating at less than 60 percent.

New inventions and genetic engineering breakthroughs coupled with more efficient computerized machinery will bring agriculture out of the decline before the rest of the economy. As we enter the 21st century, agriculture will once again be seen as a priority, not an expendable part of the economy. The planet earth could well be populated with over 6 billion people by the year 2000, and the only industry that can feed them is agriculture.

Seely G. Lodwick (1983, 517–521), former under secretary of agriculture for International Affairs and Commodity Programs, has some insightful ideas on the direction of U.S. agriculture in the years to come:

> The other certainty, along with taxes, is that the world's people will want to eat better than they have in the past. Those who are hungry and malnourished want to have adequate diets and the world must find ways to meet that need. Those people with only adequate diets want to have food that is more nutritious, more varied, richer in protein. Not only do they want

more protein in their diets, they need it. As developing countries increase their consumption of poultry, dairy and livestock products, their people become stronger, healthier and longer lived—more capable of contributing to the advancement and development of their countries and ours too. We can no longer afford to squander the energy and talent that are lost in people who cannot fully perform because they are not well fed. The problems of the world are too numerous and too large and we need the capabilities of all the world's people. This invites innovation on the part of American farmers and traders to find ways of serving those needs. We have the opportunity to expand exports of processed foods and other high-value products that increase dollar returns to this country and also create non-farm jobs in processing and food manufacturing. We also have the challenge to find new methods of trading—barter and countertrade, for example—and the linking of trade with development projects that make imports possible for the poorer countries. All this adds up to a growth opportunity for those Americans who produce food. Food producers will be the key to progress towards a future world of peace and plenty.

The old proverb, "The only thing that is permanent is change," comes to mind as we observe agriculture moving through the long-wave cycle. Farmers must look beyond the current situation to the next advance of the K Wave and realize that once again agriculture will come into its own. Within a few years, agriculture will be a more efficient, productive industry that will face the needs of a rising world population.

It appears as if in the first two K Wave cycles the fall season was more severe in many respects than in the most recent cycles in terms of bankruptcy and business failure. This was because agriculture made up a far greater portion of total economic activity during these periods. In the last cycle decline of the 1920s and 1930s, agriculture made up less of the total economic activity than previous cycles, but the winter season of the 1930s was far worse than the fall season of the 1920s. Agriculture was certainly a far larger portion of the economy in the 1920s and 1930s than in the more recent fall season of the 1980s and early 1990s. The 1980s fall season of the K Wave decline was mild because agriculture and raw materials represented the smallest portion of the total economy in history. The bottom line of this line of thinking is that a larger portion of the total economy appears set up to take a hit in the latest winter season than occurred in K Waves of the past.

I am sure that during the recent hard times many are wishing for the good old days on the farm, but there is really no more exciting time to be alive than when the world is going through major changes. As we pull out of the latest K Wave decline and enter the next advance, these will be very rewarding and fascinating times to be involved in agriculture. Many will be saying, "We never had it so good."

Works Cited and Additional Sources

Bernstein, Jake. 1991. *The Handbook of Economic Cycles.* Homewood, IL: Business One Irwin.

Lodwick, Seeley G. 1983. "Are Farmers on the Way Out?" *Vital Speeches,* June.

McCormick, John. 1984. "A Riches-to-Rags Story" *Newsweek,* 2 April.

Sheets, Kenneth R. 1985. "Farmers up in Arms" *U.S. News and World Report,* 11 March.

———. 1985. "Ailing Farm Economy—Damage Spreads Wide" *U.S. News and World Report,* 29 July.

Wall, Wendy L. 1986. "U.S. Agriculture Faces Still More Shrinkage, Many Economist Say." *The Wall Street Journal,* 24 December.

12

TECHNOLOGY AND INVENTION

"Truth as old as the hills is bound up in the Latin proverb, 'Necessity is the mother of invention.' It is surprising what a man can do when he has to, and how little most men will do when they don't have to."

Walter Linn

Most of the greatest life-changing inventions and ideas, typically born in the hard times of a K Wave decline, bear their economic fruit when fully capitalized in a K Wave advance. The electric light, cotton gin, steam engine, and automobile were all products developed during K Wave declines and fully capitalized during the ensuing advances. Winter is a time of hibernation, reflection, and planning. In spring, the plans begin to bear fruit.

Kondratieff began his review of K Wave theory by stressing that capitalist economies progress in a cyclical pattern and not in a linear or constantly advancing manner. He concluded that this cyclical pattern is always progressing to new heights. Each new cycle of the K Wave starts out further along in the development of the global economy. Great technological advances help a civilization move into new phases of growth.

12.1 Surges in Major Innovations, Worldwide (Hochgraf 1983)

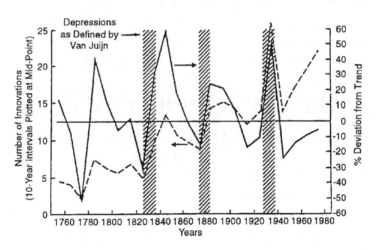

The development of technology and the introduction of new inventions play a major role in the character of the K Wave cycle. If it were not for innovation, the K Wave would just continue to turn over in one place, and society would make no real progress towards higher standards of living and better ways of doing things.

There has been a great deal of speculation and discussion on just how new inventions and technology contribute to the rise and fall of the economy. Kondratieff's research attempted to show that there was an increase in the number of inventions during a decline because people were looking for more efficient and effective ways of production to get their particular industry moving in a profitable direction. Kondratieff emphasized heavily the effect of inventions in the areas of communications and transportation on the K Wave.

There is the possibility that during hard times we tend to be more thinking and contemplative creatures and thus spend more time considering our predicament and how we intend to better our condition. It is difficult to study the effect of invention on the K Wave due to the complexity of both the inventing process and the implementation of new ideas.

The problem with just totaling the number of inventions during the decline and comparing it to the total during the upswing is that inventions have different qualities and characteristics and fall into different categories. Some inventions are in the capital goods area and are developed in an effort to minimize the cost of producing consumer products; these inventions are usually developed in research and development (R&D) departments of industry and government. Other inventions are in the area of consumer goods and new retail products aimed at improving the life of the general public rather than efficiency in industry. These inventions come from both the private sector (the freelance inventor) and the R&D of industry.

For the past 200 years, there has been a steady increase in the number of inventions each year, while it would seem through the research of a number of individuals, including Kondratieff, that some of the more important inventions that had enormous economic impact were developed during major economic declines.

Gerhard Mensch assembled important evidence that clusters of basic innovations occurred in the 1820s, the 1880s, and the 1930s, exactly during stagnating K Waves. Economic history, in turn, confirms that the investment outlays for the first massive applications of these basic innovations generally occurred 10 years later, after the turn from the depressive K Wave to the expansionist K Wave had already taken place.

It would seem that the time of invention is not as important to understanding the dynamics of K Waves as is understanding the economic forces causing capital to flow into the new innovations so that they are integrated into the next upswing of growth and expansion.

Ernest Mandel (1980, 41), a long-wave theorist of Marxist origins, pointed out that J. Schmookler (1966), "has tried to prove that the patent cycle is closely related to the business cycle in general and does not precede or anticipate it." This is to say that the actual use of new inventions will increase with the advance of the K Wave and decrease with its decline.

Mandel continues (1980, 41),

> Although the argumentation seems convincing, it does not distinguish between qualitatively different types of patents and thus it cannot provide an answer to the question we pose. What is decisive is the phenomenon of patents permitting radical innovations, not the patent cycle in general.

It is easy enough to understand that everyday-type patents are facilitated by major developments that increase communications and transportation.

John D. Sterman (1985, 21–22) of the system dynamics program at M.I.T. made the following insightful observations about technological innovation and the long-wave cycle.

> In contrast to the innovation theories of the long wave, the National Model suggests a long-wave theory of innovation better describes the situation. The NM shows how fundamental physical processes in the economy can create the long wave without any variation in innovation rates. The bunching of innovations can thus be explained as the result of entrainment of the innovation process by the long wave (Graham and Senge 1980, p. 283–84): `The long wave creates a shifting historical context for the implementation of new inventions. Midway into a capital expansion, opportunities for applying new inventions that require new types of capital become poor. The nation is already committed to a particular mix of technologies, and the environment greatly favors improvement innovations over basic innovations. During a long-wave downturn, basic innovation opportunities gradually improve, as old capital embodying the technologies of the preceding buildup depreciates. Near the trough of the wave, there are great opportunities for creating new capital embodying radical

new technologies. The old capital base is obsolescent, bureau-cracies that thwarted basic innovation have weakened, many companies committed to producing old types of capital are bankrupt, and traditional methods are no longer sacrosanct.' Though innovation is not necessary to explain the long wave, there is little doubt that each long wave seems to be built around a particular ensemble of basic technologies, including particular forms of energy, transport, communications, and materials. These ensembles evolve synergistically and, like species in an ecosystem, compete against other candidates for a limited number of available niches.

Sterman's observations indicate the great impact of technology and innovation on the economy and the K Wave. Lower interest rates and wages, as well as cheaper raw materials, greatly increase the profit picture as the economy enters a new advance, thus creating more investment capital and an overall more favorable environment for the implementation of the new technology.

When the financial markets reach their peak at the end of the fall season and as winter begins, industry is caught in the same squeeze that has been plaguing agriculture for 10 years. The slow-down of investment in expansion will be profound. When the general overexpansion and overcapitalization of industry with expensive debt begins to take its toll and the buying power of the world is eroded, prices tumble. When prices fall below what it costs to produce, the screws clearly tighten on the economy.

For a while, companies will still operate to cover fixed costs, but soon prices will drop too far and companies will begin shutting their doors. Unemployment and bankruptcies will reach new highs, and the entire economy will slow. As we move deeper into the decline and companies are no longer expanding—that is, the ones that make it through the first years of the decline—there begins to be a buildup of capital. Interest rates, wages, and payrolls fall. Costs fall. The profit picture begins to improve, yet com-

panies with the newfound tendencies towards risk aversion are
extremely slow to expand or spend money on major outlays.

A natural place for the investment of the company's excess
capital during this time is in R&D. This new research expenditure
coupled with the psychological factor of seeking solutions during
hard times breeds new products that can help pull the world out of
its economic slumber and into the next upswing of the cycle.
When the old ways crumble, it frees us to see in new ways.

Kondratieff concentrated heavily on inventions in transportation and communications and their impact on the expansion
of the K Wave. Transportation and communications are extremely important fields of development in that they have a triple
effect on growth during the expansion period of the K Wave.
First, they create new industries of their own for investment and
profit. Second, they generate more trade among nations and continents and in effect stimulate the development of the global
economy. Third, stimulus to world trade helps to encourage
development and capitalization of other less important inventions and products that are not necessarily in the fields of communications or transportation.

The act of inventing and the process of development and
implementation of inventions is all part of what we consider the
growth of technology. It is said that humanity is now doubling its
knowledge of the universe every few years. This increase in
knowledge and the explosion of technology that accompanies it is
opening all sorts of avenues for business and science. These new
avenues are creating wonderful opportunities to build a better
world and are providing for the possibility of a more peaceful
coexistence among nations.

What one doesn't notice readily is the impact this technological advance is having on our global community and marketplace.
Chapter 4 touched briefly on the technological impact on the
money system of our global community, but I would like to discuss this a bit further here.

The vast network that has been created through the new technology in communications, which links every corner of the world through an electrical impulse, could be viewed as the central nervous system of the global economy. The impact of this money system has yet to be fully realized by its millions of daily users. Walter Wriston (1985, 28), former chairman of Citicorp, discussed the technology of the financial system in an article in *The Wall Street Journal*:

> The new system was not built by politicians or economists. It was built by technology. In some respect the new world financial system in the accidental by-product of communication satellites and of engineers learning how to use the electromagnet spectrum up to 300 gigahertz. In the same manner that Edison failed to foresee that his phonograph would have any commercial value, the men and women who tied the world together with telecommunications did not fully realize that they were building the infrastructure of a world marketplace.
>
> The convergence of computers with telecommunications has produced a world trading system, which in turn has allowed creation of a new international monetary system I call the Information Standard. Because this world market is something different in kind and not just a change in degree, it has truly revolutionized the world. Political, regulatory and economic concepts and compact suddenly lose some of their relevance and everyone from business people to politicians has new issues to worry about. The new Information Standard, unlike all prior arrangements, is not subject to effective political tinkering . . .
>
> Prior to the advent of the Information Standard, if a country did not like the gold standard or the gold exchange standard or the Bretton Woods arrangement, it could opt out of the system. A finance minister would call a press conference and explain that the current international arrangements were unsatisfactory and that his nation would no longer play. This was the fate of the gold exchange standard and the Bretton Woods

fixed exchange standard. Today, there is no way for a nation to opt out of the Information Standard. There is no place on this planet to hide.

This massive reordering of the international financial system has been largely overlooked because the scientists who created the technology did not focus on their creation of the world marketplace and the central bankers and governments weren't trained to anticipate the impact of technology on currency values. But ready or not, the technology won't go away, the market won't stop making judgments every minute and the Information Standard is here. Like other forms of free speech, government will have to learn to live with it.

Wriston is extremely accurate in his interpretation of the character of our new monetary system, but he fails to see the even more dramatic changes that will occur in the latest K Wave decline. What he has described are the ever increasing capabilities of the hardware of the emerging new money system. We have yet to see what sort of software package will be introduced as the solution to an inevitable financial crisis. There is a day of reckoning coming in international financial markets. There will invariably be major innovations in the global financial system.

Kondratieff and others have explained, and we have seen in this chapter, that communications and transportation are the leaders in pulling the economy out of the contraction and into the expansion. What innovations will pull us out of the current contraction and into the next economic expansion?

Consider the enormous impact of the space shuttle and other space advances. The next stage of space flight will fall into the innovation category of transportation and will be accompanied by great breakthroughs in communications. Space travel developments may help propel us into the next K Wave advance. One such development will be a space plane that will take off horizontally.

We will see great advances in all areas of space in the years ahead. Space flight will be as common in the next peak of the long-wave cycle as air flight is today. The construction of a U.S. space station and an eventual moon base during the next advance will create hundreds of new ideas, products, and manufacturing processes. Before the next advance is over, it is likely that millions of jobs will be created as a direct result of advances in space technology.

Space is only one area that will see enormous advances during the next expansive upswing of the K Wave. Biotechnology and genetic engineering will open new frontiers for industry. Artificial intelligence and the use of a new generation of robotics will bring numerous avenues of growth to the economy. Magnetically levitated trains will drastically change ground transportation. New batteries will be invented that will make widespread use of electric cars common during the next advance. The mechanical flywheel battery may well change transportation as we know it.

The collapse of computer prices in this K Wave decline is leading to their widest possible use in all types of research and engineering. A whole wave of new technology and products will be traced to the mass distribution of powerful computer systems that are being placed into the hands of almost anyone who wants them. The future is being created on computer systems in garages, bedrooms, offices, and in the research departments of major corporations. New products, processes, and materials will be developed during this decline and will propel us into the next advance.

But first we must survive the challenging yet stimulating decline, during which the impurities and inefficiencies that have built up over the past 50 years will be purged from the system. The result will be a prospering and expanding global economy built on pooled individual talent challenged to survive a long-wave winter season.

We have come to see that technology and invention do indeed play a major role in the rise and fall of our global economy. It is important to remember that without a severe decline that shakes the system and its participants, many of the new advances of the next K Wave economic expansion would never come about. Necessity will force the changes that must be made to insure our future success.

Works Cited and Additional Sources

Dula, Arthur M. 1985. "American Business: Heading into Orbit." *Saturday Evening Post,* March.

Hochgraf, N. 1983. "The Future Technological Environment." *11th World Petroleum Congress*, London: John Wiley and Sons.

Mandel, Ernest. 1980. *Long Waves of Capitalist Development.* Cambridge: Cambridge University Press. 41.

Reynolds, Alan. 1985. "In Search of a Money Standard" *The Wall Street Journal,* 12 November.

Schmookler, Jacob. 1966. *Invention and Economic Growth.* Cambridge: Harvard University Press.

Sterman, John D. 1985. "The Economic Long Wave: Theory and Evidence." Working Paper 1656–85 at M.I.T. Cambridge, Massachusettes.

Wriston, Walter. 1985. "In Search of a Money Standard" *The Wall Street Journal,* 12 November. 28.

13

ON POLITICS

"I hate all bungling as I do sin, but particularly bungling in politics, which leads to the misery and ruin of many thousands and millions of people."

Goethe

"I place economy among the first and most important virtues, and public debt as the greatest of dangers to be feared. . . . To preserve our independence, we must not let our rulers load us with perpetual debt . . . . We must make our choice between economy and liberty or profusion and servitude. . . . If we run into such debts, we must be taxed in our meat and drink, in our necessities and our comforts, in our labors and in our amusements. . . . If we can prevent Government from wasting the labors of the people, under the pretense of caring for them, they will be happy."

Thomas Jefferson

There has been a great deal of debate over the centuries as to which force is more dominate in molding human destiny: economics or politics. In relation to the Kondratieff long wave there is no doubt that the location of the economy within the cycle has great impact on what sort of political rhetoric or ideology will get you elected.

Few would argue that what gave Franklin Roosevelt victory in 1932 was the pain of the Great Depression and his promise that government would take care of the people and bring the speculative and dangerous market forces under control. His promise to more closely regulate the banking industry and the financial markets, which were perceived as catalysts of the crash in 1929 and in turn the Great Depression, were major factors as well. By the same token, few would question that Ronald Reagan's promise to get government off people's backs and to give industry more freedom in the marketplace through deregulation played a large role in his being elected in 1980 and reelected in 1984.

Why two totally different positions yet victory in both cases? There should be no doubt that the location of the economy within the K Wave and its impact in all areas of life is the chief reason.

The 1992 elections present another example. The weakness of the U.S. economy in 1992, due to the beginning effects of the shift from fall to winter seasons in the global K Wave and the drag it created, was what got George Bush turned out and Clinton elected. We were in a short-term 3 1/2 to 4 year Kitchin cycle or regular business cycle recovery; it just wasn't strong enough, due to the declining global K Wave forces at work.

Clinton advocated government action and intervention as the solution to virtually all the country's problems until the political wind began to howl in the other direction. Government could end up taking the blame for developments in this K Wave winter. The timing of this phase of the cycle makes for possibilities for radical government reform.

In his working paper at M.I.T., "The Economic Long Wave: Theory and Evidence," John D. Sterman (1985, 26) made the following observations on political and social values:

> Substantial evidence exists that political and social values in Western nations fluctuate with the period and phasing of the economic long wave (Namenwirth 1973, Weber 1981). Independent content analyses of political tracts in the U.S. and

Great Britain revealed statistically significant 50-year value cycles in both countries which coincided with each other and with the phasing of the economic long wave. During periods of long-wave expansion, material wants are satisfied, and social concerns turn to civil liberties, income distribution, and social justice. During the later phases of the expansion, foreign-policy concerns predominate. As the expansion gives way to decline, conservatism grows, and political attention returns to material needs. Economic policy takes center stage in legislative agendas. During the downturn, the accumulation of wealth becomes the overriding concern, at the expense of civil rights, equity, and the environment. The most dramatic example of this cycle is, of course, the rise of fascism in the 1920s and 1930s. The student rebellion of the 1960s and growing conservatism of the 1980s in many Western nations are also consistent with the current long-wave cycle. . . . The variation of political values is primarily the result of entrainment by the economic cycle.

It would be foolish to try and link every world leader or U.S. president from George Washington to the present with the position of the economy relative to the K Wave. The theory does not attempt to do so. It is, however, possible to make such a link during the critical turning points of the cycle. These prove to be the most volatile periods for the economy and thus the most predictable periods in the struggle for power within the political system.

There are powerful forces at work in the years leading up to the K Wave peak, during the fall season, and during the first few years as the economy slides into the K Wave winter. The left had no chance for victory as we moved into the seeming prosperous and speculative laissez-faire climate of the K Wave fall season.

In the late 1920s, Hoover was a president with a hands-on managment style—just like President Clinton. Like Clinton, Hoover believed the government rather than the market should fix things. The fact is that Hoover and Roosevelt did a great deal to make the depression far worse than it had to be. We will always have the K Wave decline. We don't have to turn it into a devastating and lengthy depression. Many have argued that if government had gotten out of the way in the 1930s and let prices, wages, banking, and business adjust naturally, the decline would have been far less severe.

I'm a bit hesitant to criticize President Roosevelt. Grandmother Barker never hesitates to inform me that I wouldn't be around if it hadn't been for President Roosevelt seeing to it there was food on the table during the Depression, even though my grandfather never turned down a day's work. I like to think that free markets would have been even more compensating of hard work, but you shouldn't argue with your grandmother.

Paul Johnson (1991, 240) in his book *Modern Times,* reading I highly recommend, had some fascinating insights into the economic events of the Great Depression and the political responses by Hoover and Roosevelt. Looking at an honest assessment of what occurred in the 1930s reveals the forces that were at work in the 1930s and reveals how things will have to be different this time around:

> The credit inflation petered out at the end of 1928. The economy went into decline, in consequence, six months later. The market collapse followed after a three-month delay. All this was to be expected; it was healthy; it ought to have been welcomed. It was the pattern of the nineteenth century and of the twentieth up to 1920–1921; capitalist 'normalcy'. A business recession and a stock-exchange drop were not only customary but necessary parts of the cycle of growth: they sorted out the sheep from the goats, liquidated the unhealthy elements in the economy and turned out the parasites; as J.K. Galbraith was to put it: 'One of the uses of depression is to expose what the auditors fail to find.' Business downturns serve essential purposes. They have to be sharp. But they need not be long because they are self-adjusting. All they

require on the part of governments, the business community and the public is patience.

Many wrongly assume that Hoover maintained the laissez-faire policies of Harding and Coolidge up until his defeat by Roosevelt. The fact is that when the economy got weak and the market crashed, Hoover blinked. He turned to intervention early on in his administration. The idea of letting the free market heal itself was thrown out the window. Hoover was educated and trained as an engineer before he entered the political arena. He tried to use government to engineer the country out of the crisis—thereby exacerbating the economy's decline. Johnson (1991, 244) observed:

> When the magnitude of the crisis became apparent, Andrew Mellon, the Treasury Secretary, at last repudiated his interventionist philosophy and returned to strict laissez-faire. He told Hoover that administration policy should be to 'liquidate labor, liquidate stocks, liquidate the farmers, liquidate real estate' and so 'purge the rottenness from the economy'. It was the only sensible advice Hoover received throughout his presidency. By allowing the Depression to rip, unsound business would quickly have been bankrupted and the sound would have survived.

Government attempting to stop the depression guaranteed its severity and longevity. The interventionist direction taken by Hoover has been the blueprint for government ever since. Ronald Reagan tried to change this, but his advisors got the best of him. Johnson's (1991, 244–245) account of Hoover's early action should be a lesson for getting government out of business this time around:

> From the very start, therefore, Hoover agreed to take on the business cycle and stamp on it with all the resources of government. 'No president before has ever believed there was a government responsibility in such cases,' he wrote; '. . . there

we had to pioneer a new field.' He resumed credit inflation, the Federal Reserve adding almost $300 million to credit in the last week of October 1929 alone. In November he held a series of conferences with industrial leaders in which he exacted from them solemn promises not to cut wages, even to increase them if possible—promises kept until 1932. . . . It is true that Hoover ruled out direct relief and wherever possible he channelled government money through the banks rather than direct to businesses and individuals. But that he sought to use government cash to reflate the economy is beyond question. Coolidge's advice to angry farmers' delegations had been a bleak 'Take up religion.' Hoover's new Agricultural Marketing Act gave them $500 million of Federal money, increased by a further $100 million early in 1930. In 1931 he extended this to the economy as a whole with his Reconstruction Finance Corporation (RFC), as part of a nine-point program of government intervention which he produced in December. More major public works were started in Hoover's four years than in the previous thirty.

Hoover was spending a pile of money to try and save the economy from depression; therefore, he decided government needed more revenue to continue pioneering his new government endeavors. It is difficult to believe that anyone could be so foolish as to think that any form of tax could help the economy when it is in decline. The deficit was drastically increasing in the early 1930s due to the explosion of government programs. Johnson (1991, 245) tells us how Hoover decided to pay for his doomed government ventures.

> . . . the 1932 Revenue Act saw the greatest taxation increase in U.S. history in peacetime, with the rate on high incomes jumping from a quarter to 63 per cent. This made nonsense of Hoover's earlier tax cuts but by now Hoover had lost control of Congress and was not in a position to pursue a coherent fiscal policy.

Government intervention in the economy only makes matters worse. Recent protectionist sentiment should be viewed in the context of government engineering during the Hoover administration. Johnson (1991, 246) tells us the consequences of trade policy during the period:

> The final crisis came when America's protectionist policy boomeranged. The atrocious Smoot-Hawley tariff of 1930, which sharply increased import duties, more than any other positive act of policy, spread the Depression to Europe. In the summer of 1931 the collapse of Austria's leading bank, the Credit Anstalt, pushed over a whole row of European dominoes ... and a series of debt-repudiations ensued. What remained of America's exports to Europe vanished, and her policy of foreign loans as a substitute for free trade collapsed.

Looking at the close of the Hoover era, Johnson (1991, 246) observed that, for all his effort, Hoover's policies did nothing to stop the depression and, if anything, made it worse:

> By that time Hoover's interventionism had prolonged the Depression into its fourth year. The cumulative banking crisis had, in all probability, the deflationary effect which Hoover had struggled so hard and so foolishly to prevent, so that by the end of 1932 the very worst of the Depression was over. But the cataclysmic depth to which the economy had sunk in the meantime meant that recovery would be slow and feeble.

Looking at the transition from the Hoover to Roosevelt administrations, we see that there really was no significant difference in the policy of the two presidents. They were both planners and interventionists. Roosevelt went for direct relief, while Hoover distrusted this approach. Quoting Johnson (1991, 255):

> Roosevelt's legislation, for the most part, extended or tinkered with Hoover policies. The Emergency Banking Act and the Loans to Industry Act of June 1934 extended Hoover's RFC. The Home Owners' Loan Act (1932) extended a similar act of the year before. The Sale of Securities Act (1933),

the Banking Acts (1933, 1935) and the Securities and Exchange Act (1934) merely continued Hoover's attempts to reform business methods.

Johnson (1991) concluded that the Hoover-Roosevelt interventionism was a continuum. By leading government involvement in the economy and markets, "they impeded a natural recovery brought about by deflation."

An interesting note on politics and insight into the fact that Japan is the leader of this K Wave decline is that in 1992, in the midst of the collapse of the Japanese stock market, the Japanese government created the Securities and Exchange Surveillance Commission (SESC). This agency is modeled after the SEC, which was created by Roosevelt at the same point in the last K Wave decline and along with the same political rhetoric of controlling the markets. And some say history doesn't repeat itself! It would appear that Japan and this K Wave decline are right on schedule in many respects.

The economy has never returned to the growth levels seen before the Great Depression and especially during the great economic advances of the 19th century. Since the Great Depression, government has continued as a yoke around the neck of the economy. While government and the public sector of the economy have grown, the private sector and the free market have shrunk relative to the total economy. Shrinking the pie is not the way to feed a growing, more-demanding crowd.

The trend of bigger government doesn't have to continue. Indeed, all trends must come to an end. We have evolved into an interventionist system that doesn't come close to resembling the economic system envisioned by America's founding fathers. We saw the Soviet Union collapse due to the failure and folly of central planning and government intervention. For years the United States has been moving in the same direction.

As we go into this decline, the economic facts are different from those of the 1930s. Instead of having a balanced budget at the beginning of this decline, the government is drowning taxpayers in trillions of dollars of red ink. The public will not go for another Roosevelt-style solution. Sure a few will want to take the disastrous road of even more government spending, but most Americans have come to realize that with deficit spending the government is throwing away their future as well as the future of their children and grandchildren.

The American people will pay down debt during the winter season, and they will want their government to do the same thing. During this decline of the K Wave, the political turmoil and demand for change in the United States will be greater than at any time since the Civil War, if not the revolution. We are already beginning to see signs of this overdue reality rock the system.

It may well be that the bulk of the American people are going to look for another way out this time around. The 1994 elections were indicative of a new trend against the flow of power to Washington. Polls show that voters distrust the existing two-party political process more than at any time in history.

Typically under the two-party political system in America, the obvious tendency would be for the election of Republican presidents in the laissez-faire fall season phase of the K Wave and the election of Democratic presidents during the winter. During a majority of the years of the K Wave advance, it would be hard to predict the political party elected to power—since economic growth makes politics less important in the minds of the public. But basic K Wave political rules may not hold this time, due to public anger and distrust of Washington. The fact that there was a Democrat in the White House before this decline hit will also change things. Clinton could become the Hoover of our day, blamed for the K Wave winter.

The real standard of living of the middle-class family in America has fallen since the 1970s, and that is with two people working instead of one. The American people are angry with the deterioration of the situation and with government. This anger is not limited to America. We can see the same anger coming from the public around the globe—even if it is more pronounced in the United States.

Government is failing to serve the people effectively—even with spending a billion dollars more every day than it extracts from the producing individuals and companies in the economy. The middle class is in a squeeze. A major political revolt of the middle class could erupt, forcing major changes in the political system in America.

The sweep of Republicans in the 1994 elections could be the beginning of this revolt. However, if the Republicans don't deliver, and fast, they will likely be sent packing as well before the K Wave winter is over.

Due to the economic and financial mess that Washington will be in during the K Wave winter, we may well see a viable third party emerge on the American political scene over the next 10 years. Many politicians of existing parties may even switch to a new party.

The Ross Perot phenomenon in the 1992 elections was a reflection of the frustration on the part of the American people with the two-party system. However, it is possible that an independent candidate's victory would not bring the degree of change desired. An independent bid is based more on personality than on principle. Once the personality is gone, you have the same old two-party system left.

The Republicans will probably not go far enough for the level of anger that will permeate and drive the middle class. It may become a viable argument during this decline that what America needs is a new political party that seeks to return America to the principles of individual economic, financial, and religious freedom it was founded upon. The American people are much more intelligent than politicians give them credit for being. Voters have been pushed almost to their limit and are aware of the inability of government bureaucracy to perform effectively.

President Franklin Roosevelt inherited a government that had low debts and therefore a degree of flexibility. During this K Wave winter, government will not have the options that were available to Roosevelt. Government is out of ammunition after running up debts of trillions of dollars. This time around, the public may well demand that government get out of the way and let the market and the resilience and hard work of the American people get the country back on track. Government cost control and privatization will likely be the most popular political themes in the years ahead.

All the problems that government promised to address and correct since Hoover have done nothing but grow worse. Poverty has increased, crime has surged, education has suffered, banking is in crisis, and the economy has underperformed. The costs to taxpayers for this great service from federal government increases every year. The social forces at work are demanding drastic change, and this mood will grow.

Robert Prechter, Jr. (1995, 8), made the following observations on the likely political trends of this K Wave winter season in a recent issue of his newsletter:

> . . . the Democrats will almost certainly get the blame for the initial decline because they hold the White House, and most people associate the country's leadership with the President. Clinton will undoubtedly veto some Republican legislation between now and the election. Presuming any such vetoes are upheld, it will be simple for Republicans to blame Democrats for falling markets. In fact, there is precedent for this outcome. Democrats picked up 53 Congressional seats in 1930, which gave that party a majority in the House. (They narrowly missed a Senate majority, by two seats.) The Supercycle collapse in stock values or over 75% from that election was blamed on the Republican president, so in 1932 Democrats gained another 97 seats, nearly double the 1930 number, giving them overwhelming majorities in the House and Senate. The same thing should happen in 1996, but the guidance of alternation is favoring Republicans this time.

However, the whole story today is not so simple, which is why EWT in 1989 called for "a multi-decade setback, a radical change or dissolution for at least one, if not both, of the current major parties. The developing bear market is at least of one greater degree than the one that began in 1929. While Republicans may reap a large benefit initially, it will probably be temporary. By the final stock market bottom, which according to my Kondratieff cycle analysis is due in 2003 + or − 1 year, voters should be thoroughly disgusted with both major parties.

Polarization on major issues will be dramatic as the low apprcaches, and the old centrist parties will be unattractive to most voters. A third party is likely to win in either 2000 or 2004, and be either fascist in nature or radically freedom oriented. By the guideline of alternation, the latter is more likely, but hardly assured.

This K Wave winter may bring more political change than the 1930s, but in the opposite direction. Government will be downsizing and spining off its role in many sectors of the economy to the private sector. Cost control and increased quality will be the goal. Health care, in terms of Medicaid and Medicare, will be prime examples. Government will seek to save billions by turning its management role over to the private sector. We may see the privatization of the post office and other government institutions.

Radical change will come on the state and local level as well. Municipal governments are bleeding communities dry with giant unnecessary budgets as well as benefits and fat pensions for government employees that dwarf the private sector. At some point, the public will not be willing to take any more.

In looking at the political consequences of the K Wave, we cannot avoid the subject of nationalism. As economies are in trouble and nations are looking inward, there is a surge in nationalism around the globe, just as in the 1920s and 1930s. This is not necessarily a bad thing in and of itself, but there is a danger of it becoming economic isolationism and being carried too far.

Isolationism could threaten the life of the global economy and could possibly cause the decline to be far more lengthy and devastating than it has to be.

This new wave of nationalism has been powerful in the United States as in the rest of the world. It has been a positive force in that it has given America a new pride in quality and a job well done. At the same time, this nationalism could lead us down the dead-end road of protectionism. There will no doubt be enormous pressure for the world's new nationalism to bring increased economic isolation as the economy moves deeper into the decline. We will need leaders who can convince the people with authority that this is not the road to take.

We cannot look at politics without considering a major danger threatening the global economy and our future prosperity. There is certainly the danger that during this K Wave winter we will not go in the direction of freedom but into the arms of even more government and bureaucratic tyranny.

There has been a great deal of talk in recent years about a new world order. It is often mentioned in conjunction with a more powerful United Nations. In the midst of the crisis of this K Wave decline, the situation may force major mistakes by national leaders in a state of panic.

Instead of turning away from the failure of big government and back to the market system envisioned by America's founding fathers, the leaders of the world may think that uniting under a new form of world empire is the solution. This world empire would be managed and administered at the level of the United Nations. Such an empire would be reminiscent of Rome.

Remember, more government is the problem, not the solution, when it comes to countering the forces of a K Wave decline. A global government or world empire would simply be one more level of bureaucracy that has to be paid for with higher taxes. A global government may survive for a few K Wave cycles, but in the end it would choke off the economy, destroy markets, and suppress individual freedoms. We could enter a decline bigger than Rome's, which led to the Dark Ages.

A United Nations where the sovereign nations of the world can get together to try and settle their differences and share ideas that are beneficial for all is reasonable. But to give up even more individual freedom for one more shot at government as the solution to our problems will be the greatest mistake America could ever make.

Individual nations must remain sovereign within the global system, just as the individual must remain sovereign within the national economy. The result of a new world empire would be a global bureaucratic nightmare that is doomed to failure.

As a reaction to crisis, the United Nations could be offered more funding and more power to exercise over the nations of the globe. A sort of "global New Deal" will be the cry—if you will allow the comparison with our last K Wave decline. A new global money system will likely be part of a global New Deal.

We will discuss this more at length later as we review the two paths out of this global decline. Most of those who will offer global solutions mean well. They are hard-working, basically good people who want to help the situation—they are just wrongheaded when it comes to the political and economic facts and the cure needed.

They will likely not succeed in pulling off a world-empire political coup. The nationalism brought on by the social, economic, and political forces at work in a K Wave decline will be too great to overcome and will counteract such attempts.

All nations will be in dire need of leaders who can stimulate great domestic faith in the years ahead. National leadership will also have to deal in an insightful and meaningful way with the forces at work in the global political and economic environment that will seek to usurp national power. This will be true of every nation in the international arena—where such visionaries will be in short supply.

Works Cited and Additional Sources

Prechter Robert Jr., 1995. *The Elliott Wave Theorist.* Gainesville, GA.

Sterman, John D. 1985. "The Economic Long Wave: Theory and Evidence." Working Paper 1656–85 at M.I.T. Cambridge, Massachusetts.

Johnson, Paul. 1991. *Modern Times.* New York: Harper Collins.

Part III:
The Intelligent
Investor

14

INVESTING AND
THE K WAVE

"When prosperity comes, do not use all of it."

Confucius

*"I thatched my roof when the sun was shining, and now
I am not afraid of the storm."*

George F. Stivers

The first matter to be covered when considering the Kondratieff
long wave's effect on investments concerns timing. An economic cycle of 50 and 60 years duration is questionable as a precise
investment-timing instrument. You cannot use the K Wave to say
what will happen next month or even next year with precision in
any market. However, the K Wave's long-term trend impact on
financial markets is critical information. The K Wave's impact
can make or break an investor's long-term returns—and even
determine a company's survival. Investors should incorporate
the most important elements of K Wave theory into their general decision-making process. These are the overall inflationary
and deflationary forces at work during the seaons of the advance
and the decline.

Critical turning points that indicate the change of season in the K Wave are what the investor should seek to best understand. The seasonal tendencies in the K Wave are crucial. The end of the K Wave fall and the beginning of the winter season is the period during which history has shown a majority of investors have typically suffered significant losses. It would therefore behoove investors to position their portfolios defensively during such an important period—even if a deflationary K Wave downdraft is a once in a lifetime event.

The overall allocation of a portfolio during each season of the K Wave is obviously important. If critical turning points can be identified in the long-wave cycle within a few years, and the theory is valid, the K Wave is worth its theoretical weight in gold.

History has shown that the most successful stock investors take a long-term approach. Investors such as Warren Buffett and John Templeton have proven to be incredibly successful with their approach of finding value in stocks and holding them for the long haul. They find companies that have excellent track records and good management and that offer products or services that are in growing demand. They find these stocks when they are undervalued relative to their potential.

In my view, the Buffetts and Templetons are the heroes of the investment world and will likely continue to be so—except during only a few of the worst years of a K Wave decline. K Wave theory suggests that every 50 to 60 years it would be wise to step aside from the worthy approach of buying value for the long haul, except in a few very select companies, and concentrate on the preservation of one's capital.

Knowledge of the K Wave can be frustrating for investors, money managers, and brokers as the fall season draws to a close and in the early years of a K Wave winter. Most investors would prefer to take the approach of a Buffett or Templeton and just buy and hold solid companies with great prospects for the long haul. But the dangers of the short haul for most stocks outweigh the prospects of the long haul when the winter season of the global economy comes knocking—for example, in 1929 in the United States and 1989 in Japan.

It should be noted that some stocks will do well even in a K Wave winter. These will be companies that have low or no debts, have strong balance sheets, and are in high-growth sectors of the economy. Some stocks will actually do better during hard times if their business helps cut costs for all other companies and they are in rapid growth areas. But stocks aren't the only investment that must be considered. We must take a broad look at all investments and the K Wave, including stocks, bonds, gold, and real estate.

First we must refine our definition of the K Wave cycle in terms of investments. The K Wave is a global cyclical inflationary expansion and deflationary contraction of economic activity at its very heart. The inflation and deflation of the cycle fluctuates between inflationary periods of economic expansion and deflationary periods of economic retrenchment. The K Wave's effects on financial markets and investments are based on these basic trends. Extreme swings of investor psychology or the basic mood of the public help create and define these different periods of inflation and deflation. Economic expansion and contraction and the financial investment activity and speculation that surround the four seasons of the K Wave are the backbone of the theory.

The periods of inflationary expansion and deflationary contraction must be broken down to the seasons to be useful for the investor. P.Q. Wall has done groundbreaking thinking on the key periods of price movement within the K Wave by applying Spengler's notion of seasons to the K Wave and investment markets. The first phase is early inflation, which is the spring season of the K Wave. Late runaway inflation is the second phase, which can be equated with summer. Early deflation is the third phase, also known as the fall season of the cycle. The fourth and final phase in the K Wave is a period of runaway deflation, the winter season for the global economy in the K Wave cycle.

In the same way that human efficiency is highest in the spring and fall of the year, so, in the economic K Wave, corporate efficiency is greatest in the spring and fall. Stock prices obviously perform best when corporate efficiency is the greatest. Let's briefly evaluate these four seasonal periods to see how they could affect the investor. In this chapter, we will cover the basics. The following chapters will go into more detail on how particular investment instruments are affected by the cycle.

Early inflation takes place in the first half of the advance of the K Wave, which is the spring season. In the most recent long-wave cycle, this would represent the period from the late 1940s to the mid-1960s. Prices of raw materials, commodities, real estate, and stocks rise during this period. The level of general price increases during this period tends to be slow and steady—except for stocks, which trend up fairly strongly and make for great investments by outpacing inflation. Global stock markets did fairly well from the early 1950s until the mid-1960s. This was basically a period of slowly rising real prices and steady economic expansion. You won't make a killing buying real estate early in this period, but patience will pay in the long run. Stocks would have bottomed in the previous K Wave winter long before the spring period had begun and would have entered their K Wave climb. Interest rates also trend slowly upward during this period, so bond prices tend to turn down in a K Wave spring and under-perform other investments.

The summer period of late runaway inflation comes when the K Wave economic expansion has heated up significantly. The generation that experienced the pain of the last decline is being replaced with a new generation of managers and investors. They have their hands on the controls of the engines of economic growth and finance. The latest K Wave summer lasted from the mid-1960s to the late 1970s. Prices of commodities, real estate, and raw materials rise sharply during the overheated summer season. Look at what the price of oil, coal, gold, coffee, and lumber did during the last K Wave summer. Investment in farmland, timber, oil wells, advanced agriculture production, construction, and energy production would make good investments early in this period.

Stocks tend to experience bear markets during this period. In real terms, the bear markets are more severe during spring, but don't look as bad because of inflation. Stocks will sharply underperform real assets in the inflationary K Wave summer. Inflation accelerates during this period, rising most rapidly in the last years, as was the case in the late 1970s. Everyone jumps into business because they believe the advance and prices are going to constantly increase, bringing ever-rising profits. Final spikes in raw materials and commodities come as the K Wave summer period of late runaway inflation draws to a close; in the late 1970s, wheat, gold, and oil had inflationary blowoffs. Interest rates rise sharply during the summer phase and reach their final highs at the end of the summer in late runaway inflation. This means bond prices decline sharply during a K Wave summer, especially at its inflationary ending.

The primary recession of the K Wave is what brings this runaway inflation phase to an end. The shift from late inflation in the K Wave summer to early deflation in the K Wave fall is taking place. The primary K Wave recessions in the early 1920s and early 1980s are classic examples of this final price peak that ends the K Wave summer period of fast-paced economic expansion and runaway inflation. The price of commodities, raw materials, and farmland reach their peak at this time. Raw material and commodity producers such as farming and energy enter depressions when the runaway inflation ends.

This new third phase is the fall period of the K Wave, which is really the beginning of the K Wave decline. You would never know it because it is a period of positive feelings and is rife with financial speculation. All the money floating around in the global economic system after the summer inflationary expansion phase has to go somewhere; it pours into global stock markets and paper assets. Prices of raw materials and commodities are falling during this period, while wholesale and retail prices still rise—even if not as fast as they did in the runaway inflation phase. Speculation also hits residential and commercial real estate along with the stock markets of the globe during the early disinflation and deflation phase of the K Wave fall season.

Interest rates fall during the early deflation of the fall season. There is typically a brief rise in interest rates and prices late in the fall season when the speculative manias take full effect and actually create significant demand for expansion. The activity at the end of the fall season, which appears to be an improving global economy, is the ultimate Indian summer boom. At the end of the early deflation fall phase, commercial and residential real estate reach their speculative peaks, and the global economy is set up for the runaway deflation winter phase of the K Wave decline. We witnessed this real-estate price peak in Japan and America in the late 1980s just as we saw in the late 1920s. Since interest rates typically decline during the fall season, bond prices rise during most of the fall.

The next phase is the one remembered in the history books. The most fascinating thing about the runaway economic deflation of the winter phase of the K Wave decline is that virtually no one sees it coming. The generation driving the system has come to believe first that inflation and then that low inflation is a permanent fixture in the system. Even as prices sink lower in deflation, the press and public are looking for inflation just around the corner—as falling prices accelerate. Virtually all U.S. prices were crashing in the early 1930s. Consider Japanese real estate in the early 1990s or in the United States in the early 1930s. There are intermediate price rises that produce hope, but they soon give way to deflation.

Looking back over history, we see distinct phases of runaway K Wave winter deflation following third-phase fall seasons in every K Wave decline. Governments always try to step in and prop up prices because deflation destroys the basis of the financial system. In the early 1990s the Japanese government was doing just that as prices sank lower and lower—just as Hoover and Roosevelt tried in the 1930s. But not even government is bigger than the K Wave and global markets.

Virtually all prices decline during the runaway deflation winter phase of the cycle. At some point, in the panic, chaos, and crisis of the runaway deflation, gold becomes a great investment because of the banking problems that always develop. The problem is that gold may get caught in the deflationary downdraft for a while before it shines as an investment. Real assets such as real estate and commodities also fall in price during the K Wave winter. Interest rates continue their downward trend, although they may spike up in a short-lived scramble for funds as the crisis accelerates in the beginning of winter. Interest rates don't reach their bottom until the end of the runaway deflation winter phase just prior to the beginning of the next early inflation spring phase of the K Wave; therefore, bond prices rally in winter. In general residential and commercial real estate, stocks, commodities, raw materials, and farmland have a tendency to decline in price as the K Wave winter season works havoc and chaos on a global economy that is going through major restructuring in preparation for the next spring season.

There will always be brief inflationary rallies during K Wave economic deflationary declines that in time give way to more economic deflation. Stocks and oil will have strong rallies in overall declines. The deflationary phase may last a decade or longer. If 1990 marked a beginning of the transition from fall to winter in Japan, we may not see the bottom in real prices until the late 1990s and the early 2000s in many sectors of the global economy.

It should be obvious that you don't want to own most stocks and real estate during the runaway deflation phase of the cycle, although there are exceptions to every rule. A few industries and numerous companies will do extremely well even during a K Wave winter. High-quality corporate bonds and stable government securities will do well as interest rates decline in a K Wave winter.

The problem with timing is that the bottom in each area of the economy will come at different times in the decline. The lowest levels in prices in stocks and real estate may come years apart. By the time it is clear that the economy has entered the next advance of the K Wave, the latest spring cycle phase of early inflation, the best buys will have already been snatched up in most markets by savvy investors. The best buys in stocks will come many years before the next spring season begins. Many final lows in stocks will come early in the winter season. Investors aware of the K Wave will have to be on their toes and ready to act contrary to popular opinion. When the public thinks the world has come to an end and is throwing in the towel, it means that we have most likely reached bottom and that a new advance of prosperity and expansion has already begun in the global economy.

Even though the different inflationary and deflationary phases of the K Wave cycle give overall direction for different investments, you never want to cast your views in stone. In the different seasons of the cycle, there will always be particular cases that move against the general trend. Some commercial real estate did great in the late 1980s and early 1990s when the general trend was down. Some Japanese stocks have gone up during their vicious bear market, and a few U.S. stocks are buy-and-hold investments even though a severe bear market is likely. There will be a few buy-and-hold stocks in every bear market. Always be open to rare opportunities in every area of investment: stocks, bonds, gold, and real estate.

Certain areas of every country will not be hit as hard as others, and some cities within those general areas will fare better than most. Specific areas in a specific city will often do better than the entire city or region.

A word about market timing is important at this point. It has already been stated that the K Wave can't be used for exact timing. Kondratieff himself said there must be a several-year margin of error when observing the turning points in the cycle. He was looking back at the history of actual events. Looking forward is even more difficult. Investors face the daunting task of looking into the future for what will happen to the economy, financial markets, and their investments. This is where the four Kitchin cycles that come within each season of the Kondratieff Wave are helpful.

Investors should look at the powerful forces of the Kondratieff Wave for general guidance in asset allocation. When the signs of the major K Wave seasonal turning points are flagrant in the marketplace, one should invest accordingly.

There is another critical consideration for investors in relation to the K Wave cycle. During the fall and winter of the cycle, there is a drastic increase in failures of financial institutions. Many banks, insurance companies, and brokerage companies face major trouble in the fall and winter seasons—especially during the runaway deflation of winter. Banks collapsed in 1933, and Roosevelt declared a banking holiday. Many brokerage firms failed in the early 1930s. Many financial institutions have and will fail during the latest K Wave decline. It is very likely that government bailouts will be curtailed, shut down completely, or simply fail by being too little too late. Budget constraints will be far more important this time than in the 1930s. The money just will not be there. The trend in Washington has already turned more restrictive in terms of federal government responsibility for all the country's problems. This trend appears to be accelerating.

Millions of investors will likely suffer because financial institutions that they do business with will go belly-up. Anyone who has money on deposit with a financial institution should check the safety of that institution. This principle should apply at all times, but especially when faced with a fall and winter decline of the long-wave cycle.

There are a number of companies that rate financial institutions such as insurance companies, brokerage companies, banks, and savings and loans for their stability and safety. These companies have different approaches to rating and different product and price structures. Appendix A at the end of this book lists the primary companies in this field along with their addresses and phone numbers. It would be wise to use one of these rating services to rate the financial institutions you do business with. Compare the pricing and services offered by each rating service, because they occasionally change rates and special offers. You should also learn to ask the right questions of management and to read a balance sheet of the financial institutions you use. Most major financial institutions will survive, but many will fail in a K Wave winter. During an advance, few financial institutions fail, but it is nevertheless wise to use safe and stable financial institutions.

Eventually, we might have a true market-based financial system where financial institutions survive on their market and business merit and not with government props and bailouts that encourage bad management. It will be important to be able to decipher the safety of the institutions you do business with. Independent rating agencies should replace taxpayer funded government insurance for financial institutions. Depositors could find out the risk they are taking before they put money in. Risky banks would pay higher returns, while safe banks would pay lower returns. If a bank failed, it wouldn't cost taxpayers a dime. The system would be self-cleansing, not glued together with extorted funds from taxpayers to pay for bailouts, which make the banking system corrupt, weak, and inefficient.

Identifying the new opportunities of the spring season of the new K Wave advance is just as critical as being cautious and conservative during the winter season. There will be an abundance of opportunities available, but it will take astute investors to identify the new trends and investments that will capitalize on the new economy that will emerge.

We now understand more fully that investors always face tough decisions, but especially during critical periods in the K Wave. The years immediately ahead are just such a critical time. At this time, we should remember the work of Raymond Wheeler (Zahorchak 1983), who said you should go back two K Waves for guidance. If he is right, the K Wave of the first half of the next century will look more like the advance and decline of the early 1900s: the boom that culminated in the 1920s and the depression of the 1930s. In the event you have found this book on a back shelf and dusted it off long after that period has passed and its history has been written, the 2020s and 2030s should be in for some exciting and rough sailing as well.

To summarize the investment implications of the seasons of the K Wave, the following review of the general tendency of markets should be helpful. In spring you have stocks up, commodities up, and bonds down. The summer season sees commodities up and stocks and bonds down. A K Wave fall season sees stocks and bonds up and commodities down. During a K Wave winter, bonds are up while stocks and commodities are down.

This chapter was meant as an overview of investments relative to the distinct seasons of K Wave theory. The chapters that follow are more specific in looking at the effect of the Kondratieff long-wave cycle on specific types of investments. But first, a discussion of inflation versus deflation is necessary to clarify a few K Wave fundamentals.

Works Cited

Zahorchak, Michael, In Raymond A. Wheeler, 1983. *Climate: The Key to Understanding Business Cycles*. Linden, New Jersey: Tide Press.

15

INFLATION VERSUS DEFLATION

"The real price of everything is the toil and trouble of acquiring it."

Adam Smith

Throughout this book, I have discussed both the inflationary expansion and deflationary contraction of the Kondratieff long-wave cycle. It is critical that I more clearly define K Wave inflationary advances and deflationary declines—since these are the basic trends that create the long-wave cycle.

Typically, the K Wave "economic" inflation in the advance and the "economic" deflation in the decline have been mirrored by prices. By "economic" inflation or deflation, I mean what is going on in the real economy adjusted for price changes—how *many* houses, refrigerators, and manicures are being produced and demanded regardless of their price. Basically, "economic" inflation and deflation refers to what the economy is doing, not the prices in the medium of exchange charged to do it. It is important to note that there is a big difference between real "economic" inflation and deflation and "price" inflation and deflation.

By "price" inflation and deflation, I mean the amount of a particular currency it takes to purchase desired goods and services such as houses, refrigerators, and manicures with dollars, yen, marks, pounds, and so on. Unfortunately, you can have rising prices and still have a deflating economy. In this chapter, I will discuss the fact that the true meaning of K Wave inflation and deflation runs far deeper than just prices.

The heart of the Kondratieff long wave is the direction of global economic activity in terms of real productivity, real income, real gross domestic product, real global product, and, in the end, the real standard of living—all adjusted for rising or falling prices in the economy. These components, which are the central forces of the economy, are expanding year after year in the K Wave advance and contracting year over year during a K Wave decline, particularly in the winter season.

Perhaps far more important than even these economic factors is the critical K Wave component of human psychology. The K Wave advance is a period of expanding or inflating material human expectations and demands: The mood of humanity is positive. A K Wave decline is a period of contracting or deflating human psychological expectations and demands of the material world: The mood of humanity is negative.

The underlying inflationary and deflationary economic forces and the trends of individual and social psychology are critical to long-wave cycle theory. They are far more critical than price inflation during the advance and price deflation during the decline. Strip away the direction of prices in any particular currency and there would still be a clear boom and bust in the real economy of the long-wave cycle. Prices usually reflect what is going on underneath the surface of the economy—but they don't have to.

In most K Wave advances and declines, prices have also gone through inflationary and in turn deflationary trends along with the real economy. However, in a more fundamental sense, this does not have to be the case for K Wave theory to be valid. Without price observations, K Wave theory goes a long way to explain what is happening in the global economy. Prices are just the more obvious icing on the economic cake. This brings us to an important point of observation on the K Wave theory and its influence, particularly when it comes to investments.

The economic inflation advance of the K Wave, the spring and summer seasons, typically see rising prices—price inflation as in the cost of houses, refrigerators, and manicures. The greatest price inflation follows spring and comes in the summer, such as we saw in the late 1960s and the decade of the 1970s. The disinflation and actual deflation, falling prices, come in the fall and economic deflation winter season of the long-wave cycles. This was evident in the 1920s and the 1930s. It has also clearly been the tendency in the 1980s and the early 1990s. However, it is important to clarify that these price trends are surface reflections of the more fundamental economic inflation and deflation of the long-wave cycle. Once again, that is to say that the key to the long-wave cycle is not inflation and deflation in prices, but in the developments within the real economy.

There has been a lot of discussion in recent years as to the nature of the economic crisis the global economy will face in the years ahead. Basically, two schools of thought have emerged.

The largest camp has always been made up of those who see a hyperinflationary crisis in the cards. This group thinks the United States and other major economies are headed for a banana republic style economy of hyperinflation. They certainly have solid arguments favoring their view. Government debts and disturbing inflationary central bank policies are their best arguments. I must concede that the central bankers around the globe have shown a tendency to bail out economic problems by printing money, which has obvious inflationary implications.

The smaller school of thought has argued, most of us quoting Kondratieff, that falling prices and deflation is the most likely direction for the global economy during the most difficult years of this latest K Wave winter decline.

In my mind, it is questionable whether governments truly can print their way out of the deflationary forces that are weighing on prices in this K Wave decline. This especially goes for economies with dominant global currencies that are less controllable by central banks. There are a lot of financial black holes to fill in a K Wave decline, such as the S&L bailout and commercial real estate debacles, long before real price inflation is created.

The real demand for money is declining in a fundamentally deflationary economic K Wave descent, which makes creating price inflation a real effort for the central banks and the printing press at the Treasury. Every segment of the economy is overproducing, so it is difficult to force enough money into the system to ignite prices. Competition is incredible. It takes significant effort to create price inflation in a K Wave decline.

It is a testament to the underlying power of a K Wave decline that the incredible amounts of monetized debt—the billions in new money created by the Federal Reserve in recent years by buying government debt and pumping dollars into the system—has not created a big jump in inflation. The hawks at the Fed are waiting for this to happen; they never met Kondratieff. The new dollars aren't creating inflation because we are in a K Wave winter that is oversupplying everything from toothpaste to luxury autos. This oversupply is keeping a lid on prices. Producers and retailers have trouble raising prices in a glut—even if there are more new dollars sloshing around in the system. There is another reason we see no real inflation while the Fed is making billions in new money: On top of the glut of goods, consumers are "maxed out" on debt and can't afford to buy the excess goods at the beginning of a K Wave winter. The consumer is retrenching in a big way and becoming price conscious. This principle of consumers being "maxed out" financially and psychologically is a key to the inner workings of the K Wave clock that ticks full circle.

The lonely new dollars of monetized debt must find a home. In the early 1990s, these new dollars were chasing financial assets

15.1 Historical Data Consumer Price Index (1967=100)

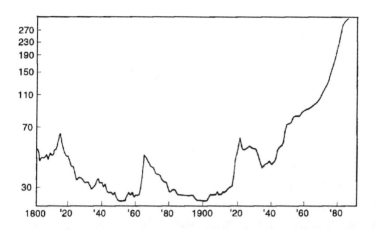

Source: Sterman, John D. 1985. "The Economic Long Wave"

and pouring into stocks and bonds. They were perpetuating the K Wave financial bubble in global stock and bond markets. All the Fed has to do is look at falling producer prices and the stagnant consumer price index and then look at stocks trading at 30- to 40-plus times earnings to know where the new dollars were going. The 1990s aren't the 1970s and 1980s, when consumers were still starry-eyed and looking for a good time on plastic. They are now far more realistic in their expectations. The new dollars the Fed was creating were producing financial inflation instead of goods and services price inflation.

A K Wave fall is ending in financial markets, while a K Wave winter has arrived for the average American, German, Japanese, and British family. The Fed knows it cannot feed the fires of financial inflation forever without destroying its credibility and in time the entire financial system. It knows that new money-financed bubbles do not exhale in an orderly fashion. They bust. The Fed's new money creation will ultimately hurt the dollar. Those who believe we are in for hyperinflation are making a simple judgment call. They believe the Fed will support the declining economy and try to save the imploding debt structure over the dollar. They believe the Fed, as the lender of last resort, will monetize at full throttle, creating new money by buying as much debt for as long as it takes to stimulate the economy, even at the risk of hyperinflation. This won't happen. The Fed is not stupid and will not destroy itself. It will cut its losses, end the financial inflation, and support the dollar, taking the deflationary exit rather than the hyperinflationary route. Indeed, it has already begun taking this exact route.

The only way to hyperinflate and avoid a currency crisis in the sort of trouble that's brewing would be an international hyperinflation effort, with all central banks in perfect agreement and working in unison in the midst of a global panic. Right. Just like the Serbs, Bosnians, and Croats can agree on national borders. Nationalism and introspection will be on the rise in a K Wave winter. *P.Q. Wall Forecasts, Inc.* (1994) has used the term *fortress America* to describe the emerging mentality in the United States. This is a trend we are seeing in nations around the globe. In the real world of economics and finance, nations tend to give up global cooperation in a K Wave winter in order to address domestic realities and necessities. All nations turn inward to correct the many problems created by a K Wave decline.

The complex plan and agreement it would take to create hyperinflation in leading nations will never come about. Gridlock happens. By the time they all agreed on the plan, we would be registering the coldest day of the emerging Kondratieff winter. This might happen, and a new international money, run by an all-powerful World Central Bank, could rise from the ashes, but that's another subject.

I personally believe that the resolution of the global crisis we face will be price deflationary, that prices will fall along with the real economy. In many respects, it already is deflationary: falling real-estate values in Japan, England, the United States and other countries; falling farmland prices and commodity prices; and many falling consumer prices. However, if a government or its central bank is dead-set on creating inflation during a Kondratieff Wave decline, it is certainly conceivable that it could be done, even if historical examples are few and far between. There are signs that central banks are trying their best to inflate during this latest K Wave decline—or to at least stop deflation.

Please note that it will not change the underlying K Wave economic deterioration and deflation of the real economy if prices are inflated by debasing a currency such as the U.S. dollar or currencies from other nations. The economy can deflate in real terms while prices rise or explode and go even further to destroy the social fabric of society.

As the global economy is entering the K Wave winter, central banks and national governments walk a narrow path between price inflation and price deflation. Imagine a narrow path running along the center of the face of a huge cliff. For most of the fall season, the path is fairly wide. But the further the economy moves into the real K Wave economic contraction and fundamental deflation in terms of real income and real growth, the harder it is to balance the emerging economic forces pulling between price deflation and price inflation.

As the K Wave takes the global system further into the fundamental long-wave economic decline, monetary and fiscal policy walk an increasingly narrow path. Eventually, the path simply disappears into the face of the cliff. There are no alternatives left. Prices have to move sharply in one direction or the other. But remember, the real economy will take its predestined, contracting, deflationary direction no matter what prices do.

You cannot have stable prices or no price changes while on one hand incredible and powerful deflationary forces such as bankruptcy, overproduction, and declining asset values are pulling the system into contraction and on the other hand central banks are monetizing debt and printing money like there is no tomorrow, trying to inflate enough to patch the system together so it will keep expanding. One or the other will win out in terms of prices. No central banks are talented enough to do a balancing act on a path that doesn't exist. And there is no turning back to where the economy began. Time pushes the global economy ever forward. One direction or the other must be taken: hyperinflation or deflation.

The bankers and politicians want to print enough money to pay for the mistakes of overshooting the economic target during the K Wave advance. However, they don't truly want inflation. This is why they usually fail to inflate prices. They don't realize the magnitude of the deflationary forces and don't go far enough with the inflation.

History has shown us that bankers and politicians have never been able to move quickly enough on monetary and fiscal policy stimulus to counter the deflationary forces of a K Wave decline. They are also restrained by global market forces more than ever before, forces that limit their options. We have always seen price deflation as well as economic deflation during K Wave winter declines of the past. It is legitimate to ask whether they can create inflation during this decline since they have never done so before. I'm betting on history, which suggests they won't be able to inflate their way out of the latest K Wave decline either.

The German economy during the fall season of the 1920s and the early 1930s is one of the few examples of hyperinflation when the global K Wave was in its decline phase. The central bank and government of Germany were able to create inflation by monetizing debt and printing currency. One positive aspect of this was that their WWI debts were inflated away, which may have had something to do with the policy.

A question obviously worth asking is whether the United States will be the Germany of the 1990s and early 2000s. They could attempt to avoid the inevitable consequences of the real economy in a natural K Wave winter deflation.

I personally don't think they will pull it off. But I'm keeping my eye on central bank and government policy. They probably won't move fast enough, and the deflation will kill their efforts. However, I don't claim to be infallible, and I intend to pay close attention to the price data to see if the U.S. central bankers and politicans are crazy enough to take the route of hyperinflationary Germany. If I had to place odds, I'd say an inflationary price Kondratieff Wave winter resolution in the United States this time around is a 20 percent probability. Still, the German hyperinflationary lesson is one that should not be forgotten.

I can certainly make the inflationary argument. The greatest argument against deflation and in favor of inflation is that the central bankers and politicians are more powerful than ever before. The government is also a more dominant player in the economy than ever before. With the Monetary Act of 1980, the Federal Reserve can monetize all debt—even the local sewer bond debt of towns in Zimbabwe. The political and monetary tools for inflation are more powerful during this decline than at any time in history. This basically means the Fed can create, at the drop of a hat or the stroke of a computer key, an incredible amount of dollars to chase goods, services, and assets. However, this doesn't mean they will use their power effectively to create inflation.

If central banks take the inflationary route, it only means there are more dollars, yen, or pounds in the system. It doesn't create a growing economy in real terms. Price data only measures the economy in debased terms, not real terms. Remember, the real economic and psychological contraction is still going to go on during the K Wave decline. To a real extent the old cliché is accurate: The governments and central banks that chose inflation would only be pushing on strings. They may create a pile of string—higher prices—but no real economic growth. They would not stop the K Wave decline, only shift perceptions of what is happening. I have serious doubts as to whether the real price deflation can actually be stopped by such monetary antics. We will all know the outcome soon enough.

It is important to note that such moves to create inflation if pushed to an extreme could potentially create hyperinflation. By their very nature, such inflating efforts in a K Wave decline would have to be pushed to incredible extremes to actually take hold.

Once again, I don't think there will be enough agreement within central banks and government on the action to take to avoid price deflation. The new trend in Washington is for fiscal conservatism. At this point in the K Wave, these are nothing more than fancy words for deflation. Government is finally considering reigning in its inflationary spending as a deflationary abyss looms larger. You have to enjoy the irony a bit. The natural deflationary direction of the K Wave decline will overcome the policy makers and swamp their efforts.

We could possibly see a situation where price inflation hits a few countries in the global economy such as the United States and Japan, which may have aggressive inflationary policies. Germany, Switzerland, and other nations with more conservative fiscal and monetary policy this time could see deflation. I doubt this division will occur and I think we will all see price deflation in varying degrees before this K Wave is over. Even so, I'm not willing to say price inflation cannot occur in a K Wave winter if the bankers and politicians go over the deep end and totally embrace inflationary mechanisms in a state of money-printing panic. Russia is the best candidate for a hyperinflationary depression like Germany the last time around, and the political fallout could be similar. Russia is already in bad shape and has proven it is willing to destroy its currency for political purposes. Russian efforts at reform could backfire. The people may endorse totalitarian rule in an effort to fix the crisis.

This book has obviously presented a case for price deflation in a K Wave decline. The following chapters on different investments also take this approach. Obviously, if I'm mistaken and we do see hyperinflation in a K Wave decline, it will change some of my investment philosophy. However, I believe it will be easy enough to see inflation coming and to make the necessary changes. There will be clear signs that inflation and hyperinflation are on the way in any particular country. The consumer price index will see occasional rises during the K Wave decline and real economic deflation but they should never spike to double-digit levels during the duration of the decline. If double-digit inflation or even levels over 5 percent annualized hold on the consumer price index or producer price index for more than a few months, a red flag should go up immediately: Banana republic style hyperinflation could be coming to the first world. All thanks should be sent Congress and to the Federal Reserve in Washington.

Obviously, bonds would be a lousy place to be in an economic environment of hyperinflation. Real estate would perform much better, and gold would do far better in price inflation or hyperinflation. Stocks in real terms would not be attractive. Short-term debt instruments would be attractive—but watch out for the potential default of governments or world markets rejecting the government debt of the nation that has chosen the hyperinflationary path.

Another possibility is that we could see global deflation for a few years in the decline and then a drastic change. Bankers and politicians could then use the crisis to consolidate their power and resolve to inflate the system. We could see a global effort on the part of central bankers to inflate the system. We could come out of the decline and into the next K Wave advance with much more inflation than previous cycles or even see inflation in the last few years of the decline. This would produce deflation–inflation whiplash. Once again, the politicians would be fighting last year's battles while the markets move on into the new economy.

In the final analysis, some of the arguments for an inflationary or even hyperinflationary price-action resolution to the building global economic crisis are compelling. In response, I can only say that 200 years of K Wave history would argue that the politicians and bankers won't have that much control over developments. If they do, the change-in-price trend will be fairly obvious, with price inflation heating up while the global economy languishes in what could be called a hot Kondratieff winter.

16

STOCKS

"What mental grasp, what sense have they? They believe the tales of the poets and follow the crowd as their teachers, ignoring the adage that the many are bad, the good are few."

Heraclitus

"He who wishes to be rich in a day will be hanged in a year."

Leonardo da Vinci

Global stock markets have long been barometers of the world's economic and business activity—as well as measurements of swings in human emotions and expectations. As an investor begins to fully realize the great impact the K Wave can have on the global economy and financial markets, questions as to its effects on stock prices are typically the first to be asked. The stock markets of the world hold the future to the lives of millions of people whose retirement and sustenance are dependent on the performance of individual stocks, mutual funds, pension funds, and personal investments in global equity markets.

Before reviewing stocks in light of K Wave theory, it is important to note that to sell all stocks based on the K Wave or any other theory would be foolish. There will always be a few great opportunites for stock investors, even during a K Wave winter. Some of the industries that will lead the next K Wave advance have already been formed and are emerging. The key is to find the diamonds in the K Wave rough. The key isn't to sell all stocks in a K Wave winter, but to own, hold, or buy only the right stocks.

In general, global stock-price trends in the K Wave are fairly simple. Each K Wave experiences two great bull markets: in the spring and fall seasons. Each K Wave experiences two periods marked by a number of bear markets: the summer and winter seasons. Stocks rise during the K Wave spring along with a slow rise in inflaticn and improved corporate efficiency. They experience a few corrections along the way. In the summer season, stocks have major problems due to inflation and rising interest rates that destroy corporate efficiency. Stocks boom in the K Wave fall as disinflation and corporate costs—wages and raw materials—stagnate and decline, thus boosting corporate efficiency. In the winter, it is severe deflation that harms corporate efficiency and creates bear markets in global stock markets. Note that these are general trends. The exceptions will still offer reward to investors.

Remember that the K Wave represents what is going on in the real economy. The constant-dollar Dow, which adjusts stock prices for inflation, actually experiences a crushing bear market in a K Wave summer. In real dollars, the K Wave summer bear-market, during the season of high inflation, may well be worse than the K Wave winter bear-market during the season of deflation. The summer bear-market in real stock prices is hidden by inflation. In winter, the deflation makes the bear market feel worse than it actually is in terms of the real prices in the economy, since the dollars that represent stock prices are typically increasing in purchasing power.

Stock prices rise more slowly in nominal and real terms in the spring but explode upwards in nominal and real terms in the fall season, spiking to new highs in the last few years of fall. The price of a majority of stocks decline during the bear markets of the K Wave winter. Fortunately, bear markets occur far more quickly than bull markets. The sharp bear markets in a K Wave winter will present incredible buying opportunities for long-term investors. By the time investor psychology has reached bottom, most stocks will already have begun their next K Wave advance in new bull markets.

To understand how the K Wave winter will unfold, it is important to closely observe the three- to four-year Kitchin cycles. These are the three- to five-year regular business cycles that often run in sync with elections. What is important is where these cycles come within the Kondratieff cycle. Remember, there appear to be four Kitchin cycles in each of the four seasons of the K Wave. That means there are 16 Kitchin cycles in one K Wave. Identifying and paying attention to where a market is in the three- to four-year Kitchin cycles will greately assist investors in timing buying and selling opportunities.

Many are under the illusion that a major bear market in stocks could never happen again because of new rules, regulations, and government safety nets. They point to increased margin requirements, close SEC regulation, welfare, and government financial insurance. K Wave theory, however, with the weight of 200 years of history on its side, would tend to say that a bear market in stocks is not only possible, but has already begun in Japan.

The turn of global stock markets mark their slow realization and acceptance that the global economy really is entering a protracted economic decline that could last for more than a decade. However, financial markets are smarter than the individuals who drive them, and it takes investors a while to catch on to the new facts of life. A few of those who only become aware of the K Wave economic winter as global stock markets accelerate their descents, and who can't handle the new realities, are seen jumping from the windows of tall buildings.

So how does this K Wave in equities really occur? In Chapter 7, I briefly explored the generation gap and demonstrated that as old pessimistic blood is drained from the leadership in the economy, a new generation and breed of risk takers take over. The great pendulum of pain and pleasure takes its rhythmic course, and the pain is long forgotten. The belief and illusion that the economy can only expand takes precedence. The liquidity created during the K Wave advance has to have some place to go. It moves into stocks.

When the bullish psychology takes over, everyone believes markets will hit a pothole on occasion, but no one really believes we could ever skid off the road. This creates a natural upward bias in stock markets based on what one could call the pendulum power of the generation gap. The upward momentum of the markets becomes somewhat of a sporting event, and everyone truly wants to see the score get higher and higher. The only problem is that in a real sense the forces and people driving the market are all on the same team, creating the illusion that everyone can be a winner.

It was humorous to listen to the great variety of reasons put forward for the bull markets of the latest speculative fall season. One day it was interest rates, the next day it was earnings, then came falling oil prices. Sure, there are the intermediate cyclical conditions and the technical factors that all play an important role in the market, but the most important and overriding element comes from the sweeping effect of the Kondratieff long wave as nothing—including the Dow Jones Average in New York, Nikkei in Tokyo, Hang Seng in Hong Kong, FT100 in London, CAC 40 in Paris, DAX index in Frankfurt, and all other global markets—can escape its path.

The forces driving global stock markets in the 1980s and early 1990s were the same forces that were at work in the 1920s. Remember, the United States was the leader of the K Wave last time around, while Japan has assumed financial leadership this time around. On August 21, 1921, the Dow Jones Industrial Average was sitting at 63.90. In just over eight years, on September 3, 1929, the Dow hit 386.1. This height was not seen again for 25 years, late in 1954. In the interim, the Dow bottomed at 40.56 on July 8, 1932. The parallels with the Japanese market in the 1990s are ominous. In the 1950s, the Japanese market was less than 500; in the 1980s it started out under 7,000. It rose to over 39,000 in December 1989 and has since plunged (see Exhibit 16–1).

The Nikkei followed the exact pattern sketched by the U.S. market during the fall season of the 1920s when it plunged in the K Wave winter of the Great Depression. The worst in Japan could be over, but the Japanese market could easily see a decline of 80 to 90 percent or better before this bear has finished its mauling. There will always be bear-market rallies of 50 percent retracement or better between each stage of the bear-market decline.

Many would like to attribute the entire crash in the markets in the 1930s to speculation and lenient rules and regulations that led to the boom and therefore the bust. This was of course a factor but is itself a reflection of the psychology of the K Wave. The forces at work that arise every half century or so had far more to do with the collapse than investors buying on margin. An article (Feinberg 1987, 226–227) that quoted Robert Prechter discussing a crash to come during the latest K Wave decline had exceptional insight into the foolishness of faith in today's margin requirements:

> Those hoping that any future collapse will be cushioned by post-1929 safeguards are misguided, Prechter says. Like fellow doomsayers James Grant and Jim Rogers, an investor, Prechter believes that today's 50 percent margin requirement, as opposed to 10 percent in 1929, offers only illusory protection. 'These days,' he says, 'with options and futures and second mortgages, you can get much more than 10-to-1 leverage. And at the top, people will be tremendously leveraged.'

Although many who invested in the market in the 1920s were wiped out, there were numerous astute investors who became quite wealthy during the period. There are a number of cases of people in high corporate positions whose companies and banks were boosting the market but who were personally selling

16.1 The Constant Dollar Dow with K Wave Seasons

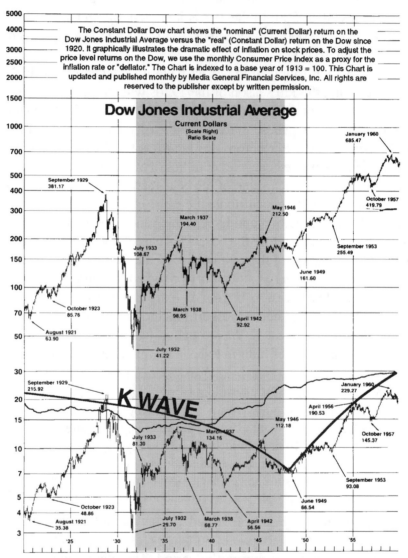

The Constant Dollar Dow chart shows the "nominal" (Current Dollar) return on the Dow Jones Industrial Average versus the "real" (Constant Dollar) return on the Dow since 1920. It graphically illustrates the dramatic effect of inflation on stock prices. To adjust the price level returns on the Dow, we use the monthly Consumer Price Index as a proxy for the inflation rate or "deflator." The Chart is indexed to a base year of 1913 = 100. This Chart is updated and published monthly by Media General Financial Services, Inc. All rights are reserved to the publisher except by written permission.

Information provided by Media General Financial Service, Inc. Richmond, VA. 23293 1-800-446-7922.

16.1 The Constant Dollar Dow with K Wave Seasons (cont.)

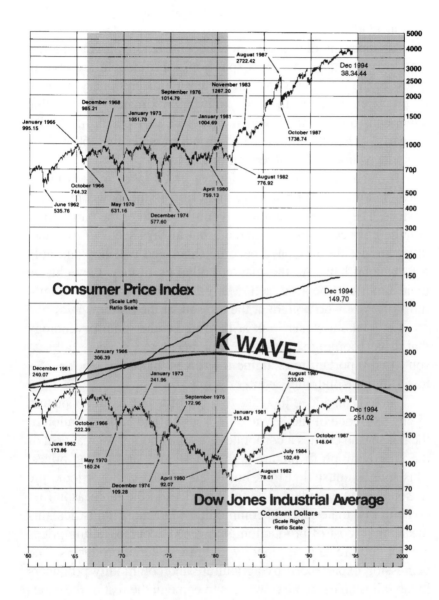

out or going into short positions. They made vast fortunes while the rest of the world was in panic. The situation is the same this time around.

As upper middle-class society becomes more and more afflu-ent during an upswing and expansion, more people are able to invest in the markets with their increasing discretionary income. In the United States in 1952, only approximately 6.5 million Americans owned stock, which was close to 1 person in 20. By the early 1990s, this number had grown to better than 60 million by some estimates, or more than one in four.

The sad fact is that the axiom of greed takes over in the K Wave fall season, and a large majority of the newcomers are novices. They always want to stay until the end of the party. After volatile corrections in the market, that always seem to rebound, investors decide they have become smart and will buy and hold for the long haul. As the market collapses further, they change their minds and begin to sell. Many ride the K Wave down until most of those who bought at the top sell, at the bottom.

Let's take a closer look at the forces other than psychology that drive booming stock markets higher in the K Wave fall sea-son. It is important to examine the forces that drive stock prices lower in the Kondratieff winter decline.

There is an added increase to the profits and earnings picture by the existence of the K Wave fall season. The early deflation of the fall season creates a corporate efficiency boom. A great deal of the improving profit picture is due to sagging and falling prices. This sounds unusual at first, but when we take a closer look, the reasons become evident. The falling prices in the fall season first come in raw materials and commodities. For most industries, this means their cost of production is lower. Of course, falling prices are not good for the commodity and raw material producers. The depression experienced by agriculture and commodity producers in the fall is an example of what is to come in the rest of the econ-omy in the K Wave winter.

16.2 Japan: The New K Wave Leader

Source: Bloomberg Financial Markets

The falling prices seen in commodities in the 1920s and the 1980s were due to overexpansion and overcapacity, which created oversupply. Raw material producers had extrapolated the growth rates of the K Wave advance into the future, but the K Wave hit the fall season first phase of economic decline. We all know that when the rest of the industrial world gets savings from the commodities and raw materials industries, it is quite some time before those savings are passed on to the consumer, and they never pass those savings along entirely.

The retail gasoline industry is a perfect and clear example. We saw a drastic fall in oil prices in the 1980s, but the consumer did not see gas prices drop the same percentage at the pump. This happens in all areas of the economy during the K Wave fall season. Costs are dropping, yet retail prices are holding their ground or even advancing. This naturally produces an increase in profits and earnings for non-raw-material producers. As the quarterly reports are released, higher earnings drive up the price of stocks. However, when the fall season has ended and winter decline begins, it is the consumer-goods manufacturers, wholesalers, and retailers who are overproducing or overexpanded and who have excess supply and space.

During the K Wave fall season a cooling of inflation and dropping prices is perceived as an improving and stabilizing effect when taking an overall view of the economy. This positive perception helps bring buying strength into the stock market. There is evidence to suggest that stocks can maintain a higher price-to-earnings ratio during a period of disinflation. Lower costs in the form of lower commodity and raw materials prices make most industries more efficient.

Because of the overexpansion, there is no need for mature companies to sink as much investment into new capital outlays. One only has to look at textiles, computers, autos, agriculture, and other industries to see that the entire world was overproducing in the latest fall season. There is certainly capital investment, expansion, and development going on, but the bulk of this is mostly by new and young companies. Many of these new companies go heavily into debt and do not survive the decline.

Mergers, takeovers, and stock buybacks sweep the markets in fall seasons of the K Wave. The true reasons are simple, while telling of the reckoning that is to come. If a company had excess capital and profits during the K Wave advance, it automatically went into new outlays and expansion of production facilities. This was because the economy was still in its rapid growing stage, and every dollar was needed for investment to keep up with growing demand. When companies no longer need to spend as much cash for expansion, you see large corporate cash positions.

The 1980s fall season was a case in point. One example was General Motors, which had a cash position of $9 billion early in the latest K Wave fall season. Much of this cash was used to acquire EDS. There were hundreds of other such instances. As corporate cash positions begin growing during this time of slowed expansion and higher profits, there is the natural tendency to start shopping around to see what can be bought. The sad situation is that debt is added to the cash in these buyouts. This causes companies to take on more and more debt when the smart move would be to existing debt. Companies should tighten the belt in preparation for more difficult times to come.

Just as in the 1920s, the 1980s saw a global explosion in acquisitions, mergers, and buyouts. The size and types of takeovers were unprecedented at their peak in the 1980s. The buyout mania that swept the globe and then ended abruptly late in the latest K Wave fall season proved to strengthen arguments of the K Wave's existence. The same thing occurred in the 1920s and will no doubt take place during the next speculative fall season—probably in the 2020s and 2030s.

The fact is that during this latest fall season the general economy was overextended. The big money was not going into new layouts and production capacity, but into the financial markets in the form of takeovers and acquisitions.

When is less more? When the number of outstanding shares on the market is shrinking while the number of dollars chasing those shares is increasing. All of these takeovers, as well as the stock repurchases by many companies who were seeing their own stocks as attractive investments, were rapidly diminishing the number of shares on the market. Estimates show that the number of outstanding shares on the New York Exchange fell sharply throughout the 1980s.

When supply is shrinking and demand is on the rise, the market has only one place to go: up. The massive global bull markets of a fall season pull hordes of small investors into global stock markets at the top for the first time since the last K Wave stock peak.

The trend toward stock buyouts changes at the top. The trend of a shrinking number of shares on the market reversed in 1990. This is because the number of shares hitting the market rises as a public hungry for gains buys up the new stock offerings and new issues at a record pace. Record numbers of new stocks were listed on global markets in the early 1990s, along with new offerings of mature companies. The number of total shares on the market soared. Shares were snapped up by the public's new love affair with stocks. Japan, however, had already made the K Wave turn in 1989, and so the Japanese public was backing away from stocks.

There will always be some winning industries and stocks that investors need to concentrate on. Some of the new companies and old ones that made new and secondary offerings in recent years are in businesses that will do well, even great, in a K Wave winter. The sectors that will outperform and actually gain will be the best-run, low-cost entertainment companies, and certain high-technology companies. Healthcare organizations, with top-flight management, which will be helping other companies cut costs in hard times, will do well. They are in a rapidly expanding sector of the economy. Other existing industries will also do well, as well as industries that will emerge as time passes.

The Kondratieff long-wave cycle is a fundamental approach to the global economy and international financial markets and does not lend itself to precise technical analysis and short-term stock market timing. You cannot look at K Wave theory and say that in this year the stock market will be up or down. The Kitchin cycle is a much better tool for this. K Wave analysis can only present general time frames. It can be utilized to say that we are in the fall season phase and headed for a stock market decline that will lead the world economy into an era of recession and depression, or it could say we are in a K Wave winter that will see stock market lows that will provide great buying opportunities. Evidence indicates that the global stock-market decline of the latest K Wave began its shift from the speculative fall season to the beginning of the winter season in Japan in 1989. While the rest of the world enjoyed the party, Japanese investors woke up with a financial hangover. (See Exhibit 16.2.)

There was evidence pointing to the disturbing fact in the early 1990s that another generation was riding the crest of the K Wave to the edge. If this is a mild K Wave winter, global equity-market declines should range from 30 to 50 percent. A mild K Wave would actually have many advantages, such as low inflation and low costs of capital. If it is a severe K Wave winter, global stock markets should find their bottoms after 50- to 90-percent declines. Since Japan had the greatest stock boom, it will most likely suffer the greatest bust. It is conceivable that Japan's market crash of 1989–1992 produced the greatest declines of this K Wave for Japan, but this is highly doubtful.

Once again, the great K Wave pendulum is ushering in the next era of purifying economic pain. Market bottoms, just like market tops in different nations, could be years apart. All global stock markets will experience a few strong countertrend rallies before reaching their ultimate lows of this K Wave decline.

It is quite difficult to pinpoint the exact peak of the K Wave in stock market advances. Anyone who attempts to short speculative peaks of a K Wave could be wiped out. Due to the undercurrents and volatility in the markets, risky investment vehicles that evolve at market tops take on added complexity. If you attempt to short a K Wave peak and miss the turnaround by even a few weeks, you could be looking at hundreds of points on the upside. The same problems will exist when a market is hitting bottom. Reverses will be powerful and wipe out short positions.

Sometime before the early 2000s are over, the K Wave economic decline will reach bottom, and another advance will begin. But there will be excellent opportunities for investors in stock markets around the globe long before this time. Global stock markets will present buying opportunities before the economy has reached its bottom. Remember, stock prices reflect future, not present economic activity.

At some point early in this K Wave winter, it is my view that it will be time to employ the investment philosophies of men like John Templeton and Warren Buffet once again. There will be incredible quality and value in global stocks, as the pendulum of human emotion will have swung back in fear. Exceptional yields and great buys on stocks will be prevalent. Unfortunately, most investors will turn them down for safety.

After a few years of violent swings that present the greatest opportunities for short-term gains in both directions, the markets will embark on a comparatively boring upswing. Out of the K Wave winter, global stock markets will embark on a rise that will last decades. A key will be knowing which industries and nations are leading the next K Wave advance. Except for in a few high-growth industries, stock price gains will be slow and steady, not comparable to the rapid profits during the speculation that energized markets in the 1920s and the 1980s.

The U.S. market could be one of the first markets to find a major bottom in prices and begin to move up, along with a number of Asian and Latin American markets. It will be important to stay in touch with K Wave fundamentals and the Kitchin cycles to know which global markets are finding their final lows in stock prices. These lows will be in advance of strong K Wave winter rallies and in preparation for the next K Wave advance.

The new global economy that lies ahead will witness the exploration of space and magnificent technological advances not presently imagined. It will be exciting and profitable for investors to become owners in the next advance by buying stocks in the companies that lead the new revolutions in communications and transportation, along with thousands of other companies that benefit from a reviving global economy. However, the greatest opportunities will exist in the midst of a K Wave winter. It will be hard to go against the trend and public mood of gloom and despair and be optimistic, buying the best companies when others will be selling. Solid research from a few of the best analysts on Wall Street, who have proven their ability through the decline, will be crucial.

If it is too late for you to miss the market declines by the time you read this book, don't despair; a new economy is on the way. There will be great opportunities ahead. There will be many bear-market rallies that will offer excellent opportunities even during a K Wave winter season.

There will be intermediate bear markets during the next K Wave advance and lengthy periods of market stagnation. The next K Wave summer will see bear markets once again. The next peak in stocks of the next K Wave fall should come in the late 2030s. We will probably see new investment products not dreamed of in the latest cycle top in the next K Wave peak.

In spite of my K Wave convictions, there are always a few great stocks that are buy-and-holds for investors. If you own excellent companies that are in a position to benefit from the cost control efforts of a K Wave winter or that are in new high-growth sectors that will outstrip all the K Wave negatives, they will make excellent long-term holdings.

There are already a few companies in the United States and other global markets that you shouldn't sell until well into the next speculative fall season peak, which is decades away. In might be smart to reduce a total portfolio to no more than 20 percent in equities at certain points in a K Wave winter season. However, after significant declines, those levels should be raised to take advantage of big market-rallies. Stocks owned in a K Wave winter should be in industries with big pluses during hard times. Service companies that don't invest a lot of capital in brick and mortar, that will deflate and lose value during a K Wave winter, have an advantage. They should be in the fastest growth sectors of the economy, have low to no debt, and have top notch management.

Works Cited and Additonal Sources

Feinberg, Andrew. 1987. "The Crash of 1989." *Gentlemens Quarterly,* February.

Leffler, George L. 1957. *The Stock Market.* New York: Ronald Press.

Malabre, Alfred L. 1986. "Kondratieff Rolls on, As Does the Economy." *The Wall Street Journal,* 20 January.

Sherrid, Pamela. 1985. "The Great Bull Market of 1985." *U.S. News and World Report,* 16 December.

17

BONDS AND
INTEREST RATES

"Every trend must go too far and evoke its own reversal."

P.Q. Wall

"The best way to suppose what may come is to remember what is passed."

George Savile

Of all the investments available, investors typically consider fixed-income securities; government bonds, notes and bills, and investment-grade corporate bonds to be the safest. The overall return on fixed-income securities tends to be lower than stocks over time since the income investor assumes less theoretical risk than does the stock-market investor. It is thought by many that fixed-income investments are immune from the effects of the business cycle, but this is far from the truth.

To begin our look at fixed-income investments and the long-wave cycle, we should first state the obvious. Generally speaking, when interest rates go up, the price of fixed-income instruments goes down, and when interest rates go down the price of fixed income instruments goes up. In this chapter we will review the impact the K Wave has on bonds.

Kondratieff (1951) stressed the relationship between interest rates and bond prices and the flow of the long-wave cycle. He saw emerging from his analysis a very distinct K Wave pattern for bond yields and prices. Kondratieff concentrated his study on government bonds, which are more stable than most corporate issues. However, he believed corporate bonds followed the same K Wave pattern of yield and prices as government bonds.

At this point in our research and study of the K Wave, it should be fairly easy to understand that the powerful economic currents that drive the long-wave cycle would also push global bond markets in a predictable direction. The predictable path of credit markets is not conjured up for the sake of the K Wave evidence, but stands on its own as an independent witness to the K Wave ebb and flow of the economy. Even so, the relationship of bond yields and prices to the K Wave is a bit more difficult to understand than other factors that we have observed, but it is nonetheless extremely important for investors.

For long-term investment purposes it is crucial to know the general pattern, interest rates and bond prices follow in the K Wave cycle. In stating that, we must first confess that the fiscal policy of government, and the monetary policy of the Federal Reserve System, both have an impact on bond markets. However, their effect is not as great as most economists would have us believe. The government and the Federal Reserve receive far more credit than they deserve as they scramble about to give the illusion that their actions are more important than the facts warrant. When we look closely, we see that the government and the Federal Reserve can only cater to the dominant forces at work as the economy takes its predictable K Wave path.

Short-term effects are all the credit we can legitimately give the budget and money supply manipulations of fiscal and monetary policy. It would perhaps be safe to say that the K Wave doesn't react to policy, but that policy reacts to the K Wave. The long-wave cycle is a market force far greater than any government and is beyond the scope of government to affect in the long term. These are important considerations in relation to the bond markets. Bonds owe their short-term activity to government policy and Fed action. Long-term bonds are guided by the inflationary and in turn deflationary long-wave cycle. This observation has proven to be critical information to the long-term bond investor.

Kondratieff's research indicated a clear pattern for bond prices and yields emerging from his data. It became very clear that bond yields and interest rates reached their lowest levels during the low points or troughs of the K Wave, around 1848, 1896, and 1940. Yields began an upward movement in 1789 and peaked around the years just prior to the first downturn of the K Wave. The downward pressure continued on yields and interest rates in the first K Wave decline until we moved into the next upswing of the K Wave in the mid- to late-1840s. This next rise in rates began in the 1840s and continued until the early 1870s, as the economy prepared for the next fall and winter seasons of the K Wave.

The evidence clearly shows interest rates declining from their peaks in 1870 to the next trough of the K Wave around 1896. From this time on, most investors are more familiar with yields and rates. During the 20th century we recall that yields and interest rates were slowly rising to their peak in 1922, from here they turned sharply down, but then picked up slightly in 1928 and 1929 and then began to fall sharply as the K Wave decline set in during the Depression and until the mid-1940s.

The comparisons of recent years with the last long-wave cycle are all too clear as we saw interest rates rise once again from the early 1940s to their peak in 1981. We saw them fall off sharply during the early 1980s just as they did in the 1920s. They rose slightly in the late 1980s and then began to plunge. The Federal Reserve was forced to begin slashing rates to stimulate the economy as the global K Wave began its fundamental shift and the economy was no longer demanding money. Interest rates are nothing but the price of money. The Fed is ultimately controlled by the market and therefore the long-wave cycle.

The Federal Reserve cut the discount rate drastically in the early 1990s. Japan was also forced to cut rates drastically as it led the global economy into the latest K Wave decline. Past declines have effectively brought interest rates down to almost nothing. Demand for capital vanishes as the economy slides into K Wave depression and deflation. This lack of demand for money causes interest rates to collapse.

There is a brief period as the economy shifts from the fall to the winter season when interest rates spike up. We saw this severe credit crunch in 1931 and 1932. This spike appears to have begun this time in the fall of 1993.

Poor quality rates on BBB and lower-rated bonds and risky-mortgage and business loans ultimately rise the most in this crunch and prices of fixed-income securities tumble. The rates on quality AAA-corporate and solid government interest rates ultimately rise the least in this transitional spike phase.

This spike comes partly from an Indian summer boom at the end of fall before the winter season, but more importantly this occurs as individuals, companies, and governments in poor financial shape scramble for funds for their survival. It is the last few months of the spike when participants in debt markets begin to appreciate the magnitude of the economic problems and speculative excesses that must be wrung out of the system.

After this short-lived spike in interest rates, as winter turns to fall, rates resume their fall and bond prices rally. Only the bonds issued by companies and governments that are going to survive the K Wave winter resume the rally. The long-term K Wave decline rally in bond prices that began with the fall season after being interrupted by the spike, lasts until the bottom of the K Wave winter.

It is during the spike of the credit-crunch period when the survivors, individuals, companies and governments, are separated from those that will fail the test of a K Wave winter. This was the case for the 1931–1932 spike. Many will panic, thinking it is a new upward trend in interest rates, and will make the wrong moves.

Over the past 200 years of history we have clearly seen price increases in bonds, and therefore falling interest rates from around the peak in K Wave expansion as the summer K Wave season turns to fall, until the end of the winter season. Bond prices peak and interest rates bottom just as the K Wave winter is turning into spring and the demand for money begins to rise. The greatest bond rally in history was from the early 1920s until the mid-1940s. We have witnessed the same phenomenon since the early 1980s and it should last until the early 2000s. There have been and will continue to be intermediate fluctuations of yields and prices. K Wave theory concentrates on the overall trend in both yield and price, an area where the existence of a K Wave pattern is all too obvious.

17.1 The K Wave in Interest Rates

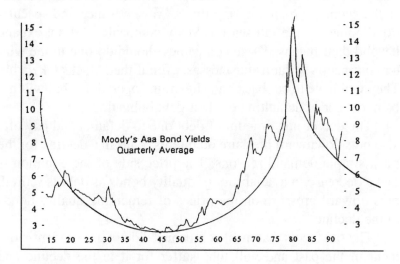

Source: P.Q. Wall Forecasts, Inc.

The role debt plays in understanding the K Wave is very important and is closely related to bond prices and interest rates in the bond markets. Outstanding debt is lowest as we begin a K Wave expansion in the economy and highest in the peak of the financial markets at the end of the fall season and the beginning of winter. Debt drys up in the winter phase. A new generation becomes converted to financial conservatism. It is not important that "all" debt be flushed from the economy during the decline, but that the debt which is unproductive and nonperforming be eliminated. This includes the outrageous debt built up for Third World nations: leveraged buyouts, needless expansion, and excessive agricultural supports, as well as all types of corporate, government, and individual debt.

This debt is flushed out in part by simply being paid off and in part because of the bankruptcies and failures taking place during the Kondratieff winter. Individual, corporate, and state debt is at unsustainable levels as the world enters another K Wave winter. There are many companies that kept their heads about themselves as the economy roared during the K Wave advance and speculation boomed in the fall season. Many companies did not expand beyond their means. These companies should do fine in the winter contraction as far as businesses, even if their stocks take a hit. They will have to cut back and streamline operations, but will not be in danger of defaulting on their debt obligations.

The decreasing amount of debt due to defaults and pay offs also puts downward pressure on interest rates in a decline for the most simple demand reasons. The price side of the equation is that a decrease in availability of quality bonds as debt is retired, puts upward pressure on the prices of remaining quality bonds in the decline.

The sad fact is that most companies did not use prudent judgment in the past and will thus suffer for it in the decline and depression. Debt is a useful instrument for business at the right time. However, too much of a good thing can be fatal.

The latest K Wave contraction will force companies, which are inefficiently structured, into default and bankruptcy. As we move deeper into the decline, an increasing number of companies will be forced into submission. The banks which made the foolish mistake of loaning to companies, real estate projects, and individuals, beyond the creditors means to repay, will be forced out of business. Default will purge inefficiency out of the global economy. Only the financially fit of the business world will survive.

The bonds that survive the K Wave winter, those issued by stable governments and prudent companies at fairly high interest rates, will turn in their best price performance in years. However, investors must realize that any company with competent enough management to maintain a strong position in such a volatile and reckless economy will be smart enough to call in these high-yielding bonds and issue new debt at the new low rates. Such a potential development should be taken into consideration when mapping a strategy for the years ahead.

So why do interest rates and bond prices follow these K Wave trends? The inflation of the advance and the deflation of the K Wave decline are critical to understanding why interest rates rise during the advance and fall during the decline. When companies and individuals believe prices will always rise they don't mind borrowing and having debt on the underlying assets of loans. They believe inflation will bail them out of their debts if they have to sell. The inflation of the advance therefore increases the demand for borrowed funds. The opposite takes place during the decline, as no one wants debt on assets that are falling in value—because eventually you will owe more than they are worth. The deflation of the decline decreases the demand for borrowed funds.

The reasons that debt is productive in a K Wave advance and destructive in a K Wave decline for individuals and companies are fairly easy to understand. A simple example would be helpful. If you borrow 90 percent of the value of a house, say $90,000 on a $100,000 house, and the house doubles in value, you now only have 45 percent debt instead of 90 percent, or $90,000 on a $200,000 house, and some of the debt would have been paid down. This concept applies to farmland, factories, machinery, and commercial real estate. Enough inflation bails out debtors and therefore creates more demand for money and therefore higher interest rates.

Eventually the cycle runs its course and runs in reverse. The global economic system is overbuilt with homes, factories, and wheat fields. Prices begin to fall. No one wants to borrow money if prices are falling. The person who borrows 90 percent on a home, say $180,000 on a $200,000 home and watches the price drop to $100,000, now has 180 percent debt on the home's new market value. If the borrower has to sell, he or she is now most likely a bankruptcy statistic. Instead of inflation bailing the borrower out, deflation is destroying the borrower and most likely his or her foolish lender. This is happening around the world during the latest K Wave decline as it has in all declines of the past. And it is not just the home buyer but the factories, oil rigs, and wheat fields that are falling in value. You can especially see the effects of deflation in Japan, Australia, England, and the United States; Japan is by far the best example since it experienced the greatest speculation. Apply the principle to stocks bought on margin and the picture becomes even clearer.

Once you comprehend the inflation and deflation of the K Wave, you understand why no one wants to borrow money in a K Wave decline. Just ask how many Japanese want to borrow money to build commercial buildings in Tokyo in the 1990s since prices collapsed. Major markets in Europe and the U.S. are experiencing or facing the same deflation—and they will again some 50 years hence. If no one wants to borrow money then the price of money, i.e., interest rates, naturally falls. The Federal Reserve can lower interest rates all it wants. It is the fool who borrows money when prices are falling. The economic lessons of the decline decrease the number of economic fools walking around looking for a loan. In the late 1930s, short-term interest rates were under 1 percent and virtually no one wanted to borrow. The process becomes a vicious cycle in both the advance and decline that must play itself out.

Investors realize that there is something different going on when the Fed can drastically cut interest rates and no one shows up at the banks applying for loans. The whole process and the reasons behind it are really quite simply if you think about it. The K Wave and therefore this book are only pointing out the obvious human tendencies for swings from one extreme to the other.

The effect of supply and demand for money becomes obvious as the economy enters the spring of the K Wave. When the new expansion or next upswing in the global economy begins, there is once again a demand for money. This naturally puts upward pressure on interest rates and yields—the price of money. Interest rates will begin and continue to rise until the next peak of the K Wave and changing of seasons from summer to fall—that is once we find the bottom of the latest decline. Just as with any commodity, when the demand for money increases so does the price we pay for that money in the way of interest rates. We saw this phenomenon as real interest rates started to rise in 1789, 1846, 1896, and in the 1940s. We will no doubt see it again in the late 1990s to early 2000s.

Another major consideration when planning bond investment strategy based on the K Wave is the psychological changes taking place as we enter a major world economic decline. Bonds have a safety factor since they take priority over stock, if the time ever comes for liquidation of the issuing firm. Bonds receive a safety premium over stock. As the decline sets in, the psychology of the marketplace is changing from one of extreme optimism to one of extreme pessimism.

The demand for safety in a decline produces a strong upward pressure on the price of bonds and a downward pressure on interest rates and therefore yields. At the same time, we see a great decrease in the demand for stocks. There is growing strength in the minds of investors toward risk aversion as the new era of pain is ushered in.

The debt of the U.S. government has been considered one of the safest investments in the world for years. In a K Wave winter, government securities will have increasing prices brought on by the safety factor. I say this with caution. Rising prices should also be the case for the bond issues of stable foreign governments whose people will participate with citizens of the United States in the rush for security—this I also say with caution. This may startle many people, but I believe that even though government bonds may offer great investments, I would place greater faith in AAA and AA corporate debt over U.S. bonds. I would recommend AAA and AA corporate investment over any public debt. The balance sheets of AAA companies look better than most governments.

The one avenue of government investment that should definitely prove to be safe and liquid is Treasury bills. Treasury bills are the government's short-term borrowing instruments. The government must keep this market liquid otherwise Washington would have to shut down. Without a liquid T-Bill, market politicians won't get their paychecks. Count on government T-Bills remaining a liquid and safe investment. Most direct treasury U.S. government obligations should survive, but I would keep an eye on the deficit in the event Washington opts for a hyperinflationary solution. I would avoid all U.S. government-agency debt obligations, i.e., nondirect Treasury government debt, during this decline and the next. If Uncle Sam does have to stop payment or reshuffle its debt portfolio in a crisis, agency debt will be the first to get the ax.

It should be pointed out that the rally in bonds that will come with a K Wave decline will be greatest in high-quality instruments. Low-grade and junk bonds will vaporize with the companies that issued them. A wise and prudent move would be to steer clear of any poorly rated bonds during a decline. The street-wise and astute investor will be able to pick through the rubble and find some incredible winners in the junk bonds of companies that end up surviving. But this game will not be for inexperienced investors or the weak at heart.

I cannot emphasize enough that, when facing a K Wave winter decline and looking at corporate bonds, the only ones you should consider are the highly-rated issues from stable, blue-chip companies. Other, lesser-quality companies could be considered if they are closely analyzed and have secure market positions with low debt-to-equity ratios. Keep in mind when investing in bonds that most are callable by the issuer after five years and that you could be caught by having your bond called.

For speculative investors, there are excellent profits to be made in bond futures and interest-rate futures at critical K Wave turning points. Such investment instruments are, again, not for the inexperienced investor.

In reviewing bonds and interest rates, we see that they do indeed follow, both in price and yield, the flow of the K Wave cycle. It should be noted that mortgage rates and bank-CD rates will tend to track the government and corporate interest-rate patterns discussed in this chapter.

The investor should be aware of the K Wave effect on his or her corporate and government bond holdings. Investors should be clear on the position they want to find themselves in during the coming years. The risk-averse bond investor as well as the risk-taker have a great deal to gain by observing the Kondratieff Wave in relation to bonds and interest rates. Quality bonds tend to rally during K Wave declines as interest rates fall and the demand for borrowing dries up.

The 1990s appear to be another global K Wave winter decline that looks attractive for quality bonds overall, even if the greatest gains have already been realized. However, when the economy begins to move into the next advance beyond the year 2000, the bond investor would be wise to take note. The demand for money, and therefore interest rates, will begin their next K Wave ascent.

Works Cited and Additional Sources

Homer, Sidney. 1963. *A History of Interest Rates:* Rutgers University Press. New Brunswick.

Kondratieff, Nikolai D. 1951. "The Long Waves In Economic Life." *Readings in Business Cycle Theory.* Translated by W. F. Stolper. Homewood: Richard D. Irwin.

18

GOLD

"The greatest gift is the power to estimate correctly the value of things."

Francois, Duc de La Rochefoucauld

"Divers weights, and divers measures, both of them are alike abomination to the Lord."

King Solomon

Gold has always played an important role in the K Wave. But before we try to project how gold should perform throughout the cycle, we need to take a quick look at its history. It is important to understand why gold is a unique commodity.

"What makes gold the noblest of metals?" asks writer Timothy Green (1981, xvi–xvii).

> Its greatest strength is its indestructibility. Unlike silver, it does not tarnish and it is not corroded by acid—except by a mixture of nitric and hydrochloric acid. Gold coins have been recovered from sunken treasure ships after two centuries beneath the sea, looking bright as new. . . . Its beauty and versatility swiftly recommended it above all other metals. One ounce of gold can be beaten into a sheet covering nearly 100 square feet. It is also so ductile that one ounce can be drawn into 50 miles of thin gold wire. It is such an excellent conductor of electricity that a microscopic circuit of liquid gold 'printed' on a ceramic strip saves miles of wiring in a computer.

It is estimated that in all of recorded history about 107,000 tonnes of gold has been mined. This may seem like an enormous amount, but consider that, because of its density, this entire amount if melted down would measure less than 19 cubic yards—which is less the volume than three average-size houses. This total world supply of gold if priced at $350 per ounce would come to just over one trillion dollars. A sobering thought in light of this fact is that all the gold in the world couldn't pay off less than a quarter of the U. S. government's debt. The fact is that gold was in very short world supply before the middle of the 19th century and has only been available in large amounts for some 130 years.

Russia was producing some three-fifths of the world's output of gold in 1847, just prior to the discovery of gold in California. Mines, near Mongolia and the Lena River east of Lake Baikal and on the Amur River, discovered in the late 1940s were producing over 40 tonnes in 1880 and over 50 tonnes in 1914. The "Age of Gold" was ushered in by California in the rush of 1848–1849. Up until that time, it is estimated that only about 10,000 tonnes of gold had been mined in all of history.

It all began one afternoon in January of 1848 when James Marshall, a carpenter, found small specks of gold at John Sutter's mill at the junction of the American and Sacramento Rivers. The United States was in the process of completing the purchase of California and New Mexico from Mexico for $15 million in early 1848, just as the news of the gold find was spreading. By 1852, tens of thousands of fortune hunters and adventurers had flocked to California and had mined well over $81 million in gold in 1852 alone. California was probably one of the last good investments made by the U.S. government.

Australia was the nation next hit with gold fever when, in 1850, there was a major gold find in New South Wales that yielded 26 tonnes in 1852. Gold was discovered in a number of places in Australia, but the world's largest finds were yet to come in South Africa where production reached 120 tonnes by 1898.

One last big strike before the end of the century came in the Klondike in 1896 as a couple of salmon fisherman saw a glimmer of gold on the bottom of a stream. The Klondike rush yielded over 75 tonnes of gold in the last three years of the 19th century, the biggest century for gold discovery in history.

Gold poured into the money centers of Europe in the mid-19th century, producing dramatic effects on the world's economy and monetary systems. This was during the upswing of the second long-wave cycle, and the gold discoveries did a great deal to boost the world economy and stimulate global trade. These great discoveries of gold paved the way for the introduction of the gold standard, which became an international basis of money. A majority of currencies were attached to a fixed amount of gold from 1879 to 1913. Most of Europe abandoned the gold standard in 1913, and the United States finally followed suit during the banking crisis of 1931 after suffering a great drain on gold reserves .

On April 5, 1933, under the leadership of President Franklin Roosevelt, it became illegal for U. S. citizens to hold or own any form of monetary gold, either coins or bullion. The government was doing this in 1933 in an effort to relinquish its responsibility to repay in gold. Today the government has no such obligations, and should not find such a policy necessary.

In order to get a feeling for the present situation of gold in global markets, we must go back to the Bretton Woods agreement of 1944. The international banking collapse of 1931 left the world monetary system in shambles. Countries were unable to control and carry on fiscal policy without seeing their currencies depreciate in terms of gold, their capital flee the country, or their credit markets crippled. This led to a meeting in Bretton Woods, New Hampshire, and the creation of an international monetary agreement that would, because of its inherent contradictions, come crashing down 25 years later, at least the exchange rate aspects of the agreement.

The basis of the agreement was that the dollar would be redeemable in gold—but only by foreigners. United States citizens and banks were not allowed to exchange dollars for gold. The price of gold would be fixed at $35 per ounce for the foreigners. The foreign currencies would be required to maintain fixed exchange rates with the dollar. They were allowed to rise and fall by only 1 percent from their fixed rates.

This had the effect of treating the dollar as gold, at least in relation to foreigners. The United States Federal Reserve had the U.S. Treasury print more and more money. Naturally, the dollar became extremely overvalued against foreign currencies. Foreign governments were forced to print large amounts of their own fiat currencies in order to buy the excess dollars. The dollar was overvalued by all measures. Being convertible into gold, the dollar was being traded in for gold almost as fast as it was being printed.

Foreign governments very much preferred gold locked away in their vaults rather than owning overvalued dollars. The dollar was convertible by both foreign commercial banks and the central banks of foreign nations. And converted it was, as the gold reserves peaked at 701 million ounces in 1949 and plummeted to 296 million ounces in 1968. During this period, the United States Air Force was said to be making constant flights with cargo planes loaded with gold from Fort Knox to Europe.

Because of the significant devaluation of the dollar, as the presses rolled on during the Bretton Woods agreement, there began an upward pressure on the market price of gold during the early 1960s. In order to stop this upward pressure, the central banks had begun open-market efforts to hold the dollar up and hold gold down. These open market efforts were mainly composed of the United States selling large quantities of gold in an effort to keep the price of gold down.

At the realization that gold could not be held down indefinitely, a meeting was called in Washington in 1968 during which a "two-tier" market was established where central banks would continue to operate in gold at the official level of $35 per ounce, and the free market would be allowed to find its own price.

Central banks were forbidden to participate in the open market. This of course did not stop the erosion of the dollar. All European currencies were coming closer to pushing through their limits set in the 1944 agreements. This was clearly because the gold dollar was losing its shine.

England was the first to violate the agreements and devalue its currency. All of Europe soon followed suit. This caused a massive flight into gold, but the United States still honored its gold dollar at $35 per ounce. In 1971, United States gold reserves were getting extremely low and were pushing below their 25-percent backing of reserve notes (dollars).

Rumors began to spread that the United States was going to close the gold window. No longer would gold be exchangeable for the dollar. This would cut the dollar loose from any backing and allow the devaluation of the dollar to go unchecked. This rumor caused a new-style gold rush, and in one week some $4 billion in gold left the country for European vaults.

On Sunday, August 15, 1971, rumor became reality as President Nixon in a televised address announced the closing of the gold window; no more gold would be given in exchange for U.S. dollars. The only market that now existed for gold was the free market, and gold prices took off with a vengeance. When the gold dust had settled, U.S. gold reserves had fallen from over 22,000 tonnes to under 8,300 tonnes, while European gold reserves had exploded to over 17,000 tonnes.

We have seen gold prices soar from a low of $34.75 in 1971 to their high of $850 per ounce in 1980. Gold has since dropped to the $300-per-ounce range, then rebounded. After the agreement collapsed, foreign banks could sell the gold they had heisted from the United States under the Bretton Woods agreement on the open market. Not a bad take since they got over 14,000 tonnes of gold at less than $35 an ounce, gold they could now sell for over $350 an ounce on the open market. Don't ever think the European bankers don't know what they are doing. They saw the U.S. politicians coming on that deal and are still laughing about it.

The Europeans now own most of the basis to the new money that could emerge during this K Wave decline. It should be noted that just after this gold heist was complete, the European banking community created the European Currency Unit (ECU), which is partially backed in gold. It is obvious that America was taken to the cleaners at Bretton Woods. Now Europe has most of the world's gold and the only currency backed in gold. This means it will very likely come to the international monetary forefront during a financial crisis in the K Wave winter.

One of our main objectives in K Wave analysis is to determine what effect it will have on investment instruments. The obvious question concerns what is in store for gold in coming years.

In the mid- to late-1970s, there were many financial advisors running around saying to buy gold at any price—the sky was the limit. Indeed the sky was the limit, at which point gold abruptly plummeted. This advice cost clients dearly and could continue to cost them until international financial panic pushes the monetary qualities of the precious metal back into the limelight at some point in the future.

There are a number of wonderful ideas on gold. Many attach gold prices to a strict inverse relationship to the dollar. There is a good reason for this assumed relationship, but many put far too much faith in gold performing the opposite of the dollar. This is what I call the "window on the fingers syndrome," created when Nixon slammed the gold window down on quite a few fingers. The fact is that as you enter the major turning points of the K Wave, tendencies in financial markets are quickly broken; we have seen the gold-dollar inversion law broken on a number of occasions.

I am sorry to inform these inversion die-hards that gold is now an investment considered to be an industrial commodity as well as a safe haven or store of value. Of course, the collapse of the dollar would be extremely bullish for gold. In fact, in the very long run, gold could surpass U.S. savings bonds in safety. Such safety considerations for gold make it react to international economic conditions accordingly.

On a number of occasions in recent years, we have seen gold move up in reaction to negative financial/economic news and move down in reaction to positive economic news. We will see this very clearly at some point in the decline.

The wise investor will wait until attractive purchasing opportunities present themselves in gold. You should not rush in just for the sake of buying gold. Gold could be trapped in the deflation and falling prices of the decline far longer than most anticipate. At some point, it will break away from the crowd of nonmonetary commodities and perform very well because of its monetary qualities and characteristics.

Even if the price of gold does not explode upward, its purchasing power will rapidly increase as other values collapse, which would still make gold an excellent investment. Gold will always be accepted as a form of payment even if it must first be converted into the latest fiat currency.

Kondratieff related the buying power of gold and the production level of gold very closely to the K Wave cycle. Since production prices reach their peaks as the K Wave expansion peaks, it becomes extremely expensive to mine gold. At the same time, the purchasing power of gold is declining. This tends to slow production as we enter the peak of the industrial expansion of the long-wave cycle.

The opposite occurs in the decline, with production costs falling and the purchasing power of gold increasing. As the decline deepens, the cost of labor and the price paid for mining equipment gets cheaper, while the purchasing power of gold is on the rise. This naturally leads to greater production efforts and output as the K Wave reaches its low point in the trough of the decline. The confusion in the markets and the crash of the banking system will create a rush for the safety of gold. The free markets we have today in gold will put great upward pressure on the price of gold at some point during the coming decline.

The investor would want to hold a position in gold during the entire inflationary advance of the long-wave cycle. In a free market, it should perform well during the advance. Gold makes an especially good investment during the late runaway inflation seen during the last decade of the advance phase of the long-wave cycle. This was the case in the 1970s. However, during the fall season and the first few years of the K Wave winter, gold should be avoided because of the deflationary forces of the long-wave cycle. A few years into the decline, a global financial banking crisis tends to hit that makes gold important for investment insurance and as a disaster hedge.

Throughout history, those who have held a portion of their portfolio in gold have always come out on top when times get really tough. The buying power of gold has consistently gained while all else has fallen by the wayside in K Wave declines. Paper money supported by nothing can only last for a season and in time will come to nothing. Like everything else that has no foundation, it will in time be washed away. Gold will have a double advantage in the latest decline. It increases in purchasing power in a deflationary economy, and it may emerge as the basis to a new national or international money system.

A major factor to consider when looking at gold is the impending changes and potential collapse of the international monetary system as we know it. We have seen an international banking shakeout in every decline of the long-wave cycle. This has always led to major changes in the money and banking system that include a changing role for gold. Evidence indicates that the global monetary and banking system today faces a major shakeout. It may have already come by the time you are reading this book.

In the midst of the decline, a new international monetary system will likely emerge that will lead the global economy into the next advance. One of two likely monetary systems will emerge— gold will play a role in each and is therefore an important part of an investor's portfolio.

One money system would be a single international currency unit backed fractionally in gold and run by the World Bank under the authority of a more powerful United Nations and very likely modeled after the ECU. This system would be limited in its economic potential, although the economy would still move into the next advance. The other money system would be a true free-market gold-based banking and money system that would be the engine of an explosive new economy that could perform far better than the economy of the last K Wave advance.

Either system could bring us into the next advance of the cycle. We will take a more in-depth look at the two new money possibilities in the final chapters. One thing is certain, change is coming as the failed fiat money and banking system that has lasted since the beginning of the latest cycle crumbles.

It would be wise to hold some gold in one's readily available possession as the decline could be more severe than anyone could anticipate. Gold could be used to acquire what you need in a worst-case situation of total financial shutdown for a lengthy period of time. Personally, I hope the global financial situation will not come to that, but it is worth considering and planning for such a development.

I typically don't recommend more than a 20 percent maximum position in gold, and 10 percent may be sufficient for most investor's portfolios. Gold should be seen first and foremost as insurance against worst-case financial scenarios and secondly as an investment. The view of gold as insurance makes a down market easier to tolerate. I always urge investors not to become extremist and go too heavily into the gold market.

All gold holdings should be divided between ingots or widely circulated coin and solid gold stocks. The Canadian maple leaf would be a perfect coin to hold because of its purity and acceptability. The maple leaf comes in one-ounce, half-ounce, quarter-ounce, and 1/10-ounce coins. An IRA can be invested in U.S. gold Eagle coins, which is a consideration for many investors. All gold other than what one keeps in one's immediate possession should be stored in a safety deposit box with an institution the investor knows well. Of course, extremely large holdings should be held by well-established firms with excellent long-standing reputations, such as are available in Switzerland.

Gold stock mutual funds may be an attractive form of investment in gold for the small as well as the large investor. This should be closely considered. It may be smart to divide your gold investments between gold stocks or gold mutual funds and actual physical gold holdings. One-half in stocks and one-half in coin, ingots, or bullion bars would perhaps be the best mix. This all depends on the amount of investment you plan to put in gold and your personal preferences. The tendency for gold stocks to move up more on a percentage basis than gold itself should be kept in mind. Gold stocks may perform better than the actual gold in an international financial crisis. Once the K Wave decline is over and the financial crisis is a thing of the past, a gold position should be held as an inflation hedge as the next K Wave expansion begins.

There is always the possibility that the government may once again seize private gold holdings as it did in 1933. We certainly hope that won't occur, but sufficient steps should be taken to protect oneself against such a possibility. This confiscation of bullion clearly presents the advantages of holding gold mutual funds or gold stocks.

In summary, we see that the K Wave suggests gold as an important part of monetary policy in our financial past and future. It would indeed be a good idea to include it in your personal plans and objectives when considering your investment position for a long-wave cycle. History has proven that gold has survived what nothing else can and that only gold is as good as gold.

Works Cited

Green, Timothy. 1981. *The New World of Gold.* New York: Walker and Company.

Paul, Ron. 1982. *Case for Gold.* Washington: Cato Institute.

19

REAL ESTATE

"Humanity does not profit by experience . . . . We should say: Profit by history; because the life span is too short to permit more than one ride."

James M. Funk

The reality that the value of a home, apartment, or office building, and an acre of farmland can go down in price just as easily as it goes up casts a revealing light on the idea of an economic K Wave passing though the global economy every half century or so. You might even say it makes the K Wave theory "hit home." So much for my K Wave humor.

A major concern for average homeowners and investors alike is the effect the K Wave has on the value and price of residential real estate—mainly their own home. This has proven to be especially true over the past few years as real-estate values have dropped in many major economies around the globe.

In the mid-1980s when I predicted real-estate values would soon drop significantly, I had numerous conversations with individuals in California and New England who said in effect, "Sure, real-estate prices might fall in other places, but not here. Prices are booming." The same thing was said about Japan—Tokyo in particular. Well, we now know that the commercial and residential real-estate bubble of the last K Wave advance has burst. California and New England have been some of the worst hit thus far. The United States, England, Japan, France, Canada, Australia, and even Switzerland, along with numerous other countries, have seen real estate falling in price.

The world became addicted to rising real-estate prices and was blindsided by the deflationary impact of the long-wave cycle. Although prices were falling in many areas long before then, it is likely that the history books will look at 1989 as a peak in global commercial and residential real-estate prices that will hold for decades.

The erosion of global prices that we have seen during every K Wave decline has also been seen clearly in the value of real estate. This is of utmost concern to the homeowner who has taken on enormous debt over the last few decades of the upswing in the K Wave. Many homeowners are faced with large monthly payments on an asset that is decreasing in value. Over the past few years, we have seen the erosion of home values for the first time since the Great Depression.

In terms of commercial real estate, the reason so many banks are in trouble around the world is due to the falling values of commercial portfolios.

For many years, if a family came on hard times and came up short on payments, they could sell their house for a gain without much effort. This was unfortunate but not financially devastating. Things have changed. In increasing numbers, families are finding that their homes will not sell on the open market for what they have in them. Under such circumstances, many are finding it is wise to simply allow the bank to foreclose and take the home. We are also seeing situations where it is the seller who writes the check at closing instead of the buyer. Such situations were unheard of during a K Wave advance. Owners simply walking away and sellers writing the check at closing are occurring with increasing regularity as the latest K Wave decline proceeds along its predictable path.

Early in the latest K Wave fall season, the worst-hit areas for real estate were in the central United States. The problems in the heartland spread quickly to both coasts as the fall season progressed. Prices on both coasts began their plunge in 1989. Real-estate prices in Los Angeles, Boston, and other cities plunged by 30 to 40 percent in many cases.

The changes occurring today mark the need for tremendous strategy changes on the part of families and businesses involved in real properties. This is of course a majority of the families and most businesses. Average prices could fall from 20 to 90 percent before the declines are over, although just as in the stock market there will still be opportunities and periods of strong rebound in real estate.

Many who use real estate as a tax shelter and a hedge against inflation are finding in this K Wave decline that the game is being played on an ever-tilting playing surface. This calls for positions to be closely analyzed and restructured if it is not too late. Vacancy rates in commercial real estate are reaching unheard-of levels. In many cities, development will come to a screeching halt.

Most real-estate owners and investors believe this is a short-term phenomenon. They don't want to accept that major shifts are going on in the structure of the global economy, brought on by the long-wave cycle. The K Wave is right on schedule, and deflationary developments in real estate haven't surprised anyone who understands the fundamentals of what the forgotten Russian, Nikolai Kondratieff, observed about capitalist free-market economies. Many who were once skeptical of the K Wave are beginning to change their tune as they observe the real-estate evidence, which is overpoweringly in favor of the K Wave hypothesis.

To gain direction for what position the home owner and investor should be taking concerning real estate, we must first take a close look at what has created the situation in which we now find ourselves. When the economy initially moves into the spring expansion of the long-wave cycle, inflation is just beginning to show its face. Prices, including real estate, which have been in decline for as long as several decades, are beginning to move in an upward direction. The economy is digging itself out of the K Wave decline and into the next advance. Demand is rising across the board. As the new upswing begins, interest rates begin to pick up from the lows they reached in the trough of the decline of the K Wave. These factors all have the effect of moving real-estate prices in a steady upward direction throughout the entire K Wave upswing of the economy.

Inflationary pressures are increasing as the economy moves further into the expansion phase, making real estate extremely attractive as a hedge against inflation. A rising money supply increases the amount of money chasing real estate and therefore chasing prices higher. The further we move into the expansion, the easier it is to forget that prices will eventually come down. Eventually, the generation that created the last speculative bubble in real estate retires. A new generation of infinitely optimistic investors and developers drive capital into global real-estate markets during the advance of the K Wave and into the fall season.

We know that inflation subsides as the K Wave summer comes to an end. There comes a point during the fall season of the K Wave where there is no longer the rush into real estate as during the extremely inflationary period through which the global economy had just passed. The 1970s and 1980s were a classic global K Wave real-estate bubble that had to burst.

Farmland is the first real estate to take a hit. We only have to look as far as the average family farm in America to see the K Wave having its effect on real estate in the 1980s. The average price of farmland, as mentioned earlier, dropped approximately 50 percent between 1981 and 1992. That is serious deflation. The effect this has on the agricultural industry was all too obvious as we witnessed failure after failure in all parts of the country.

This real-estate situation was created by oversupply and over-expansion built into the system during the advance. The head of steam in the system just overshot the true needs of the economy. The growth and price trends in the K Wave advance were simply projected into the future by investors and developers—a classic K Wave expansion overkill.

No trend runs to the sky. There is always an equal and opposite reaction in economics just as in physics. Too many buildings were built, creating a real-estate glut. Further, the K Wave advance created too much liquidity, chasing those prices higher; therefore, prices had to come down in a bust, as illiquidity spreads as a K Wave decline deepens.

What happened to farmland in the fall season is an excellent example of what is in store for the rest of the real-estate market in the later years of the decline. Residential and commercial real estate was overbuilt. Japan was the most inflated this time around and is therefore experiencing the greatest real-estate crash and its consequences.

If you have ample liquid assets during the winter season of the K Wave cycle, you will be able to pick up real estate at rock bottom prices. There is a good chance, based on cycle analysis, that the bottom in real estate in the United States, and possibly Japan, will be at the bottom of the first Kitchin cycle of this K Wave winter. That will likely come in the 1997 to 1998 time frame. Some areas may bottom even sooner, and many will later.

The late 1990s and early 2000s will offer fire sales, not seen since the 1930s, in real estate. These bargains will represent excellent buy-and-hold investments for the next K Wave advance. Deals will be everywhere, in farmland as well as in commercial and residential properties. Real estate becomes a buyer's market that reaches its best deals in the K Wave winter season before the next advance of the cycle begins.

Investors who don't care to invest directly in real estate and manage it themselves would be wise to find a solid real-estate investment team that will acquire and manage for them the exceptional commercial, residential, and raw land properties that will be available in the worst years of the decline. Excellent returns and long-term investments will be available before the 1990s are over.

There are exceptions to every rule for investing based on the K Wave. Some real-estate investments purchased during the previous advance and fall season will do well during the K Wave winter season. But these properties and opportunities are extremely rare. The real opportunities for real-estate investment based on K Wave theory come in the winter season when prices have collapsed and the excesses are being wrung out of the system.

I don't advise everyone to go out and sell all their real estate before a K Wave decline. It is too late during this latest K Wave to get top dollar anyway. Some investors will choose to hold real estate right through the decline and will do just fine. However, they will have to be liquid and have little debt. But there is no investment that has the permanent safety value of real estate. This includes raw land, farmland, homes, office buildings, and apartments. Investment in real property protects the investor from what I consider to be the K Wave unpredictables.

There are any number of complications that can arise during a severe economic downturn that will affect other investment instruments but not real estate. Stocks, besides decreasing rapidly in value due to overall economic conditions or individual corporate failures, are subject to complexities in transactions and in the brokerage end of transfer of ownership. If you were flawless in your market picks and your overall timing, your broker could still make a mistake that could cost you dearly. Many will find that their brokerage firms themselves are in financial trouble and will be forced into bankruptcy because of their own foolish market transactions. So even without making a wrong move yourself, you may find your investment washed away by another's mistakes, or you may find your assets frozen for years while litigation drags on and you are left helpless. Bonds could face the same problems as stocks. You may also find your banking deposits frozen during the restructuring of the banking system. No one knows for sure what will happen to the money and banking system in a K Wave decline. An absolute worst-case situation would be the default of the U.S. government on its obligations. It could happen. On the other hand, if the government chooses to hyperinflate its way out of their debt and create an inflationary depression, real estate will be a great hedge.

These sorts of market and transaction problems will not affect an investment in real estate. As long as the title was thoroughly searched by an experienced, dependable lawyer, you will not run into the predicament of suffering for someone else's mistake. Real estate is something you can jump up and down on, grow or saw a tree down on, see with your own eyes, and walk on with your own two feet. A debt-free family farm saved many families from starvation in the Great Depression as members of the family returned home. The key is to be sure that rents or cash is available in a worst-case situation to pay the taxes.

I recently read of the president of a bank who resigned and bought a farm in the country because he didn't want to be in the city for the K Wave winter that is coming. He obviously didn't buy his farm for price appreciation.

Taxes on real estate that is losing its value is an important consideration for anyone looking at the pros and cons of owning real estate in a K Wave winter. In Chicago in the 1930s, rents would not pay the taxes in most cases. Debt should be avoided on real-estate positions that are held during a decline. This gives the owner options and flexibility so that hard times don't dictate action. It may be advisable to use debt to buy real estate at the bottom of the decline before the next inflationary advance phase of the K Wave. Debt should always be used with moderation so that the debt works for the investor, not the other way around.

When ultimate safety is a consideration, real-estate reigns supreme. This would bring us to the conclusion that the investor should be concerned with far more than selling at a gain during the decline. The investor must realize that even though real estate will probably not rise in price, and will most likely even fall, it possesses a quality no other investment has: permanence. The short of it is that there are reasons other than profit for owning real estate. Even so, some profitable, well-structured, real-estate deals will be put together prior to and during the worst of times.

Another word of caution on the matter of real estate comes under the topic of debt and concerns your personal residence. The first and foremost investment of anyone during this time would be to have your principle residence debt-free, with no liens or claims outstanding from any source. This is tall order for most families and individuals. You may choose to rent to avoid the real-estate price declines. You could then find a bargain in the worst years for real estate.

The most serious drawback to the new tax laws in the 1980s was that due to the elimination of the consumer interest-deduction, a lot of homeowners shifted their consumer debt to their home equity lines of credit. During this decline, many a homeless family is going to wish they had never heard of the home-equity loan. Again, one of the smartest moves any family could make before a K Wave decline is to get their home as debt-free as possible.

It should be noted that certain cities in the United States, and around the globe for that matter, did not become nearly as inflated as others during the K Wave advance. Property values could hold up quite well in the K Wave decline in areas that didn't experience drastic price increases in the advance. Areas that will be hit the hardest are the resort locations of the wealthy and other properties that do well in times of general prosperity. Areas that experienced the greatest price booms usually experience the greatest bust. Well-established and historical neighborhoods should suffer the least. The price of real estate in different countries, regions, and cities around the globe will bottom and begin the next K Wave advance at different times.

Property-tax bills could prove to be a major issue for real-estate investors in coming years. Since all prices will be adjusted downward, we should see a substantial drop in taxes on real property as we move into the decline, due to the falling value of real estate. Of course, local governments may just raise tax rates to compensate for falling prices. Doesn't that sound like the logic of a politician? You should be quick to have your home or other property reassessed at the new lower values for property-tax purposes.

In summary, we must emphasize that there is no investment with the physical security of real estate. However, real estate will continue to decline in price into the K Wave downturn and winter season. The bottom of a deflationary K Wave decline is a great time for investors to buy real-estate bargains and hold on for the next inflationary advance of the long-wave cycle. Above all, it is real estate that provides a roof over your family during the good times as well as the bad.

Additional Sources

Waldman, Peter. 1986. "Severe Deflation Hits Commercial Properties in Many Areas of U.S." *The Wall Street Journal*, 4 September.

Part IV:
Looking to
the Future

20

CYCLES: THE
FINGERPRINTS OF TIME

"What experience and history teach is this—that people and governments never have learned anything from history, or acted on principles deduced from it."

George W.F. Hegel

"If men could remove cycles from the world they would destroy themselves. Fortunately men have no such powers. But they are indelibly convinced they do, which is why cycles will work forever."

P.Q. Wall

The primary subject of this book is clearly the Kondratieff long-wave cycle and its four seasons. It should be evident that I agree with the late Harvard economist, Joseph Schumpeter (1939), who observed that the Kondratieff long wave is the single most important tool in economic prognostication.

My reason for this thinking is simple: The K Wave's length is approximately 50 to 60 years. It therefore allows most of us to experience only one complete cycle in a lifetime. Longer life expectancies allow an increasing number of people to experience two booms or the unfortunate pleasure of two K Wave busts, but few live the 100-plus years necessary to experience two complete long-wave cycles. Certainly, no one is actively engaged in the economy and financial markets for two full cycles.

This single full-cycle experience says a great deal about the Kondratieff long wave. The K Wave and its seasonal stages have proven to have the greatest bearing of any economic or financial cycle on the life and investments of a given individual.

A key to personal development and worldview is at what age an individual experiences a K Wave winter. If experienced at a relatively young age, it will mold an individual's perceptions and views for the remainder of her or his life. If experienced late in life it can be traumatic and drastically alter an individual's remaining years—especially if major financial loss is suffered in retirement.

Other seasons of the K Wave have a significant impact on an individual, but the K Wave decline and winter clearly draw attention to themselves. The worst years of K Wave declines inevitably become mile markers on the road map of history that are remembered and spoken of with awe and respect for several generations. A generation born in the summer, spring, fall, or winter of a K Wave has its own unique way of looking at the world and reacting to it, which molds and influences the economy and all of society in future years. For example, the generation born in a K Wave advance and inevitably spoiled by the wealth created by their parents' generation is sure to drive the system over the edge, without the experience of the past decline to provide financial and economic sobriety. Clearly the K Wave is the key to any cycle research related to social development and investments. In my view, the Kondratieff long wave is the most important cycle—bar none. But what of the other cycles. Over years of cycle research, it has become increasingly obvious to me that the K Wave is but one wheel in the clock of time. This book would prove remiss if it didn't at least briefly discuss a number of other cycles. Even Kondratieff (1951) wrote of a few of these cycles, as already briefly mentioned in Chapter 2.

Other cycles can have a major impact on the way a Kondratieff long-wave cycle is realized in society and can influence its impact on investments. The following discussion of other cycles is food for thought.

A good starting point for a review of cycles is Schumpeter's (1939) classic work, simply and appropriately entitled *Business Cycles*. The three cycles that were the focal point of his research were the Kitchin, Juglar, and Kondratieff cycles. Schumpeter does an excellent job of discussing all three.

The Kitchin cycle is named for its earliest advocate, economist Joseph Kitchin (Schumpeter 1939), and is often called simply the regular business cycle. It is typically considered a three-and-one-half year (42-month) cycle. Many observers see it as ranging from as short as three years to as long as five. Clearly you should not attempt to establish rigid parameters for any cycle.

It should be noted that presidential-election terms fit nicely within the parameters of this business cycle. The Kitchin business cycle is greatly influenced by U.S. presidential elections and has a great deal to do with what is called the economic theory of elections. Presidents try to boost the economy for election years and don't mind taking a recession early in their first or second term because it will be forgotten by the time the next election rolls around. They like a growing U.S. economy in the last year of their second term, if they get a second term, to be remembered fondly and to boost the chance of their party keeping control of the White House. The regular Kitchin business cycle in the U.S. economy in turn has had a big impact on the global economy.

It is my conviction that after the Kondratieff long wave, the Kitchin cycle is the most important cycle for economic and financial market analysis. The work of market analyst and philosopher P.Q. Wall (1993) must be credited with what I believe is an important discovery in the relationship between the Kitchin cycle and the Kondratieff cycle (P.Q. Wall Forecasts, P.O. Box 15558, New Orleans, LA 70175–558). As an integral part of his prime family of cycles, Wall has observed that there are four Kitchin cycles in each of the four seasons of the Kondratieff long wave. Therefore, there is total of 16 Kitchin cycles in each K Wave cycle.

P.Q. Wall's (1993) work is built on concepts of an inherent threeness and fourness within all cycles. He has found that divisibility by the number 144 [(3 squared × 4 squared) or (9 × 16)] is important to the structure of cycles. Each Kitchin business cycle can be divided into three subcycles or Kitchin thirds. Wall goes further and divides each Kitchin third into three distinct spokes; so that there are nine spokes in each Kitchin cycle. An approximate 20-week Kitchin spoke-cycle, what we will call a Wall cycle, is therefore 1/144th of a Kondratieff cycle.

In 1929, the U.S. stock market appears to have peaked in the third Kitchin cycle of the fall season and tumbled to its low in 1932 at the bottom of the fourth and final fall Kitchin cycle. This time around, Japanese stocks peaked in the third Kitchin cycle of the fall season, just as they did in the United States in 1929, and collapsed into the fourth Kitchin cycle of the fall season.

The Juglar cycle, named for the work of economist Clement Juglar (Schumpeter 1939), is the intermediate business cycle and is considered by most cycle analysts to range between 7 and 11 years from peak to peak or trough to trough. A Juglar cycle is likely more in harmony with commodity prices than stock and bond prices.

It is important to note that evidence indicates the Kitchin, Juglar, and Kondratieff may all be pointed down in the 2000–2002 time frame, which could be a major bottom for the global economy and stock markets, although many markets will see final lows much earlier.

The United States could see the worst years of this K Wave decline before the year 2000. The last years of a Kondratieff winter and its final two Kitchin cycles could be fairly healthy, as they were in the 1940s. We could be on the way to the next K Wave advance, especially in China and Southeast Asian countries such as Singapore, Malaysia, Burma, Indochina, and Thailand, as the new millennium begins.

China and Southeast Asia should see excellent stock-investment opportunities long before other countries. In South America, Chile and Argentina are candidates for early investment. Some of these nations are headed toward less government and more free markets, while the United States and Europe are headed in the opposite direction. Japan and most Western European nations will likely bottom out by the early 2000s. When financial markets and economies of specific nations will revive and begin their new advances is of course largely speculation at this early date.

It would be nice to stop here in my review of cycles and only cover cycles shorter than the K Wave cycle. However, there is evidence of a number of cycles that are degrees larger than the K Wave cycle. At this point, it is important to mention the extensive work on climate cycles and their impact on business cycles done by the late Raymond H. Wheeler (Zahorchak 1983) at the University of Kansas. Using over 200 researchers and over 3,000 reference sources over a 20-year period that began in the 1930s, Professor Wheeler assembled a massive data base for his study of climate and cycles. Over 20,000 items of climate evidence went into his work. In a nutshell, Wheeler found that, historically, wet weather accompanied booms, and dry weather accompanied busts. The fact that agriculture was historically the largest segment of economic activity is likely one reason for this finding. With less of the economy dependent upon agriculture, weather patterns shouldn't be as important. The bottom line for Wheeler in terms of cycles is that he discovered climate and therefore business cycles ranging from 7 years to 1,000 years. What he saw as most important were the 100-, 500- and 1,000-year cycles. Of these three, the 100-year cycle was critical to his research and findings.

Wheeler's work supported K Wave theory and the 50- to 60-year Kondratieff cycle. Wheeler (Zahorchak 1983) actually tracked what he considered to be a Kondratieff long-wave cycle going back to 600 B.C. As pointed out by Michael Zahorchak (1983), who has edited many of Wheeler's papers, Wheeler saw his 100-year climate cycle as being made up of two complete Kondratieff cycles.

Instead of looking to the 1930s for the most accurate clues for this K Wave decline, Wheeler's work would suggest we look at the decline of the late 1800s, and after that the decline of the late 1700s, for guidance as to how the latest K Wave decline will play out. Wheeler (Zahorchak 1983) basically says you must go back two cycles to find a cycle most similar to the current long-wave cycle. This effort presents mixed blessings for stock-price analysis since the bear market that bottomed in 1784 was 15 years long, came at the end of an exceptionally weak K Wave, and wiped out stock values by as much as 50 to 70 percent, while the bear market in stocks from the late 1880s to 1896 wasn't nearly as severe and wiped out only 46 percent of values.

The most encouraging thing about Wheeler's (Zahorchak 1983) work is that he forecasts climate and business conditions into the 20th century. If he is correct in his forecasts, the 1990s could be a relatively weak K Wave decline—or call it a mild Kondratieff winter. His work indicated the decline would give way to the next K Wave boom by the mid-1990s. However, his economic forecasts so far seem to be off by five to seven years in some respects and just plain inaccurate in others. Adjusting his work for recent evidence would place the beginning of the next K Wave advance in the early 2000s.

One aspect of Wheeler's work that I found particularly interesting was his (Zahorchak 1983) projection that starting around 1993 the world would be unusually wet. The blizzard of the century in 1993, the flood of the century in the United States in 1993, and floods around the globe in 1993–1995 make me wonder if he wasn't onto something. It will be interesting to see if the remainder of the 1990s are unusually wet. Once again, agriculture, and therefore weather, is less important today. The economy could be out of rhythm with weather patterns in this cycle. To look more closely at Wheeler's work, you should pick up the book of his papers edited by Zahorchak (1983), *Climate: The Key to Understanding Business Cycles.*

Also interesting is that Wheeler's work suggests that the next K Wave advance could see its primary peak around 2020 with a booming fall season in the 2020s, much like the 1920s. His work would suggest a depression in the 2030s potentially more severe than the 1930s. After a bottom in the 2040s, a new long-wave cycle would begin by the early 2050s.

Wheeler's work also covered a 1,000-year climate cycle that he seems to have uncovered. He further divided this cycle into two 500-year cycles. According to Wheeler (Zahorchak 1983), the Roman Empire began its rise around 575 B.C. His exact dates are certainly debatable. Rome peaked around the birth of Christ and declined into total collapse by A.D. 460. The Middle Ages rose from A.D. 460 and ended around A.D. 1475.

According to Wheeler (Zahorchak 1983), what we know as Western civilization began its rise around A.D. 1500 and should reach its peak in the present time frame. This is certainly debatable. Wheeler noted that at the end of a 1,000-year cycle, an old world passes away and a new one is always born. This would suggest Western civilization passes away for good around the year A.D. 2500. Fortunately, this would imply we should have a few solid centuries left, unless you have unearthed this book in an archeological dig. Just watching the evening news does make you wonder if Western civilization has reached a peak and is headed for a decline.

If Wheeler (Zahorchak 1983) is correct, a new culture will begin its rise around 2500. Given the evidence of these cycles, the time frame immediately ahead is a critical turning point. However, there is not a great deal you or I can do about it if a 1,000-year cycle really exists.

Another cycle I feel compelled to mention is one that has been introduced to most students of cycles by Robert Prechter, of the Elliott Wave International (P.O. Box 1618, Gainesville, GA 30503): the grand supercycle. Mr. Prechter's (1989) analysis of the grand supercycle removes any hope for a shallow Kondratieff Wave decline this time around. In Prechter's analysis, a supercycle is the equivalent of a Kondratieff long-wave cycle, while a grand supercycle is the next degree larger. If his analysis is correct, the advance in stocks from the bottom of the bear market in 1932, at 41 on the Dow Jones Industrial Average (DJIA), into the latest highs is the fifth and final wave of the grand supercycle advance since the market bottom in 1784.

It should be noted that we haven't seen a grand supercycle decline since the South Seas speculative bubble burst in the 1720s. This created a financial panic and economic crisis that lasted for decades and threatened to return England to the Dark Ages. The theory calls for a potential return to the 1932 low of 41 on the DJIA. Prechter's interpretation calls for a low between 41 and 382 on the DJIA. We can only hope that Prechter is wrong, but he makes a compelling argument.

Prechter's (1993) argument for the latest advance being the fifth wave of a grand supercycle is important for another reason. Elliott wave theory argues that third waves are exceptionally strong. This would explain why the K Wave decline in the late 1800s was fairly weak and stocks declined only 46 percent— since the decline came within a third-wave, grand supercycle advance. If Prechter is right, this would dash hopes for a weak decline this time, based on Wheeler's (Zahorchak 1983) argument for comparing a K Wave's prospects to the K Wave that was two waves prior. The extremes in valuations and debt levels of the latest K Wave fall season give Prechter's arguments disturbing validity. Once again, let's hope for the Wheeler outcome of a weak decline and that we have not just experienced the fifth wave of a grand supercycle.

If the idea of a grand supercycle is not disturbing enough, Prechter (1993) also has written of what he calls the millennium cycle—obviously a 1,000-year cycle. He notes that the advance since 1784 could be a fifth and final wave in a millennium cycle that began around A.D. 1000, but he hopes it is only a fourth wave. If we are in the peak of a fifth wave of a millennium cycle and facing a millennium bear market then, well, let's not discuss the possibilities. Once again, I certainly hope he is wrong.

There is the ultimate cycle, relative to world history, that needs to be mentioned briefly. Oswald Spengler (1966), in his two vast volumes entitled *The Decline of the West,* upped the cycle ante one big notch with his proposition of an 8,000-year cycle with four, distinct 2,000-year civilizations.

The Spengler cycle has been expounded upon and was first introduced to me by the writings of P.Q. Wall (1993). The present 2,000-year Spengler civilization cycle, like Wheeler's and Prechter's larger cycles, should be peaking in the present time frame around the year 2000.

According to Spengler (1966), each 2,000-year civilization breaks down into four 500-year seasons. The Western world was only moving from spring into summer around A.D. 1000 in Spengler's work. The period from A.D. 1500 to A.D. 2000 was the efficient fall season of the Western world's civilization cycle. This theory argues that Rome was turning from a 500-year fall season to a 500-year winter season around the birth of Christ, just as Western civilization is now turning from a 500-year fall to a 500-year winter. P.Q. Wall (1993) postulates that in the same way that a three- to four-year Kitchin cycle has three Kitchin thirds of just over a year each and therefore nine spokes, a 500-year civilization season has three 166 year thirds made up of three Kondratieff cycles for a total of nine 50- to 60-year Kondratieff cycles per 500-year season.

The present Spengler 2,000-year Western civilization cycle is moving from a 500-year fall season into the beginning of its own

500-year winter season in the current time frame. Most of Wheeler, Prechter, and Wall's work fits into and reinforces the Spengler framework. Spengler (1966) concludes that European-American dominance will pass to the beginning rise of a new culture around the year 2500.

The interesting thing about the notion of an 8,000-year cycle with four civilization seasons is that when you divide 8,000 by Wall's 144, you come up with an average Kondratieff cycle of 55.5 years. Wall's work takes on an even more encompassing and fascinating dimension with this fact.

But enough about specific cycles, which can become a bit overwhelming. Please allow me to turn slightly philosophical at this point. The interesting thing about cycles is that by their very nature they have beginnings and endings. Cycles are in essence and at their very heart defined by time. Cycles are the fingerprints of time. They are hung on time. Logic dictates that at some point cycles had to have been set in motion. Had cycles never begun at a specific point, they would obviously never exist.

There has to have been a starting point where cycles were kicked off within the constraints and boundaries of time—like ripples moving out from a stone tossed into calm water. Some may choose to look at this event as the big bang, others as creation. The suggestion here is that time and cycles began with the descent of the universe from its beginning or from a state of perfect balance and harmony. Regardless of your personal views on the origins of the universe, my basic suggestion here is that cycles began with time itself, whenever time began.

Time has been ticking by, and cycles have been in relentless motion ever since the beginning. The force that initiated or allowed cycles to be set in motion could not have been constrained or contained by notions of past, present, or future. The force behind time had to have reached in from outside of time and therefore started or allowed the cycle clock to start ticking. Most of the world believes a divine being was behind this event.

To say that cycles or time were set in motion without a specific beginning is only so much foolishness and gibberish. Such an idea is fraught with contradiction. This in itself is an admission that there is a force that exists beyond time that started it all. To look at it another way, there must be a place beyond time where cycles do not exist—where there is no time. After reading this book and particularly this chapter, you may consider that a great relief and a pleasant thought.

It is particularly interesting that the greatest cycle I have found discussed or written of is the 8,000-year Spengler, which is divided into four 2,000-year seasons of four different civilizations. If there is something to this thinking on cycles, we now appear to be reaching a cycle peak that has not been visited by humanity since the birth of Christ, in terms of the 2,000-year seasons.

It appears as if there have been regular peaks in civilization. In essence, humanity has reached an apex of cooperation and achievement, and key historical events have occurred, on a 2000-year recurring basis throughout history. There are those who believe and would argue, and I confess being among them, that the force beyond time, that allowed free will and therefore all cycles to go into motion, reached into the natural realm from outside of time in a very personal way some 2,000 years ago. Approximately 2,000 years before that, as the ancient civilization of the Egyptians peaked and was turning from fall to winter, around 2000 B.C., the same force from outside of time acted within time and made an irrevocable promise to always be with the descendants of a man named Abraham. It is interesting to note that historical researchers place the peak of a Mesopotamian civilization around 4000 B.C. This was a civilization whose Indo-European language appears to be the origin of many of the world's languages. Some may recognize such a civilization as a potential empire of Babel. Once again, it appears that the creative force that lies beyond time chose to intervene in world affairs. Evidence indicates that it would have been approximately 2,000 years before the Mesopotamian Empire of Babel, which would be approximately 6000 B.C., that a civilization possibly peaked and was destroyed by water. The year A.D. 2000 marks a full turn of the 8,000-year Spengler cycle.

The obvious conclusion I'm drawing here is that there may well be some form of divine motivation in the development of cycles played out in time. A duality of forces that only allows humanity to go so far with its cooperation and progress appears to be at work. If indeed a force or forces from outside of time and therefore outside of cycles has interfered with our universe in a major way in 2,000-year intervals, it could certainly happen again. You could therefore argue that we are approaching the juncture of cycles of truly Biblical proportions around the year 2000.

The idea that an 8,000-year cycle may have been further divided into 144 K Waves of 50 to 60 years each is a concept worthy of pondering for the more philosophically inclined among us. One has to note the 144 measurement dimensions to the New Jerusalem that is suggested to be outside the corruptibility of time. The philosopher in all of us has to reflect on the inherent implications that would appear to be beyond coincidence.

Whatever your own beliefs and convictions on these more lofty matters, we appear to be coming up on a critical anniversary and juncture in the universe of cycles marked and defined by time. My cycle research indicates that the worst years of this K Wave winter phase will take place globally around the year 2000. Many regions of the globe may have seen their most difficult times before this date, and some may see their worst years following this date.

I'm open to any lively debate on the role of cycles in our destiny and the final resolution of the human condition within the constraints of time. I suspect we may have a few more Kondratieff cycles or even a Spengler cycle or two before the last cycle takes a bow and the curtain drops on the cyclic stage of time.

Works Cited and Additional Sources

Kondratieff, Nikolai D. 1951. "The Long Waves In Economic Life." *Readings in Business Cycle Theory.* Translated by W. F. Stolper. Homewood: Richard D. Irwin.

Meier, Paul. 1993. *The Third Millenium,* Nashville: Thomas Nelson Publishers.

Prechter, Robert. 1993. *The Elliott Wave Theorist.* Gainesville: Elliott Wave International, June.

———. 1989. *A Turn in the Tidal Wave.* Gainesville: Elliott Wave International.

Schumpeter, Joseph A. 1939. *Business Cycles.* New York: McGraw-Hill.

Spengler, Oswald. 1966. *The Decline of the West.* New York: Knopf.

Wall, P.Q. 1993. *P.Q. Wall Forecasts, Inc.* New Orleans: P.Q. Wall Forecasts, Inc. 5, no. 2 (February).

Zahorchak, Michael, 1983, In Raymond A, Wheeler. *Climate; The Key to Understanding Business Cycles.* Linden, New Jersey: Tide Press.

21

A MODERN-DAY JUBILEE

"Times of general calamity and confusion have ever been productive of the greatest minds. The purest ore is produced from the hottest furnace, and the brightest thunderbolt is elicited from the darkest storm."

Colton

"Wealth brings with it its own checks and balances. The basis of political economy is noninterference. The only safe rule is found in the self-adjusting meter of demand and supply. Open the doors of opportunity to talent and virtue and they will do themselves justice, and property will not be in bad hands. In a free and just commonwealth, property rushes from the idle and imbecile to the industrious, brave and persevering."

Emerson

"Adversity has made many a man great who, had he remained prosperous, would only have been rich."

Maurice Switzer

The concept of the year of Jubilee is found in the Book of Leviticus 25:8–55—written over 3,000 years ago. The Jubilee was a year of celebration every 50 years. It was also a set of economic laws that would have affected all economic activity for the other 49 years.

Up to this point, we have only lightly touched on the K Wave's relationship with the Levitical laws for the year of Jubilee. In this chapter, we will shift gears and take a closer look at the parellels between the two, which are truly fascinating. Although a K Wave, particularly the winter season, isn't much of a celebration, it has an impact on the global economy similar to the Jubilee. Both, in their own way, appear to clean the slate and give the economy a new beginning. In short, Jubilee laws sought to control the primary forces that produce a regular K Wave, a phenomenon only discovered thousands of years later.

It could be argued that the Jubilee laws were a unique form of government regulation. A closer look reveals that the Jubilee reflected something far deeper than regulation or structured rules of commerce. The framer's laws seem to have understood, even predicted, the natural K Wave seasons that would inevitably be played out in global affairs:

> Every fiftieth year let the trumpets blow loud and long throughout the land. For the fiftieth year shall be hold, a time to proclaim liberty throughout the land to all enslaved debtors, and a time then all the family estates sold to others shall be returned to the original owner or their heirs.
>
> What a happy year it will be! In it you shall not sow, nor gather crops nor grapes; for it is a holy year of Jubilee for you. That year your food shall be the volunteer crops that grow wild in the fields. Yes, during the Jubilee everyone shall return home to his original family possession; if he has sold it, it shall be his again!
>
> Because of this, if the land is sold or bought during the preceding forty-nine years, a fair price shall be arrived at by

counting the number of years until the Jubilee. If the Jubilee is many years away, the price will be high; if few years, the price will be low; for what you are really doing is selling the number of crops the owner will get from the land before it is returned to you.

You must fear your God and not overcharge! For I am Jehovah. Obey my laws if you want to live safely in the land. When you obey, the land will yield bumper crops and you can eat your fill in safety. (Leviticus 25: 8–19)

The Jubilee was clearly an effort to control three areas of economy—prices, production, and debt—three areas that tend to get out of control in a market economy. There is no evidence that the Jubilee laws were ever implemented, so we have no evidence of how they would have worked to control cycles. However, the objectives of the laws are clear.

The unique laws would have had the effect of discounting prices against year 50, the year of Jubilee. The value of land was to be figured by how many years it could be used until Jubilee. The further away you were from Jubilee, the more expensive the land; the closer you were to Jubilee, the cheaper the land, which was the chief means of production in those days. It was an agricultural economy. These laws would have the effect of giving us the exact opposite of what we have been reviewing in the Kondratieff long wave. In the K Wave, we have prices beginning low in the spring season and moving constantly higher until reaching a peak in summer. Prices then collapse into the K Wave decline.

A system that incorporated the Jubilee laws would have the highest prices in year 1, the year following the year of Jubilee. Prices would constantly fall until year 50 or the next year of Jubilee. This would bring falling prices rather than inflation to the entire economic system. The Jubilee rules are followed involuntarily in a K Wave decline.

The Jubilee laws would have a major impact on total economic production. Production and expansion would be based on predictable falling price patterns and not misguided anticipation of inflation, as is the case in our global system today. The flow of capital into the forces of production in a Jubilee system would be smoother, based on predictable price movements. You wouldn't have the buildup of excess capacity in the economy.

In our system, at the peak of the cycle you have virtually every industry overproducing. This leads to trade wars, bankruptcy, and unemployment. The buildup of excess production is what eventually brings the deflation that bursts the speculative bubbles in the K Wave. The Jubilee control of production occurs naturally in the K Wave.

The third force tackled by the laws for the year of Jubilee was something we hear a lot about these days because we have a lot of it in the global economy: debt. All debts were to be eliminated in the 50th year. This prevented a buildup of inefficient and dangerous debt levels in the economy. In such a system, you wouldn't actually have excessive debt cancellation. No reasonable bankers or loan sharks in their right mind would loan money beyond Jubilee—since they knew the loan would be forgiven. Loans would not be made with maturities beyond the year of Jubilee because they would not be repaid. Debt could not snowball and be refinanced as we see in our system today.

There would be a tendency for the most debt early in the cycle in a Jubilee system, and total debt in the system would constantly decrease until the next Jubilee. In our economy, as evidenced by K Wave history, we have low debts early in the cycle and more debt late in the cycle. In fact, debt levels explode in the last years before the K Wave bust.

Outstanding debt would constantly decrease in a Jubilee system as prices decreased. Debt can be a very useful tool in our economy, but it is clear that too much of a good thing can be disastrous. Debt reached unprecedented levels in every sector of the economy in recent years. At the same point in a Jubilee system, debt would be virtually nonexistent. Debt is not inherently evil in and of itself, but when used as indiscriminately as it is in our system, it is bound to eventually create severe problems. The defaults of a K Wave winter achieve the same thing as the Jubilee cancellation with a great deal more human pain and tragedy.

Unlike the year of Jubilee, the K Wave winter, as all K Wave seasons, typically lasts from 12 to 16 years and consists of four Kitchin cycles. The last two Kitchin cycles of a K Wave winter may be very mild and have many characteristics of spring. The worst of winter will likely come in the first two Kitchin cycles that last approximately seven to eight years. Jubilee was a one-year transition while our system takes quite a few years to get out of its winter season.

Clearly, the laws for the year of Jubilee would not work in our modern system. This is not why we are observing the Jubilee law. The year of Jubilee acknowledged and constrained the end results of human nature that would cause the system to get out of control. Jubilee was to act like a safety valve. The author of the laws for Jubilee appears to have understood the generational forces and tendencies within an economy and culture.

In the modern capitalist system, the K Wave decline relieves the pressure since we have no Jubilee. The principles of the year of Jubilee give us a number of clues as to our own systems's cycles and why it expands and contracts on a 50- to 60-year basis.

By looking at the year of Jubilee, we more clearly understand and appreciate why the global economy overexpands and overproduces, has inflation and deflation, and builds up debt bubbles that must burst. By controlling prices and thus excess production and by forcing the elimination of debt by year 50, the Jubilee system would be stabilized, rather than forced to decline every half century as the free market system does. Unlike Jubilee, which was to create a new beginning immediately, the K Wave winter season is a far more painful and lengthy process that cleans the slate, forces drastic change, and out of necessity ultimately creates a new era of growth and prosperity for the system.

The unique and clear perspective on the K Wave cycle given by Jubilee is centered not in the economic laws it outlines, but in acknowledgement of the flaws in human nature itself. Humans run the system, so it is human relationships and actions that create forces that determine the economy's direction. The year of Jubilee appears to have been designed as much for the governance of our human relationships as for economic regulation.

Clearly, the year of Jubilee wasn't just another set of regulations or rules for intervention in the economy when things go wrong. They were integral laws that prevented the excesses from ever occurring in the first place. In retrospect, the Jubilee law appears to have acknowledged the natural K Wave trends and the lengths of those trends in the economy and checked them in advance.

Government regulations that try to stop the natural K Wave forces once they have gotten out of control only do more damage. This was the case in the 1930s and may be the case this time around. Once a decline is underway, regulation is futile. Jubilee wasn't a law that would bail out banks, farmers, and industry; it would have kept them from taking a good thing too far and getting in trouble in the first place.

Don't get me wrong, over the past 200 years the capitalist system has proven to be the most productive and effective form of economy. I'm not advocating new Jubilee-style regulations since I doubt a Jubilee system could ever be implemented or followed. The economic system of today has seen great advancements in wages and overall prosperity. Our system allows for anyone to work his or her way up in the system if he or she is only willing to put forth the effort and the energy necessary.

The fact that the K Wave decline is truly a Jubilee and a new beginning in our modern system can be difficult to accept, especially during the pain of a K Wave winter. The swing from prosperity to depression tills the economic soil for spring planting. A new work ethic wrought from tragedy and experience is also imparted to the average individual during a K Wave winter, so the necessary work will be sure to get done during the next advance.

A new beginning comes as the K Wave purges inefficiency and recklessness out of the economic and social system. Inefficient and excessive debt are purged from the global system due to vast corporate failures of those who used too much debt to finance operations and are contributing to overproduction. The K Wave decline produces a new beginning by forcing the implementation of new technology. It promotes more efficient corporate and manufacturing processes as companies look for new ways to ensure their survival, giving the global system new life.

There are those who believe global capitalism will one day no longer have a cycle, short or long, but will be in a perpetual state of slow but stable growth. Those who believe this have the notion of perfectibility for the economy, which appears to stem from belief in the perfectibility of human nature.

Here is where their ideas are flawed. Human nature is full of extreme tendencies, including greed and arrogance. The forces that drive the system will always be present in humanity and show a tendency to rise and fall in K Wave cycles. The system that gains its vitality and strength from this competitive nature, as does capitalism, will never reach a state of perfection or equilibrium without flaws or cycles. A system that tried to produce perfect and stable growth through government interventionism in a mixed economy would eventually be caught in the same trap that sunk Communism. It would need so many controls to maintain stability, it would produce only stagnation. Such an experiment would ultimately fail.

Government's attempts to create safety nets during and after the Great Depression only made the problems much worse. The facts reveal this. Government banking insurance, welfare, and social security have created far more problems than they solve. These programs have been and will continue to be far more costly to taxpayers in the long haul than they are worth.

Humanity must be free to fail as well as to succeed in order to produce the growth and success we have in global capitalism. As we are free to move from a state of risk aversion to a state of risk proneness, we create the business cycle. If the system ever reached a state of growth equilibrium, we would most likely find ourselves very bored.

A controlled society that sought to eliminate the long-wave cycle would have to suppress the desire to assume risk, the desire to achieve or invent something new. It would therefore stifle productivity and progress. Yes, the business cycle could be eliminated with many restrictions and regulations, but this would not be the sort of economic and political system you or I would enjoy and appreciate—just ask the hundreds of millions of former Communists in Russian, Eastern Europe, and China.

The concept of equilibrium is that we are able to move too far in one direction as well as too far in the other, and thus we tend towards the center for our own safety over time. Jubilee law simply acknowledged these tendencies and was an effort to make the results of such swings less severe. Jubilee wasn't an attempt to regulate the system as we think of regulation today, but an effort to give the market freedom within boundaries that would keep the system from driving itself over the edge.

Only by allowing freedom of movement from one extreme to the other can participants in the system have a shot at finding economic happiness. The market system must be allowed to take its course, less constrained and unregulated, if it is to be productive and competitive and provide the highest possible standard of living for all citizens of the world.

The system isn't perfect—but then neither are humans, which is why the system works. A modern-day Jubilee in the form of a long-wave winter season, which produces a new beginning for a global system that has pushed prices, production, and debt too far, is just what the global economy might need to insure its even longer-term survival.

22

SOCIALIST K WAVE VIEWS

"Marx's theory of the inevitable decline of capitalism isn't accepted by any of the influential economists . . . There is also a transition in the highest levels . . . toward accepting that the capitalist economies are self-regulating, not self-destructive."

Andrey Poletayev
Russian Economist

Most observers would question why I would even address socialist perspectives on K Waves since there is a popular assumption, due to the collapse of the Soviet Union, that socialism, especially its more radical Marxist elements, is dead. While there are very few true, hard-core socialists or Marxists left in Russia today, socialist and Marxist thinkers are alive and well in the academic and government institutions of the West.

A number of socialists have embraced their own version of K Wave theory as a means of projecting the ultimate demise of capitalism and the rise of a socialist world government. It is important to briefly examine their thinking and rebut it, since the crisis of this K Wave winter or the next will certainly bring such misguided socialist thinking to the forefront of popular discussion. Marxists will argue that the Soviet Union was not true Marxist socialism, and there will undoubtedly be a vicious attack on free markets in the years ahead. In such a time of crisis, Marxist thinking will once again assert itself in a call for socialist world government.

A number of socialist/Marxist thinkers utilize K Wave analysis in their arguments, but the one most widely published and whose thinking is most widely followed is Immanuel Wallerstein (1984). His work is indicative, but a bit more elaborate, than most socialist views of K Waves.

Wallerstein (1984) espouses that there have been three types of social systems throughout history and that a fourth is yet to develop as an "invention of the future." The first type of social system he discusses in his book, *The Politics of the World-Economy,* is the reciprocal minisystem such as the Greek city-state. The second type of the redistributive world empires, such as Rome. I'll discuss the possibilities of a redistributive world empire in more detail later on.

The present international system is an example of the third type of social system Wallerstein (1984) defines and examines. Most of Wallerstein's work examines what he calls the capitalist world economy, which he argues has been evolving since the 14th century. In his discussion of the capitalist world economy, he presents the typical and predictable two-class position that the surplus capital of the direct producers—the working proletariat—is extracted from the system in the form of profit and distributed via the market to the bourgeois capitalist class.

Wallerstein's (1984) basic thesis is that we are now in the midst of a transition from the capitalist world economy into the fourth type of social system, which he believes will be a socialist world government. This would be a system where profit and private property would be abolished, and all ownership of production would be held by the public—in other words, the state. Wallerstein sees the capitalist world economy as being in a systemic crisis that began with the Russian Revolution in 1917 and that will give birth to socialist world government at the end of a transition lasting 150 years.

Although Wallerstein fails when he attempts to show that the capitalist world economy will of necessity be replaced by a socialist world government, he does a good job of outlining the K Wave characteristics and development of the free-market capitalist system. His analysis of the inner workings of capitalism are insightful, even if they lead him to his flawed arguments concerning capitalism's ultimate demise.

Most of us would agree that capitalism is going though a period of adjustment. I would argue that this is due to the K Wave cycle decline, not a greater systemic crisis. It is far from clear, as Wallerstein argues, that the adjustments we are experiencing are terminal and will create an entirely new social system; even if Western academic socialists would like to see this unfortunate event occur.

In light of the collapse of the Soviet Union, the replacement of socialist governments in Eastern Europe with regimes friendly to the capitalist world economy, reunification of Germany, and the many losses of revolutionary (i.e., antisystemic) movements internationally in recent years, there could be a temptation to write off the work of Wallerstein and his general thesis altogether.

In many ways, it appears the capitalist world economy has turned the tide on the socialist challenge. However, since Wallerstein (1984) himself predicted some of the recent shifts and changes, especially the opening of Eastern Europe to Western market influences, it would not be wise to dismiss his thinking just yet. His work provides a great deal of radical reactionary fodder for those with socialist revolutionary tendencies, as well as food for thought for those of us who would like to preserve a free market, capitalist, international economy, and therefore need to be aware of prominent revolutionary socialist and Marxist thinking.

Critical to Wallerstein's explanation of how the capitalist world system functions and how it will meet its fate is the notion of patterns in the system. Where Wallerstein's work is most creative and insightful is when he looks at K Wave cycles. I should note that K Waves are only one of his patterns. Wallerstein (1984) believes that K Waves have been present in the capitalist world economy since its emergence in the 14th century. Wallerstein clearly sees the capitalist system as having a natural tendency to overshoot necessary supply and overproduce as the "anarchy of production" seeks to maximize profits. We have reviewed this K Wave principal and tendency of overproduction in detail in this book, although not cast it in such a negative light. The notion that all trends go too far and evoke their own reversal would be clear to Wallerstein.

Like most socialists, Wallerstein (1984) sees economic demand as strictly a "function of the sum of political arrangements." He believes that when these political arrangements supporting demand are stable for a period of time, production overshoots demand and major bottlenecks are created in cycles lasting 45 to 55 years—the Kondratieff wave.

Wallerstein argues that over the centuries, each K Wave decline and advance has deepened the capitalist system. He believes they forced the capitalist system to further penetrate the entire globe in order for the system to pull out of the K Wave contraction phase and into the next K Wave expansion. He believes that to ensure the capitalist system's survival, capital must always seek greater returns both in peripheral and in entirely new regions and countries. This is the reason most socialists believe the developed world exploits developing countries; to ensure the profitability of capital and therefore the future of the system.

Wallerstein (1984) basically argues that now, after many K Wave cycles that have driven capitalism into previously remote regions, the entire globe has basically been penetrated by the capitalist world economy. He argues that the capitalist world economy has reached or will soon reach the end of the line, a point where there are no more undeveloped and untapped regions and peoples to bring into the periphery of the capitalist system. In a sense, he is arguing that capitalism is reaching the point where it has run out of victims.

It could of course be argued that they never were victims, but were offered the opportunity to participate in the greatest economic system ever devised and consequently a better way of life. It could also certainly be argued that although most of the globe has been touched by capitalism, it has only just begun to be developed. It will take many more K Waves to get anywhere close to full development of the global economy, and even then, the system would not need new territory and people to pull out of a K Wave cycle. But Wallerstein (1984) believes the engines of capitalism have no more long-term fuel and that a systemic crisis greater than a severe K Wave decline will produce a socialist world government. He believes we have already entered this systemic crisis and are close to the point of capitulation to socialist world government.

There are many problems with Wallerstein's logic. Even he (Wallerstein, 1984) argues there are other ways for capitalism to pull out of a K Wave decline and stimulate a new K Wave era of growth. Further expansion into new regions to create a new periphery for exploitation isn't critical for free market capitalism to pull out of a K Wave decline. During much of the cold war, the capitalist system was losing territory on its borders and was still expanding nicely in a K Wave advance. There are numerous holes in Wallerstein's argument in this regard.

The reason I wanted to review Wallerstein and expose some of the general flaws in his thinking is that I believe he has something significant to contribute on K Wave analysis. He has a few insights into how the free-market system pulls out of K Wave declines, although many of his ideas borrow heavily from Kondratieff's original work. Wallerstein's (1984) observations, however, undermine his own argument of systemic crisis. He believes that since its inception in Western Europe in the 13th and 14th centuries, the capitalist system has pulled out of a K Wave stagnation phase in four basic ways.

The first way that capitalism can try to pull out of a K Wave decline is by further mechanizing to save labor costs or by simply shifting production to the low labor costs of the periphery. This basically means that industry buys more machines to cut labor costs and increase productivity or moves production to a developing region or country with cheaper labor. This is to a great extent what the North American Free Trade Agreement (NAFTA) is all about: the United States wants to shift some of its production to Mexico. This shift has been seen in other areas of the globe as well. Japan has shifted production to countries with lower labor costs in Southeast Asia. Western Europe is shifting production to the newly opened markets in Eastern Europe.

When production is shifted to countries with low labor costs, demand is stimulated in these areas. Products are produced more cheaply for the developed core countries, and demand is generated in the peripheral areas of new production due to the wages paid. What we are currently witnessing is precisely what Wallerstein (1984) expected to occur. The problem is that this process produces a drag in developed countries as good jobs in textiles, auto production, emerge elsewhere. In the early going, this process creates more of a drag than a boost because the new jobs pay a lot less than the old—deflation. The real boost to the system will come during the next advance as the periphery areas become even more developed.

Wallerstein's (1984) elaboration of some of Kondratieff's thinking is important in the present stage of this K Wave because of the massive political restructuring that has taken place globally in recent years, particularly in former socialist nations. The new markets for shifting production into Eastern Europe, Russia, China, and Latin America surpass anything ever seen in a K Wave decline. At no time in history, have so many markets been opening up with potential for stimulating demand and expanding the penetration of capitalism in general. These drastic differences with the 1930s are one reason it could be argued that we are in for a mild K Wave winter season rather than a severe one.

The vast new markets for international capitalism are critically important for how this K Wave winter season develops.

Never before in history, have so many new markets with skilled workers opened up so close together, and during a K Wave decline. The deflationary winter season of this K Wave is and will remain obvious, but many negative effects of the K Wave winter could be muted by the opening of these new markets. High costs and excess production can go to the new markets. They provide new outlets for capital in search of higher returns. Losses in one region can be made up with gains in another.

The one big potential problem is that if one of the major new markets, such as China or Eastern Europe, will be taken out of the equation. A military coup, trade war, shooting war, revolution, civil war, extreme nationalism, or any number of other events could threaten these markets. If the trend toward opening these markets reverses, this K Wave winter could easily be more severe than the 1930s. If one or more of these markets are shut down in this K Wave winter, the consequences could be disasterous for a global economy that is on the edge of crisis.

The second way Wallerstein (1984) sees capitalism pulling out of a K Wave winter crisis he takes directly from Kondratieff: the innovation and new technology that invariably arises during a decline to set the stage for an advance. By creating new businesses and industries around new innovations, overall demand is stimulated in the economy. The new technology and new industries that come with it create the new jobs for the next K Wave advance in the developed core countries. These new jobs replace the jobs that were shifted to the periphery in the decline.

A third way Wallerstein (1984) sees the capitalist system pulling out of decline is with redistribution of world surplus in both core and periphery areas of the capitalist system. This is a unique contribution to K Wave thought and is a late 20th-century phenomenon. This redistribution is an effort to increase demand and stimulate the system. Wallerstein sees this as the planned bourgeoisification of the proletariat. This could be seen as the central effort of the New Deal during the Great Depression. Redistribution of wealth is an attempt to stimulate the system by shifting wealth from the few to the many. Even though I argue that the attempt fails and actually hampers recovery, Wallerstein is correct in observing that it is one way governments of capitalist states have tried to stimulate the system to move out of a K Wave decline.

Finally, Wallerstein (1984) argues that demand was stimulated in past K Wave declines by expanding the outer boundaries of the capitalist world economy. New periphery countries were created, areas previously untouched by Western capital. It should be noted that as Wallerstein sees the globe as being pretty much fully absorbed into the capitalist world system here at the close of the 20th century, in his thinking this final option for pulling out of decline no longer exists. This is the primary reason he believes the capitalist system has entered its systemic crisis.

Only one of Wallerstein's (1984) four observations on how capitalism pulls out of crisis depends upon the borders of the capitalist system being expanded, at least on earth. The other three can come internally and dynamically and do not require exploitation of new land or peoples.

The capitalist system is less dependent than ever upon the capital/labor relationship with which socialists are obsessed. There is also the final frontier—space. Expansion into space doesn't take more room on earth. Elbow room in this regard is unlimited, and new lands and peoples have to be exploited. Call it expansion without exploitation. However, avenues for deployment of capital are limitless on earth, even in old markets that can be rejuvenated. Capitalism will not die because it runs out of room even if the space industry doesn't pan out.

However, after saying that, I will concede that Wallerstein's (1984) thinking is very important in terms of increased activity in peripheral markets in the former Soviet Union, Eastern Europe, China, Mexico, South America, and Southeast Asia as we move into this Kondratieff winter. Expansion of capitalism into these markets is laying the groundwork for the next K Wave expansion and could dampen this decline. Economic growth and development in these areas as a means to reduce production costs and to provide an outlet for capital as well as markets for surplus production are one reason we could manage a mild K Wave winter this time around. Finanical markets appear to be expecting the benefits of this dramatic turn of events. If something unforseen closes these markets—such as an international crisis: civil war in Mexico, Russia, or China, or an upheaval such as a global trade war—then a mild K Wave winter could turn nasty—and fast.

Wallerstein's (1984) strongest argument for his dream of the emergence of socialist world government was his observation of the increasing socialization of the means of production. This was taking place up until the late 1970s and early 1980s. Socialism, the public ownership of production, was expanding, and many believed it was working in some countries. However, this trend reversed when socialism appeared to have hit a wall.

Privatization seems to be the fundamental new trend globally. It is hard to conceive of a socialist world government coming about when the global system is rushing toward privatization. The reversal of socialist movements that had taken power, primarily in the Soviet Union and Eastern Europe, casts serious doubt on a socialist world government evolving. But at the same time, we are seeing a push for more central control and renewed calls for government interventionist programs and solutions coming from the United Nations, Washington, and the European Union.

Times are definitely getting interesting as the East rejects government control and the West appears ready to embrace it in many respects. A severe K Wave winter crisis will renew the calls for socialist solutions and could potentially reverse the global trend toward privatization and market economies in the West.

Clearly, many of Wallerstein's (1984) arguments concerning the system being in systemic crisis are having a hard time finding validity these days. Most observers are declaring that what Wallerstein calls the capitalist world economy is the victor over a socialist world government. However, dismissing Wallerstein would ignore the dangerous relevance of some of his observations and predictions.

Many of his predictions are coming to fruition as a period of economic stagnation forces the capitalist world economy to retrench and seek to stimulate new demand and open new markets. This is exactly what Wallerstein (1984) argued the capitalist system would do. The applicability and accuracy of some of Wallerstein's insights should make the reader cautious about ignoring his prognostication that proponents of a socialist world government will once again assert a claim for being the next logical world social system when hard times hit capitalism once again. Exact timing isn't crucial for Wallerstein since he allows for a transition process taking 150 years since the Russian revolution, which would be by the year 2067. With such a broad time parameter, he would seem to argue that what appears to be the receding tide of socialism may only prove to be a surface aberration in good times. A renewed call for socialist world government will emerge when capitalism's chips are down in a K Wave decline.

Wallerstein's arguments (1984) in favor of a socialist world government are certainly fatally flawed. For many reasons, a socialist world government would prove to be a greater social disaster than the Soviet Union, but on a global scale. However, during a K Wave winter crisis, people will be looking for answers, and many will undoubtedly turn to socialist pie-in-the-sky solutions. They won't buy the arguments for capitalism self-rejuvenating.

It would be wise to understand the socialist arguments and the flaws in those arguments. The K Wave cleans the capitalist system for a new beginning; it will never kill it, unless socialist theory espousing a new social system is once again taken seriously by government leaders as well as the revolutionaries.

One of the most fascinating aspects of Wallerstein's (1984) work is that he believes that in the ancient world, world economies gave way to redistributive world empires. This would be an empire like Rome or ancient China. He never clearly explains why this time around the capitalist world economy will be transformed into a socialist world government instead of another redistributive world empire. I actually think Wallerstein was onto something here concerning the possibility of a form of world empire, but his Marxist instincts led him off course.

In my view, there is a good chance that during this K Wave decline a global financial crisis will allow at least some form of a modern redistributive world empire to emerge. A redistributive world empire would have a massive international, interventionist, bureaucratic-government structure.

A true free-market and private-property based international-ism with confederated and sovereign independent nations is a much more attractive alternative to either Wallerstein's (1984) vision of a socialist world government or what appears to be the emerging redistributive world empire. More than likely, we will take one of two paths out of this latest K Wave decline.

We will either take the path of a true free-market system with limited government and extensive individual freedom, or we will take the route of a redistributive interventionist world empire. In the case of the former, the United States would look more like what its Constitution and founding fathers intended, and the world would be much better off. In the case of the latter, the world will end up looking a great deal like the oppressive and ruthless Roman Empire, with its despotic all-powerful Caesars, who ultimately exploited the system and pushed the world into the Dark Ages.

Wallerstein's (1984) prediction of a socialist world government does not have a realistic chance. Socialists will once again be disappointed and not see their dreams fulfilled in crisis. The most attractive alternative for the future—less government and more individual liberty—may actually get a fair hearing in the years ahead. Whether it will emerge victorious is an entirely different matter.

Works Cited

Wallerstein, Immanuel. 1984. *The Politics of the World-Economy*. Cambridge: Cambridge University Press.

23

TWO PATHS OUT OF GLOBAL CRISIS: A WORLD EMPIRE OR THE END OF BIG GOVERNMENT

"Great occasions do not make heroes or cowards; they simply unveil them to the eyes of men. Silently and imperceptibly, as we wake or sleep, we grow strong or we grow weak, and at last some crisis shows us what we have become."

Bishop Wescott

The political, financial, and economical possibilities in the crisis years ahead are limitless. Revolutions loomed around the globe in the last decline of the 1930s. World War II, the most destructive military conflict ever known, was partially the result of the turmoil of the last K Wave winter season. As we look to the future in light of the global K Wave winter we are now facing, I think it is very fair to ask ourselves what we will become.

We should begin with the position that no matter what happens over the next decade we will emerge into another K Wave advance of economic prosperity. No matter how mild or severe this decline and the low economic tides it will bring, there is always the rising tide on the other side that creates a new more advanced economy. Therefore, the K Wave is really an optimistic theory of economic progress. My hope is that this book has communicated the positive aspects of the theory. There are great and rewarding days ahead; don't let the gloom and doom that will dominate the media get you too depressed.

Speculation on the next advance can be fascinating; however, there is a question more important than those concerning the technology that will lead the next K Wave or the particular nation or region that will lead the next global economic charge of the K Wave. A more fundamental question must be asked concerning the overall political, economic, and financial international system and/or systems that will emerge in this age of a global economy.

Communism clearly lost to the challenge of capitalism. Unfortunately, the enemies of free markets and capitalism arise from within the system and not from without. They are mostly well-meaning, lifetime political bureaucrats who simply don't understand a market economy and Adam Smith's principle of the "invisible hand." They are insulated from the life they have created for the rest of us.

The New Deal was the attempt by government to regulate and tax away the inevitable pain of a natural K Wave correction that was worse than it had to be because of government intervention. Government is still trying to cure all the ills of the system, while in reality government intervention and meddling is making things worse. An unhampered market has proven it can do anything government can do with less pain, less time, and a fraction of the costs. The New Deal turned its back on true self-regulating free markets, and we haven't looked back since.

The emergence of a more closely-linked global economy in the latest advance has brought world society to a great fork in the road. Two paths lie ahead of us. We have to choose which of them we will take out of the latest K Wave decline.

It is only during major financial, economic, and political upheavals that major structural changes in political and economic direction can take place. The population is too content during a comfortable K Wave advance. It is only in a K Wave decline that the international system is thrown into crisis and turmoil and that anything can happen. New roads are cut in crisis, and the destiny of billions of people will follow in the ruts.

The New Deal and big government would have never flown 20 years earlier—it took the Great Depression to take us down that road. It is a road that has brought us to the present era where a government out-of-control consumes an ever-growing amount of the productivity of the citizens of the globe. The average U.S. taxpayer pays over 50 percent of his or her income in taxes. In many countries, the figure is far higher.

During the crisis that lies ahead, only two real forces will be vying for power. Since the fallacy of communism and pure social-ism has been exposed for the world to see, the coming crisis is therefore limited in the direction nations can take. Evidence sug-gests that we will emerge from this K Wave winter season on one of two paths.

First let's look at the path that seems most likely at the pre-sent time. We have already discussed in this book what I call the creeping global interventionism of the 20th century, which is the natural progression of the New Deal. The New Deal was not lim-ited to the United States. It was a global phenomenon that has seen government bureaucracy expand its tentacles into every aspect of citizens' lives and economic activity around the world. The natur-al bureaucratic growth of the New Deal of the 1930s threatens to give birth to a global New Deal in the form of an interventionist, redistributive world empire under the authority of an organization such as the United Nations. If we take this route, the world empire will vastly expand its power into the new millenium.

A new world empire would be redistributive in that it would depend upon excessive taxation of property and income, in essense the redistribution of wealth, to maintain power and control over its subjects. An armed bureaucracy would be charged with keeping order, as the Roman Legions did 2,000 years ago.

Such an empire would have many characteristics of socialism but would look far more like a global police state. Individual freedom would likely be significantly restricted. Such a system would not be socialist because it would not be based on public ownership of all property and public ownership of all production. Private property would exist but would primarily be controlled by a wealthy elite class that controls the system. This was the case with the last world empire, the Roman Empire.

A new world empire would very likely be built on three solid foundations: North America controlled by the United States, Europe controlled by Germany, and Asia controlled by Japan and/or China. This trilateral approach to the world's political and economic institutions can already be seen in much of the government policy and planning in all three blocks.

True socialism is public or state control and ownership of all property and production. Many fear the rise of global socialism in the years ahead, and some, such as Wallerstein (1984), expect it to emerge. But it is simply not in the cards.

A world empire is basically an all-powerful government run in the interest of an elite super-wealthy class that controls government with quasi-governmental organizations and confidential societies. The new Caesars—U.S. presidents or the secretary generals of the U.N.—are increasingly more often than not puppets on a stage controlled by the managers behind the scenes. Through excessive taxation of the middle-class and redistribution of wealth, the world empire is held together and maintains power. In large part, it is the taxation of the middle class that funds the emerging world empire.

Those who run the system and control property and production are not taxed. Through foundations and creative accounting they keep their wealth intact and away from the reaches of their government minions. In fact, they even extract more wealth from the middle class by controlling government debt through the international banking system. It is the middle class who through taxation pay the interest on the debt that is income to the priviledged class.

In a world empire,we will witness the emergence of a new layer of government interventionism and bureacracy at the global level. It is already in place, but it lusts for more power and legitimacy. The growing global crisis that will in time appear unmanageable, as has occurred in every K Wave decline, could be the excuse for plunging the globe beyond the point of no return into a redistributive world empire. During the emerging crisis, under this new world-empire scenario, the United Nations will increasingly be given more power and authority, and the nations of the world will lose power and sovereignty.

Many would argue that there is no turning back from this path. Call me an optimist, but I believe there is one other possibility that cannot be ruled out: the end of big government. It is increasingly evident that a majority of the citizens and taxpayers, not only in America but around the globe, are fed up with the hollow promises of government at every level. They have been promised education, prosperity, healthcare, increasing living standards, happiness, financial security, banking insurance, and a lot of other pie-in-the-sky utopian nonsense. The results of government attempts to create a perfect world are sad examples of good intentions gone bad. Government has increased its appetite for the hard-earned productive resources of the people of the globe, always needing just a little bit more of the total pie to solve our problems. Government has failed miserably at every turn in the road.

The government cut of GGP (Gross Global Product) has constantly increased in recent decades, while the standard of living of the majority of hard-working people has continued to decline. Decade after decade, government has made promises and failed to deliver the goods. Not because government hasn't tried—it has tried. Government simply cannot do what only a true free-market system motivated by self-preserving individuals is capable of doing. This fact is becoming obvious to a growing number of people in a growing number of nations.

Individuals must be accountable for their actions for better or worse. Government can't level the playing field, holding up the losers and holding back the overachievers, and expect the system to produce its best or even second best results. Such a system will in time only produce failure and misery across the board.

Roosevelt rallied the people into believing that government could lead the way. Government intervention has been a yoke around the neck of not just the economy, but all individuals ever since. Government has consistently expanded its influence. From those with the greatest ability to those with the least ability, we have all been held back by the noble intentions of misguided politicians who have tried a grand experiment. Now we are facing the next horrifying specter in the experiment of big government: a new world empire.

There are those who still hold the old-fashioned view that America is the leader and last hope of real freedom from government tyranny in the world. If Americans don't demand a return to freedom and the road of the private sector and free markets to solve the problems faced by the accelerating global crisis, I have my doubts that any other nation or nations can carry the torch. However, it must be noted that there are nations and regions that are definitely moving away from government and toward free markets and private solutions to society's problems. Southeast Asia is an excellent example of this trend.

The trend away from government intervention and toward private solutions is one of the primary reasons I believe Southeast Asia will lead the world into the next K Wave advance. They appear to already realize that government does not have the power to solve problems or improve living standards. The little tigers of Southeast Asia are building what could be the foundations of the private rather than public path for the new economy. The only question is whether these new nations can survive the onslaught of global government if the United States doesn't change its ways and join in the trend away from government. Maybe these nations can make it without the moral support of the United States and will prosper and pass the United States in many respects for the simple reason that they embrace the principles that made America great.

The backlash against global New Deal interventionism is spreading. A tiring of government intrusion and a weariness of the self-interest-motivated folly of politicians is a global phenomenon. The Clinton administration may represent what history will view as the last stand for big government. The tide seems to be turning with the 1994 elections. We may be just seeing the tip of an iceberg of popular revolt against government intervention in society that will rise to the surface in this K Wave winter.

A true revolt of the middle class is a real possibility in a number of countries, but would likely transpire over a decade or more. The political situation will be exciting in coming years as the K Wave unleashes major new forces in the political debate and process. The grass roots revolt that is now waiting in the wings is not a typical political revolt for some new grand political scheme, schism, or "ism."

We are seeing the beginning of what appears to be a revolt against political interference across the board and at all levels. Ross Perot only scratched the surface. What we are seeing is not a revolution for a cause, but a revolution against government, an anticause.

As already discussed in Chapter 13, government has set itself up to take the blame for this K Wave decline by claiming to have the solutions. The backlash against government failure could be close to revolutionary. A global political climate change not seen since the American revolution may be in the wings during this K Wave decline.

The battle lines are clearly beginning to be defined for the choice of paths to be taken out of this K Wave decline. The proponents of a return to free markets and private sector initiatives are certainly the underdogs at this point. As the next decade unfolds and the failure of government intervention becomes more obvious to the masses, look for an acceleration in the call for the path of free markets and private sector solutions.

A popular revolt may call for an end to the trend toward a U.N. dominated world empire and global welfare state. The curtain will be jerked back, concealing the true nature of the land of Oz in Washington, D.C., Tokyo, London, Peking, Moscow, Paris, Bonn, Brussels, other capitals around the globe, and the United Nations. The political wizards will be seen for the fakes they are, and the revolt will swell.

The new economy created by the next K Wave advance may well blow right past government interventionists and world-empire builders, leaving them wondering what happened to their control of the system. The new economy will create information and communication systems, along with prosperity, that governments will not be able to control.

We are likely to see a rekindling of the vision of America's founding fathers—this time internationally. It was a simple vision. The early American government was seen as a necessary evil created for defense and to maintain the domestic peace. It was understood and accepted that a free people, free to work hard and succeed, could handle the rest. Freedom from the tyranny of government was the vision that inspired people to come from every nation on earth to the new world.

You may doubt the feasibility of this potential path developing out of the latest K Wave decline. You might be right! Such doubts have a solid basis. Maybe society has gone too far in the wrong direction to turn back. Maybe a new world empire is inevitable. A little doubt is certainly warranted, but the potential return to America's political roots and freedom from excessive government intervention is a far greater possibility than most realize at this point. In coming years, this truth will become more obvious.

The pendulum has only recently swung far enough in the direction of government control and potential tyranny of a world empire to begin its swing back to liberty and individual account-ability. The voters may well demand that government get out of education, child care, art, lending, bank insurance, the postal ser-vice, and so on and turn these roles over to the private sector. In certain instances, these things will be managed by the private sec-tor for government and in others jettisoned from government involvement completely.

We can't really talk about the two paths that lie ahead in this book without at least briefly discussing the likely global monetary and financial outcome of each path. Obviously, each path will pro-duce a major difference in the money system.

The monetary system advocated by the path of the world empire will most likely be run by the World Bank as a subsidiary of a more globally powerful United Nations. Central banks of the globe would work closely in concert with the World Bank under new international laws and probably an emergency U.N. Security Council resolution. A U.N. resolution would force the new money system on the nations of the world without choice. A precedent for forced acceptance of U.N. resolutions was set with Iraq and Saddam Hussein: there are severe consequences for not following U.N. Security Council resolutions to the letter.

In the worst years of the K Wave decline, potentially during a banking crisis, the internationalists who advocate a world empire will take bold steps. World leaders, probably the G–7, could get together and offer a new global money system as a solution. The trilateral currency blocks of the U.S. dollar, the Japanese yen, and the German mark or European currency unit, the ECU, would be the foundation of the system. The goal would be to merge these three currency blocks in time, poten-tially immediately, but probably within a decade, into a single international currency unit. The first steps in such a money and banking system would be created in the midst of a global banking crisis. Personal privacy would be gravely threatened by such a system.

The only way the people of the world would accept such a system in a crisis would be if it were tied somehow to the perceived stability of gold—even if it was not a true gold system. Keep in mind that during K Wave declines, nationalism is a powerful force. Rising nationalistic movements would likely have to be crushed to see a global New Deal type of money system implemented. This system would have a model in the present European currency unit, which is backed fractionally in gold. The likelihold of a gold basis to such a system makes owning some gold a wise move. However, eventually gold could be dropped from this system, and we would have a single international fiat currency backed in nothing but faith in the world-empire bankers and politicians. If we take this path, the economy would still enter the next K Wave advance, but under such a new monetary system there would be much slower growth than without it. Controlled by the all powerful world-empire, human potential would be restrained. There is a much better way.

In the worst years of this decline, we may well see the forces for globalism and world empire become disarrayed and even dissipate. The European Union is showing signs of strain already. We may see the nations of the globe recoil from recent trends toward world empire. We will likely see a new wave of nationalism, even micronationalism and isolationism not seen since the 1930s. Micronationalism, nationalism, and the many movements that seek smaller circles of political sovereignty and autonomy are taking the world in one direction and the forces of the emerging world empire are trying to take the world in another. Eastern Europe, Africa, Northern Ireland, Quebec, China, Southeast Asia, and India all contain examples of the trend toward smaller rather than larger circles of government power.

The second possibility for a new monetary system would come in the event that the financial crisis and economic decline gets out of the establishment's control. The forces pushing for a world empire may lose their grip. The political forces in favor of reform, less government, and freedom may begin to take control. This movement would also likely eventually turn to gold for a new money system in crisis.

The political revolt against the status quo and trends toward bigger government could become a popular movement, which might even seize political power. If political mistakes are made by the status quo establishment, which typically happens in a K Wave decline, situations could arise that are beyond the ability of the architects of the world empire to deal with. Those involved in political revolts around the globe against more government would totally distrust financial and economic solutions managed by the U.N. and World Bank. In short, we could see a wholesale rejection of the trend toward more government solutions on a local, state, national, and global scale. This trend would also include the realm of international banking and money.

Just as communism was rejected, the masses may well reject the creeping world empire. We could see wholesale rejection of the status quo in the international arena of politics and banking. This growing force would likely reject all government solutions completely for a return to the pre-New Deal era, even pre-1900s private-sector solutions. Government and its role would be cut drastically.

If this alternative path is taken, it is likely that we would see a few marriages of the antigovernment revolt with the forces of nationalism. National sovereignty would become a focal issue. National tax systems would likely be radically restructured under this scenario, and income taxes would be cut sharply and simplified.

Such a radical change would very likely also demand a return to some form of gold money in a free banking-system. A new high-tech money system based on gold could emerge in the crisis. Existing technology could be used to create and implement such a money system very quickly. By its very nature, this would also be the best international money system that could be devised—since gold would be accepted by all nations. It would still be controlled on the national level but accepted internationally.

Most people think of gold money as an old concept that could not work today. Nothing could be further from the truth. A cashless system of electronic blips backed in gold could be based solidly in a true gold money system. Encryption codes for such a system are capable enough today that the very fastest computers could not effectively break them. The technology to insure privacy and efficiency for gold money is now available.

The idea of a gold card—encrypted gold-based electronic cash—might take on new meaning in such a system. The advance of technology and the trend toward a cashless money system cannot be reversed, but its intrusion into individual privacy and its use in the world empire political power grab could be short-circuited forever.

With a true high-technology private gold money system in place, the next advance of the K Wave would be explosive, bringing prosperity and economic growth levels not seen since the 19th century. This is particularly interesting because many of the nations of Southeast Asia that are poised to lead the next advance have enough gold reserves to go to gold-based money.

The dawning world empire could be rejected by citizens of nations around the world under this sort of scenario. Out of the ashes of the latest K Wave winter decline would emerge a powerful new global economy based on less government, free markets, national sovereignty, and individual liberty, an economy that thrives on global competition with a high-tech, gold-based money controlled at the national level but that is also a smoothly operating, globally accepted international money system.

Taking either path outlined above, the global economy will emerge from its K Wave decline and enter another K Wave advance by early in the new millennium. The political, economic, and financial systems that emerge, depending on which path is chosen, will be very different. Before the current K Wave global economic crisis is over, we will know what we have become politically, economically, and financially. We will either be citizens of an all-powerful world empire that rivals the power of Rome at its apex, or we will be citizens of free nations, in a new high-tech, free market, international economy.

The world empire would likely be a highly-regulated system that would have less personal freedom and financial privacy and that would never see very high growth rates. Individual financial and economic opportunity would exist but would be limited. The standard of living would rise slowly. Large multinational corporations would dominate the economy. National governments would surrender power, authority, and sovereignty to the United Nations. Such a system would see new government-regulated and subsidized technologies and industries lead the next K Wave advance. However, in time, government would choke the system and create a major breakdown of currently unimaginable proportions, very likely in the next K Wave decline.

The alternative, a true market path, would see explosive growth and prosperity, shrinking government, and increased personal freedom and financial privacy. The system would see global competitiveness push national economies to great new heights of achievement. National sovereignty would be insured. New industries and technology would come to the market with phenomenal speed and effect. Small businesses and corporations led by visionary entrepreneurs would be the greatest economic force. The standard of living of the middle class would see drastic gains.

The path that is chosen and leads us into the next advance will see an expanding economy that will likely peak with the next primary recession around the year 2030. A drop in farmland prices, commodities, and raw materials along with a peak and decline in interest rates will be the telling signs of the primary peak. The next speculative fall season of the K Wave would then likely be the decade of the 2020s or 2030s. The secondary recession and the changing of the seasons from fall to winter will come around the year 2040. Only time will tell which path will be chosen.

Works Cited

Wallerstein, Immanuel. 1984. *The Politics of the World-Economy.* Cambridge: Cambridge University Press.

24

THE NEW ECONOMY

"In the circle the beginning and end are the same. All things come in their due seasons."

Heraclitus, 500 B.C.

"The progress of the human race is marked by periods of economic distress when want, poverty, and unemployment set the minds of men to thinking. These were periods when convictions where sharply and vigorously stated and men, by force of extremity, took their complaint to the fountain head. Great changes in government, leading to the emancipation of mankind and to the democracy which exists today were the result of movements that grew out of economic adversity."

Otto C. Lightner

This book was an effort to establish that K Wave theory has merit and warrants serious consideration and analysis. If my interpretations of the theory that were presented in this book are somewhere in the ballpark of accuracy, we are living in a critical K Wave period.

We are in the midst of major financial and economic change and dislocation in the global economy that will be fraught with danger as well as opportunity. The global economy appears to be just entering the winter season of the K Wave decline. We will not fully emerge from this period globally until the early 2000s, although a few individual nations and industries will begin the next advance years ahead of the global average.

An explosive new economy will emerge in the coming years and will offer incredible opportunity. This will be the case regardless of which path we take out of this K Wave winter: true free-market capitalism or a new world empire. A lot will happen during the emergence of this new economy that will determine what sort of international economy emerges on the other side. The years immediately ahead will determine the survivors, the new leadership, and the trends for a generation.

A few reasonable questions at this point are: What sort of new global economy will lead the next K Wave advance? What will be the engines that drive it? Which nation or nations will lead?

Just as in all K Wave advances, as Nikolai Kondratieff (1951) observed, the new economy that will emerge early in the new millennium will be driven by currently unimaginable advances in communications and transportation. No one can begin to calculate the number of technological advances already under development. Many of the new ideas are still forming in the minds of their inventors scattered in numerous nations around the global economy.

The deflation of computer prices as we have entered this decline will likely have a major impact on the next advance. Powerful desktop systems capable of tasks limited to mainframes a few years ago are getting into the hands of virtually all mechanical engineers, physicists, electrical engineers, biologist, and product designers, as well as workers in a vast number of other fields, and weekend inventors. New technology alone isn't a cure for an economy in decline, but it will be part of the fuel mixture for the propulsion of the next K Wave advance.

Lower computer prices simultaneous with a drastic increase in their power will likely change our society and economy in ways not presently imagined. One big change will be that our education system will likely be drastically altered by low-priced computers linked with the advent of fiber optics, digital video transmissions, new software, massive data banks, and new technologies that will especially cater to education.

The educational system is riddled with problems and is growing less responsive to the needs of the competitive global economic system every day. We will likely see a marriage between recent and future advances in low-priced computing and telecommunications with entirely new approaches to education. New technology will have an incredible impact on education. The failure of the existing educational system will demand such change.

Out of necessity, high-tech home schooling will be a wave of the future. Students will be able to log onto the latest computer system and connect to lectures, lessons, and question-and-answer sessions with the best teachers and minds in the world. Vast libraries, data banks and other sources of information will be available on-line. The best available school lessons on every subject will be available by computer on-line that can be downloaded periodically or logged onto live.

With less time wasted on an inefficient educational system, students will be able to spend more time in positive social settings with family and friends in their communities, developing solid interpersonal skills. High-tech home schooling doesn't mean the children of the next K Wave advance will be nerds. A sense of community will likely be a strong force in the next advance.

Some, maybe all, of these new or reorganized schools will be sponsored and supported by the free-enterprise system. Individual companies and industries desperately need skilled and well-trained workers. The private sector will get involved in education by necessity. The new schools of the future will actually teach the basics of reading, writing, and arithmetic. There will be plenty of physical schools for students to attend, but they will be drastically different than today's. They will no longer be controlled by a central bureacracy.

In short, our grade school education system has, in many ways, become obsolete. The market will respond with new solutions during this decline and during the next K Wave advance. Ten years into the future, education will look nothing like it does today. Children will receive better educations at only a fraction of today's cost. The influence this will have on the future will be astounding. But education is only one area that will see change. New forms of better education will help create the talent to drive the engines of the new economy.

The same advances that alter education will alter virtually all aspects of our working and recreational lives. Very few white-collar workers will go to work at the office when they can work from home more efficiently and effectively with computer links. This will likely alter the demographics of our cities and the development of real estate. If I don't have to go to the office, why do I have to live within an hour of the city? When I do have to go to the office, I will be able to take a super-efficient, magnetically levitated train.

These trains will travel at over 300 mph on a magnetic cushion—so why not live a few hundred miles from the office? A quick trip to the local terminal and you're in the city in no time for your weekly or monthly meetings. These forces may cause our big cities to deteriorate even further in the years ahead as technology allows workers to flee the crime and decay of the megalopolis. There is likely to be a great shift from the hassle of the cities to the security and comfort of small town life.

Other major changes to transportation will come from space research programs. A space plane will likely be a reality by early in the next K Wave advance. Fleets of these planes will follow. Manufacturing and development in space will be a primary engine of the next K Wave advance. Manufacturing facilities on the moon and Mars will likely be a reality midway into the next advance. Developments that come in the exploration of space will be applied to many aspects of life on earth. The next price peak in real estate may well see inflation on crater-front condos on the moon. Electric cars will likely outnumber gasoline-powered cars by the end of the next K Wave advance with breakthroughs in new mechanical batteries and manufacturing materials.

Whole new technologies and industries will be developed during this decline and expanded and implemented in the next K Wave advance. Job opportunities will come from sources never dreamed possible after unemployment reaches its highs in the decline. Unemployment will fall as the new economy gains momentum. People will adjust to the changes. Humans are far more resourceful than politicians give them credit for being. Take them off the free lunch line, and they learn quickly.

If needs arise and there is not sufficient talent to fill them, the market will respond and educate the needed employees who will have a powerful new work ethic after a K Wave winter. They will be ready and willing to do what it takes to succeed in the new economy of the next advance. It will be the late 1940s and 1950s work ethic and desire to achieve all over again, with tomorrow's technological advances in the areas of transportation and communication as the catalysts.

The next advance will be an exciting, fulfilling time. Since the United States was the leader of the K Wave advance and speculative fall season that ended in the depression of the 1930s and Japan was the leader of the advance and fall season that ended most recently, a legitimate question is what nation will emerge as the next leader? Looking at history, we see that the leader of the K Wave tends to move West.

You may think it inconceivable, but I believe there is a good chance that China, along with its Southeastern Asian neighbors, Malaysia, Indonesia, Thailand, and Singapore, will be the leaders of the next K Wave advance. I don't believe China will become a hegemonic power in the 21st century as great as the United States was in the 20th century, but it may well come close. In an article in Foreign Affairs, Nicholas D. Kristof (1993) estimated that, based on trends, China's economy would surpass the U.S. economy in size in the year 2002, with a gross domestic product of $9.8 trillion. This of course doesn't consider the potential damage of trade wars.

The true leader of the K Wave doesn't usually emerge until well into the advance of the cycle in terms of standard of living, national wealth, and so on. Certainly China has many changes to go through before it becomes a leader in the free market, capitalist system. The Chinese government is allowing significant free-market growth and activity at the local level. Larger scale operations are still run by the state in the 1990s, but there are signs this is changing. It appears as though the people will create a bottom-up free-market revolution in China that will peacefully overturn the communist government by the sheer forces unleashed by the marketplace.

In the Southeast Asian countries, we are actually seeing a trend toward free markets, more established property rights, and less government regulation and intervention, while the United States and Europe are going in the opposite direction.

China and Southeast Asia will suffer setbacks as the global economy moves deeper into the latest K Wave decline—along with all other nations. However, when you're close to the bottom, you don't have far to fall. You can't really talk about depression in the Western sense when a nation is only beginning to develop and build its infrastructure.

If the Chinese government cracks down on the free-market revolution taking place in that country and takes a nasty turn for the worse politically, obviously China will not end up as the next K Wave leader. However, I believe that it will be the next leader and that some of the greatest investments of the next advance will be in China—along with its Southeast Asian neighbors. Timing investments in this region will be critical.

You may think I've lost it, but the runner-up to China and Southeast Asia for the next K Wave leader may well be Russia and the Commonwealth of Independent States. If movement toward free markets continues in Russia, this will be a real possibility. Russia, in certain regards more so than China, has a talented and educated workforce ready to rebuild the economy. But Russia is likely to suffer more significant setbacks than China on the way to a booming economy. Russia is blessed with natural resources equaled only by, if not exceeding those of, the United States. In comparison to Japan, which rebuilt from the ashes of war to become a K Wave leader, Russia is having to rebuild from the ashes of both communism and the cold war. Most Russians are ready to get to work. Will we see speculation in high-priced dachas on the Black Sea before a bust at the peak of the next K Wave advance? It makes for an interesting topic of conversation at any rate.

The name Kondratieff will surely be kicked around by a few market contrarians if the Moscow stock exchange, along with the Beijing stock exchange and other Asian exchanges, is leading the globe in speculative excesses with a classic K Wave fall-season, speculative blowoff in the 2020s or 2030s. Russia may suffer its own setbacks on the way toward free markets, but I believe it will succeed in the long run and participate in the next K Wave advance—even if it doesn't lead it.

Don't misunderstand me. The United States will remain a major world power. It could easily remain the major world military power for a few hundred years. However, the United States will only remain the leader or close to the top if the right political and economic decisions are made in the years ahead. Regardless of the important decisions to be made and actions to be taken by the United States, the competition will continue to get tougher.

It may be wise to at least consider whether something could be done to prevent the extremes of the Kondratieff cycle. The question must be asked as to whether we should throw up our arms in despair over the K Wave and just accept its inevitable effects on the economy and financial markets. We should never give up on finding ways to prevent the extreme pain of the decline of the cycle. In so doing, we must acknowledge that the extremes of the speculative upswing would likely have to go as well. This might not be so bad. Still, even if we can smooth the roughest edges, the cycle will always exist.

I'm convinced that controlling or stunting the extremes of the cycle, if it is to come at all, must come internally within the free-market system, with economic and financial decisions based on knowledge of the cycle in the private sector. A true free market economy would make the cycle less severe anyway. Adjustments can't be forced by government.

The work in system dynamics on the National Model at M.I.T. would help in the decision-making process for industry. The individual participants, corporations and industry groups, and financial leaders within the economic system must make the decision to pull back or change corporate policy. With more research, the National Model may prove to be a very helpful tool. Even then, the cycle will not be eliminated, but the extremes could be avoided.

It is questionable whether such advanced thinking on K Waves will ever happen. The next generation always forgets. It is certainly too late to avoid extremes in the latest decline of the K Wave. There could be real dangers in trying too hard to control the cycle. By avoiding the pain of the K Wave decline, the growth and prosperity of the advance would most likely be stunted. It should be remembered that the K Wave is natural and healthy. You would not end the winter season of the year even if you could. The earth would burn up.

This book has illustrated that a new generation always drives the next cycle to its extremes because they didn't learn the lessons of pushing the system too far, they don't see the danger at the top and they push the system over the edge once again. At the peak of the next cycle, it is highly unlikely that K Wave theory will be any more accepted than it is today.

As we conclude our study of K Waves, it would be helpful to review the extensive terrain covered. We have examined past civilizations and looked at the factors that led to their demise. We have observed the history of the free-market system we have today, both its qualities and drawbacks. We have examined the work of the Russian economist Nikolai D. Kondratieff (1951) and what he saw in the data he gathered on the K Wave in free market economies since 1789.

The work in the System Dynamics program with the National Model at M.I.T. gave us a different perspective on the K Wave. We learned it is generated internally within a market system by decision makers in the public and private sector. We learned that the National Model is one of the few tools available for industry to look inward and make the decisions that could help to avoid the extremes of the cycle.

Field theory has had a dramatic impact on the hard sciences and on how interconnected, naturally occurring phenomena in space and time are understood. The idea of interconnected fields was examined as a possible clue to the social system activity occurring in space and time that appears to produce the K Wave phenomenon.

We have come to realize that Kondratieff could not as fully appreciate the K Wave cycle as we are able to do as a result of our experiences of this century. The emergence of an interdependent global economy has given us a unique look into the K Wave cycle and its character.

Psychology has shown a powerful relationship between the K Wave and how society relates to the economic world and what people expect and anticipate from the system. Now we will be better equipped to observe our own reaction to the different phases of the cycle.

Human conflict has been found to be directly related to economic circumstances and surroundings. War was discovered to be far more likely during a time of expanding economies than contracting ones unless one is instigated due to frustration in a decline. In hard times nations look inward, in good times they observe their neighbors possessions with lustful desire.

The banking system and the condition the system was in during past peaks and declines of the K Wave cycle and how similar those conditions are compared to the international banking system today has been reviewed. Japan is particularly vulnerable to major banking problems in coming years. The situation demands change, and we know by looking at history that major change and a restructuring of the international banking system is coming.

We have looked closely at the forces at work in the K Wave and their enormous impact on global trade. One can't help but look forward to truly free trade in an open global economy where the consumer rules at some point in the next advance.

The situation of agriculture in the most recent decline was seen as not being an isolated incident in history, but one with parallels in all declines of the K Waves of the past. Great new days are ahead on the farm once we make it into the next advance. Technology and invention have been seen as important elements to both K Wave expansion and K Wave contraction as humans seek solutions to their stagnating economic condition. We look forward to the new wave of technology, products, and ideas that propel us into the next expansion phase.

The political atmosphere of the day has been seen to have a direct relationship and to be enormously influenced by the location in which we find ourselves in the K Wave. We can only hope the right political decisions are made in crisis. Maybe this time around, the politicians will give true market reform a chance, although a new world empire ruled by a new type of Caesar is certainly a possibility. Major upheaval on the part of the middle class is a distinct possibility as the reality of K Wave pressures build.

Our study of the K Wave has brought us to the investor's dilemma in facing the cycle. Both inflationary and deflationary scenarios have been examined. We reviewed the basic investment instruments of gold, stocks, bonds, and real estate and how they typically perform in different phases of the cycle. We have speculated on how we could best profit from the K Wave cycle and its effect on the economy. We certainly hope to personally emerge in the next advance in better shape than we were when we entered the decline—ready to profitably ride the next upswing in the global economy.

Taking a look at the nature of the free-market system and its relation to human nature and the year of Jubilee gave us clues as to the real nature of the K Wave cycle that passes through the global economy on a regular basis. In the process of our review, we have stumbled upon the inherent qualities of human nature that lead our system through periods of prosperity and depression.

The misconceptions of Marxist K Wave analysis has been evaluated. It was determined that socialist world government is not a likely outcome of this decline. Finally we have considered the two paths to be chosen between in the midst of the accelerating decline faced by the global economy. We have come to realize that we will soon learn what political and economic system will dominate the next advance of the Kondratieff long-wave cycle in the new millennium. It is yet to be determined whether a new golden era of decentralized free markets or a disturbing, all-powerful world empire will emerge. The next decade will be an incredible and volatile transition into a new economy.

We have taken a look at the three foundations of evidence available on the K Wave, including Kondratieff's research, the National Model at M.I.T., and the year of Jubilee. We are now brought to a point of decision as to our acceptance or rejection of the K Wave hypothesis. The evidence is overpowering in favor of acceptance, but the true test will lie in the coming years of financial, political, and economic reality. The K Wave evidence would suggest that some form of global crisis is inevitable. What remains to be seen is whether the crisis is contained and the damage limited or whether poor political and monetary decisions allow the crisis to reach critical mass and throw international capitalism into a more dangerous systemic crisis.

In closing, I would like to again emphasize the most positive aspect of the K Wave cycle. This is the great opportunity that presents itself to the astute investor. A wise investor can use the decline, no matter how mild or severe, and the new economy that will emerge beyond to their advantage and gain. All it takes is staying in touch with the reaction of the various investment instruments in the global marketplace.

The next decade will make a great many investors extremely wealthy, while at the same time removing a far larger number from those same ranks. All who are aware of the Kondratieff Wave should be in the former group. With a good knowledge of the K Wave cycle, the coming years offer the investor the perfect opportunity to have a modern-day celebration of the year of Jubilee.

Above all, the evidence for the rise and fall of the K Wave reminds us that our world and human nature is imperfect. We will never create a perfect financial, economic, or political system. The clear evidence of human imperfection makes us aware and accountable to the fact that every individual in the global economy could use a new beginning, a personal Jubilee.

Works Cited and Additional Sources

Kondratieff, Nikolai D. 1951. "The Long Waves In Economic Life." *Readings in Business Cycle Theory.* Translated by W. F. Stolper. Homewood: Richard D. Irwin.

Kristof, Nicholas D. 1993. "The Rise of China." *Foreign Affairs,* November/December.

APPENDIX:
RATING SERVICES

These companies offer different types of safety rating services with different price structures that are subject to change. Call each to see which one best fits your particular rating needs. Ask them to describe their services and ask if they are offering any special rates or discounts. I would encourage you to stick with financial institutions that rank in the top 25 percent in the nation.

(Banks, S&Ls, Brokerage Houses, and Insurance Companies)

Weiss Research
P.O. Box 2923
West Palm Beach, FL 33402
PHONE: 1–800–289–9222

(Banks, S&Ls, and Bank Holding Companies)

Sheshunoff & Co.
One Texas Center
505 Barton Springs Road
Austin, TX 78704
PHONE: 1–800–456–2340

(Banks, S&Ls, and Credit Unions)

Veri Bank
P.O. Box 2963
Woburn, MA 01888
PHONE: 1–800–837–4226

(Insurance Companies)

A. M. Best
A. M. Best Road
Oldwick, NJ 08858
PHONE: 908–439–2200

(Municipal & Corporate Bond Ratings)
Standard and Poor's
26 Broadway 14th Floor
New York, NY 10004
PHONE: 212–208–8000

Moody's
99 Church Street, 1st Floor
New York, NY 10007
PHONE: 212–553–0546

The K Wave Report

The *K Wave Report*, edited by David Knox Barker, is a timely and concise quarterly research report for investors. The *K Wave Report* covers the ongoing developments of the global financial, economic and political issues presented in this book. Specifically addressed in each issue of the *K Wave Report* is where stocks, bonds, interest rates, currencies, mutual funds, real estate, and gold are headed in terms of the K Wave and other important cycles. Clear advice on what investment strategy you should be using to position your assets, and how to take maximum advantage of the powerful global K Wave trends, is reviewed in each issue. The latest *K Wave Report* is indispensable as a research and analysis tool for large and small investors alike. The *K Wave Report* could help you survive and prosper financially in the months and years ahead.

$25.00 For the latest Quarterly Report
$75.00 Annually (Four Issues: Mailed
   January/April/July/October.)

Send Check or Money Order To:

The K Wave Report
P.O. Box 9139
Coral Springs, FL 33075

INDEX